THE TRUMPET SOUNDETH

THE TRUMPET
SOUNDETH

WILLIAM JENNINGS BRYAN

AND HIS DEMOCRACY,

1896–1912

BY

Paul W. Glad

UNIVERSITY OF NEBRASKA PRESS · LINCOLN

Copyright © 1960 by the University of Nebraska Press
All rights reserved
Library of Congress Catalog Card Number 60–12259
Manufactured in the United States of America
International Standard Book Number 0–8032–5073–8

First Bison Book printing: September 1966

Most recent printing shown by first digit below:

4   5   6   7   8   9   10

To my father and mother

*

*   *   *

*

PREFACE

IN 1925 WILLIAM JENNINGS BRYAN, to use the phraseology of his will, consigned his body to the dust and commended his spirit to God. The passing of the man, however, did not coincide with the passing of an era, for an era had come to an end with World War I. Bryan's career had its origins in the milieu of agrarian unrest which swept the Middle West in the late nineteenth century, and from 1896 to 1912 he was his party's most important leader. Throughout his long public life he fought for principles he regarded as fundamental, and his conception of what was fundamental was conditioned to a significant degree by the environment of his youth. Yet the values, ideals, and convictions that seemed relevant when Bryan was at the height of his power were rejected twenty-five years later. Try as he might, he could not make them meaningful to the new postwar generation. Indeed, the very attempt to do so tended to warp and distort the principles he had thought immutable. Bryan then became the obstinate—and ludicrous—old man of the Scopes trial.

By the decade of the 1920's scientific investigation, together with wartime experience, had led men to question time-honored postulates. If man had descended from a lower order by evolutionary processes, then he had not been created a little lower than the angels and crowned with glory and honor; if Charles Pierce, Albert Einstein, John Dewey, and others were right, then uncertainty prevailed in the universe, and faith in an unchanging fundamental law was misplaced; if power politics and materialistic cynicism remained in spite of the war to end all war, then there was little hope of achieving the good society. The enthusiasm for an ideal social order had passed away, and in its place appeared the functionalism that came with ethical relativity; eternal verities were discarded in what Professor Ralph Gabriel calls the "Great Liberation."

When the Great Liberation reached its apogee, William Jennings Bryan, clad in his alpaca coat and baggy trousers, seemed an anachronism. He was anti-intellectual. Had he not opposed the teaching of evolution in Tennessee schools? He was a pathological demagogue. Had he not hypnotized millions with his oratory? He was politically inept. Had his record not been one of repeated failure? In the view of H. L. Mencken, certainly a leading spokesman of the new era, the basic premises of Bryan's thought and program were so much idealistic "bilge." Depreciating all that Bryan valued, stripping him of intellectual respectability, the scientific relativists of the twenties left only the memory of his golden voice.

This book, however, is not concerned with the passing of Bryan, important though such a study would be. Its theme is more heroic than tragic; that is, it attempts to place Bryan in the context of those years when his influence was great. The period from 1896 to 1912 was, to be sure, one in which he thrice met defeat as a presidential candidate. Yet it was also one in which his views and the principles on which they were based seemed meaningful to large numbers of Americans. Although he did not achieve the presidency, he did maintain his leadership of the Democratic party, and he was therefore able to serve effectively as a leader of political opposition. If there is value in such opposition (and Bryan believed there was), then he must be credited with an important contribution to American life. The significance of this contribution is the subject of the present investigation.

In preparing this book I have been guided by the notations of those who read one or more versions of the manuscript. To Professor Oscar Osburn Winther of the Indiana University Department of History I am deeply indebted for his careful evaluation and criticism of the dissertation out of which this study has grown. President Lynn W. Turner of Otterbein College made many helpful suggestions. The perceptive comments of Archie H. Jones, Assistant Director of the Chicago Historical Society, did much to clarify the argument I have attempted to present. Dr. Jeannette P. Nichols of the Department of History, University of Pennsylvania, pointed out weaknesses in my approach, and her criticism opened the way to many improvements. The astute observations of Professor Charles K. Cannon, Department of English, Coe College, have been invaluable. I have profited greatly from the comments on Chapter iv given me by Professor Richard W. Taylor of the Coe College Department of Political Science.

Professor John J. Murray, Department of History, Coe College, has given me assistance on so many occasions and in so many ways that full recognition of it lies far beyond my poor powers of description. Professor Paolo E. Coletta of the United States Naval Academy has been gracious in sharing with me his vast fund of information on Bryan. Indiana University generously provided a grant that made some of my research possible. Without the cooperation of countless librarians this work could not have been completed. I am under special obligation to the staffs of the Library of Congress, the Nebraska State Historical Society, the University of Nebraska Library, the Indiana University Library, the Indiana State Library, the State University of Iowa Library, the Iowa Historical Society, the Historical, Memorial and Art Department of Iowa, the Illinois State Historical Library, the Chicago Historical Society, the Newberry Library, the Minnesota Historical Society, the New York Public Library, and the Coe College Library. Mr. Leonard Wilson of Illinois College aided me in securing important materials in the archives of Illinois College.

If there is any evidence of sound common sense in these pages it is attributable to my most persistent and reliable critic: my wife, Carolyn. With uncommon sensitivity she managed to detect shortcomings and make me aware of them without precipitating domestic crises. And by some mysterious alchemy she was able to transform a sheaf of papers resembling the Dead Sea Scrolls into a neatly typed manuscript. This book is truly as much hers as it is mine, though I should be less than chivalrous if I permitted her (or anyone else) to share responsibility for the errors it contains.

—PAUL W. GLAD

March, 1960
Coe College

```
        *
   *   *   *
        *
```

CONTENTS

A picture section will be found following page 114.

THE TRUMPET SOUNDETH

I

*

* * *

*

PATTERNS OF CULTURE ON
THE MIDDLE BORDER

WILLIAM JENNINGS BRYAN, born and reared in agrarian Illinois, educated at home by his mother and in a small college that owed its somewhat precarious existence to missionary zeal, nurtured on an evangelical, revealed Protestantism, supported in politics by midwestern farmers ("common people" whom he loved and who returned his love), was clearly the product of a unique and puissant culture. Unlike his literary contemporaries Sherwood Anderson and Edgar Lee Masters, Bryan did not question nor repudiate the values and ideals of his environment; like his political associates Theodore Roosevelt and Woodrow Wilson, he sensed popular feelings with the politician's seismographic response to the ground swell of public opinion. Bryan, however, stands out in contrast to all these men because he was the embodiment of everything an agrarian order held dear, because—to rephrase—the "ism" he became was fashioned with forceful affection by the rural society in which he lived and moved and had his being. His influence as a political leader is, therefore, incomprehensible unless his career is set in the context

1

of a moralism derived from American Protestant Christianity, shaped by the educational agencies of the Middle Border, and made meaningful by the struggle of farmers against captains of industry and their cohorts.

American Protestantism

The story of Bryan's opposition years begins with the earliest settlers on the North American continent who brought with them their European culture complex consisting of political, economic, and religious institutions, conceptions of social classes, mechanical contrivances, habits of thought, modes of dress. On the frontier great impersonal forces were to modify, warp, and distort traditional habits and conceptions; European institutions and practices were to change after contact with what Professor Walter P. Webb has called "the abrasive frontier grindstone." [1] Religious beliefs, religious practices, religious institutions could not escape that modifying influence. Attempts to maintain traditional dogmas within the framework of a traditional ecclesiastical organization often met with failure. When religious services had to be held in cramped log cabins or out in the open air, when those exercises were conducted by preachers who were by traditional standards ill-prepared for their calling, when vestments and altars had to be discarded as unessential, when worship was sporadic as well as informal, the difficulties of preserving a sacramental system and a closely reasoned theology were insurmountable.[2]

At the same time that theological doctrines became less significant, American religious groups broke with the traditional European organizational pattern. With the separation of church and state and the winning of religious freedom they became voluntary associations.[3] Lacking the coercive power of an established church, they could widen their sphere of influence and recruit new members only through persuasion. For most of them this meant providing an emotionally satisfying program as well as concrete and tangible rewards. Much of the thrust of American Protestantism in the nineteenth century came from competing denominations and segments thereof which sought, each in its own manner, to save sinners for the Lord. Thus the way was prepared for two far-reaching and apparently contradictory developments. On the one hand, the tendency to minimize theological dogmas made possible the growth of interdenominational cooperation, but on the other, religious freedom encouraged evangelical rivalry.

Divisions within American Protestantism were in part a European inheritance; the Reformation had after all destroyed unity within Christendom. Yet the dynamics of American church history suggest by their very complexity the intensity of sectarian discord.[4] Calvinistic descendants of the Puritans were apportioned among Presbyterians, Congregationalists, and, to some extent, Baptists. But there were further subdivisions. Within Congregationalism, Old Calvinist and New Divinity factions were formed. Among the Presbyterians there was the New Light defection which resulted in the Christian Church, and the dissension which marked the withdrawal of Cumberland Presbyterians from the parent association. After 1837 those Presbyterians who remained gravitated toward New School and Old School blocs. The Baptists, too, were not without dissenting companies; in addition to Regular Baptists there were Antimission, Freewill, and Seventh-Day Baptists. Lutheran and Reformed churches were closely identified with ethnic traditions. Unitarians, Friends, Swedenborgians, Shakers, and others all had distinctive characteristics. Peter Cartwright observed that "war, and rumors of war, almost on every side" plagued even the Methodists, whose success in making converts was astounding.[5] "The whole people," thought Mrs. Trollope, "appear to be divided into an almost endless variety of religious factions." [6] There were in all more than forty independent Protestant sects and denominations in America when Abraham Lincoln entered the White House to direct a war effort made necessary by a sectional schism with religious overtones.

Pervasive though sectarian rivalry was, its influence should not be misinterpreted. Issues that divided churches were not always theological issues. The isolation of some communities, for example, could and did foster peculiar religious practices, while local pride could and did compel men to defend them. Furthermore, the theological hair-splitting that accompanied factional disputes suggests not that all churchmen thought doctrine important, but that many thought it relatively unimportant compared with a church's capacity to attract new members.

When dogmatic tenets did not square with the American experience, they were frequently modified to make them more acceptable. John Calvin's doctrine of predestination provides the most obvious case in point. Although groups within the Presbyterian, Congregational, and Baptist churches remained predestinarian, others encountered difficulty in harmonizing the rigid system of the great Genevan with the optimistic individualism encouraged by the frontier and by the vast resources of the American continent. Economic abundance created social mobility, or at least a belief in social mobility.[7] In an open society many men within the Calvinistic tradition either abandoned predestinarian views or so qualified them that the breach between Calvinism and Arminianism was significantly narrowed. The influential Lyman Beecher could go so far as to insist on the freedom and accountability of all men and to declare that "none who are not opposed" to God would be sent to hell. Thus New Divinity Congregationalists and New School Presbyterians were probably closer to the followers of John Wesley than they were to Old School Presbyterians and other orthodox Calvinists.[8]

If theological issues cut across denominational lines, it was in part because some men in all denominations made an effort to adapt their beliefs to the American environment. And voluntary churches in competition for popular support became more and more impressed with the irrelevancy of distinctions that were unfathomable mysteries to all but trained theologians. "Does not a disposition prevail to depart from the simplicity of gospel truth; to fritter away its substance; to soften down its harsher lineaments and to give it a form and features less offensive to the fastidious taste of the age?" queried the Rev. Daniel Dana, a conservative Calvinist.[9] What was simple "gospel truth" to him was not so to most Americans, but his fear that the old orthodoxy was being softened and made less offensive was well justified.

Sectarian rivalry, then, did not necessarily involve warfare between two or more ideologies. Alexis de Tocqueville found that "although the Christians of America are divided into a multitude of sects, they all look upon their religion in the same light." What he called "equality of condition" helped to account for the conception of God as Divine Monarch, governing all men by the same laws and granting to all a promise of the same future happiness. "Where men are broken up into very unequal ranks," he wrote, "they are apt to devise as many deities as there are nations, castes, classes, or families, and to trace a thousand private roads to heaven." In democratic America, where religious affiliations were voluntary, there was a tendency in all churches to make a simple, direct appeal to the average man.[10] Increasingly, churchmen centered their attention on the number of souls saved, not on what constituted salvation.

When winning converts became the chief end of evangelical activity, religious leaders evidenced a concern for the best means of achieving it. Many of them were convinced—and experience seemed to demonstrate the validity of their convictions—that the best means were also the most sensational. Revivalism, at first a backwoods phenomenon, therefore became the most favored medium for the expression of nineteenth-century religiosity in urban areas as well as on the frontier. If its popularity did not involve acceptance of the belief that nothing succeeds like excess, it did involve acceptance of the belief that good ends justify almost any means, however excessive.[11]

The revivalism of the frontier camp meeting was indeed vigorous; spasmodic twitching, hysterical laughter, uncontrollable weeping, howling, yelping, and jigging were attributed to the presence of the Holy Ghost. Such frenetic piety held few attractions for those whose faith embodied theological subtleties. In metropolitan centers of the East, it is true, enthusiasm was kept under control. But wherever the fire of revivalism burned it consumed traditional standards of doctrine and practice. Revivalism was destructive. It intensified competiton among churches and annihilated old associations.[12] On the other hand it wiped out theological obstacles to interdenominational cooperation. Revivalists were inclined to oversimplify theological problems, to reduce all issues to a choice between the two antithetical alternatives of salvation or damnation, and to welcome all who desired salvation. The appeal here was not to the intellect but to the emotions, to the heart rather than to the mind, and in the emotion-charged atmosphere of the revival those hopeful of eternal life forgot their sectarian biases.[13]

In contributing to American Protestantism a revivalistic fervor it had not known even in the days of the Great Awakening, the frontier provided voluntary churches with a technique well suited to the exuberant temper of the middle nineteenth century, and in so doing speeded the movement away from old orthodoxies. At the same time, religious associations of the East exercised a profound influence on the West. While the backwoods response to revivalism was striking, it did not obscure the fact that there was much irreligion on the frontier. General reports had it that drinking, gambling, swearing, and fighting were only the most obvious of western impieties, and metropolitan churchmen exhibited a mounting concern for their pioneer brethren.[14] This concern found expression in the missionary movement which appeared at the opening of the nineteenth century, grew in importance throughout the frontier period, and continued to flourish in modified form in the twentieth century.

The missionary impulse was directed as much toward improving the behavior of the frontiersman as it was toward enlarging his comprehension of God. Like revivalism, it encouraged interdenominational cooperation because it tended to minimize the importance of theological differences. Indeed, save for the Methodist Episcopal Church, existent church bodies had little to do with the evangelization of the frontier. Just as voluntary societies were formed to further a variety of causes such as temperance, education, or peace, others were established to carry on home missionary projects. The societies, even when sponsored by religious denominations, enjoyed more than denominational support. So Lyman Beecher in 1811 could write enthusiastically of the rapidly growing Connecticut Bible Society: "Churchmen and Democrats, Christians and men of the world, all fall into the ranks on this occasion. The thing is the most popular of any public charity ever attempted in Connecticut." [15]

At first, especially in New England, the societies were state and local in character, but with the coming of the "Era of Good Feeling" following the War of 1812, national organizations were formed. Those resulting from missionary enthusiasm, although supported from pulpits and sometimes endorsed by churches, were nonetheless separate entities. Such organizations as the American Tract Society, the American Bible Society, the American Sunday School Union, the Society for the Promotion of Collegiate and Theological Education at the West, and the American Home Missionary Society sought to place themselves above sectarian rivalries and to teach only the basic truths of a common faith.[16] Both the organization and the objectives of the missionary movement led to an emphasis on ethics and morality, not theological doctrine. Ironically, those who went to the "creedless frontier" as missionaries often went as representatives of organizations that were sometimes latitudinarian to the point of being creedless.

While both revivalism and missionary enterprises had an eroding effect upon dogmatic tenets, the latter became associated with a cluster of ideas not discernible in the former. Lacking a desire to expound a complex body of belief or an audience with a taste for theological argumentation, the missionary movement began to take on nationalistic as well as religious coloration. Because it developed out of a desire to keep the West within the Christian fold, it was vitally concerned with the fortunes of that area. In 1836, when Lyman Beecher published the third edition of his *Plea for the West,* he maintained that even the most obtuse should be able to see "that the religious and political destiny of our nation is to be decided in the West. There is the territory, and there soon will be the population, the wealth, and the political power." [17]

As time passed, the West loomed ever larger in the minds of missionary planners; with its vast potential human and natural resources, it could be transformed from a mission field to a powerful force for righteousness. This was the burden of remarks printed in the *Home Missionary* in 1839:

If the West is filled with the Gospel; if every town and neighborhood is pervaded by the doctrine which came down from heaven, and whose effect is to strengthen the authority of law, to teach men industry, temperance and justice and to lead quiet and peaceable lives in godliness and honesty, then every town and neighborhood will send forth a wholesome political influence and western representatives will be, by choice or by constraint of a virtuous public sentiment, the advocates of righteousness.[18]

Long before the nineteenth century was half over, therefore, the mission of evangelical Christianity had become intertwined with the mission of America in the thinking of many religious leaders. In 1850, when Henry Clay labored to secure a compromise settlement of problems arising out of the Mexican War and the acquisition of Texas, California, and the Southwest, the annual meeting of the American Home Missionary Society applauded a resolution "that the Gospel of Christ, brought into contact with the mind and heart of our entire population, is the only influence to which we can safely entrust the destiny of this country." [19]

To men who held such views the territorial expansion of the United States during the fabulous forties was providential; God was granting America the means to carry out her world mission. In February, 1855, the *Home Missionary* commented extensively on past developments and on its hopes for the future:

> In vain do our frontiers extend, our productions multiply, our commerce, wealth, and power increase, unless the spirit of religion keeps pace with all this growth, and rules all these elements of influence. The heathen world will be none the better for the cultivation of our boundless prairies, unless Christian hands hold the plow, and Christian hearts consecrate the harvest. . . . The West is a part of the world, a part very necessary to those who wish to save the heathen;—we must have the West. Within the lifetime of a single generation, the contributions from that portion of our land must count not by tens but by hundreds of thousands, or its operations cannot be conducted with appropriate energy or tolerable success. Within the limits of a single generation, then, a large portion of those Western states must be made to become what New England is now (and if so much, then much more) a land of churches, and schools, and charities, of pious homes, and great religious enterprises. The world is to be converted at the West. [20]

There is no sectarian bias here; this is no esoteric faith. It is "the spirit of religion"—an inclusive term—that must govern the expansion of the United States and shape her destiny. Let the hands that hold the plow and the hearts that consecrate the harvest be Methodist, Presbyterian, Baptist; it makes little difference so long as they are Christian. But the heathen will be saved and the world will be converted when the West responds to the challenge, and the mission of America will then be realized.

The McGuffey Reader

Out of the interaction of free Protestant churches and the frontier, half-developed ideas began to take on definite form. Moralistic in emphasis, they were given new dimensions by a sense of destiny which was related to the breakdown of sectarian particularism and to the movement from barbarism to civilization on the frontier. Taken together they became in the Middle West a folk belief, or a faith, more powerful than any written creed. While its elements have been present throughout all American history, perfection of the faith belongs roughly to the period from the close of the Civil War to the entry of the United States into World War I. In those years of industrial expansion and agrarian unrest, when William Jennings Bryan grew to manhood and became the "Peerless Leader" of his party, conditions on the Middle Border were ideal for the nurture and growth of a distinctive *volksglaube*. It even became a religion of the book and of the tabernacle. Its book, or series of books, was the McGuffey Reader, and its tabernacle was the Chautauqua tent.

In the years from 1836 to 1920 publishers sold more than 122,000,000 copies of William Holmes McGuffey's school Readers, a figure that attests to the fact that they struck a responsive chord in American thought.[21] Those Readers had particular significance for sons and daughters of the Middle Border, for McGuffey bent his efforts toward preserving culture and morality in the trans-Appalachian West. The tone of the Readers was bucolic; there was little or no mention of factories, iron works, or railroads. The world of the McGuffey Reader was the world of the barnyard and the village green, the old oaken bucket and the town pump, fields of corn and sylvan ponds, barefoot boys and faithful dogs.[22] But McGuffey did not deal only with the familiar, for an acquaintance with the best literature of the western world was an indication of intellectual breadth as well as a mark of respectability. He did not hesitate, therefore, to go outside agrarian America for poems, fables, essays, and stories that would illuminate the ideals he preached.[23]

McGuffey morality stressed the basic virtues of honesty, thrift, charity, and courage. He firmly believed in the dignity of labor as well as the sanctity of private property. Ambition and perseverance were praised, but so were contentment and modesty. The hero of "The Honest Boy and the Thief" was commissioned to guard the cart of a fruit seller. Successfully defending it from the depredations of one "Jack Pilfer," he was rewarded with a hatful of oranges for his faithfulness and honesty.[24] "Waste Not, Want Not" was the story of a boy who saved a piece of string in contrast to his wasteful brother. Within a few days he found countless opportunities to use his string to advantage while his brother was forced to suffer the consequences of his prodigality.[25] The exemplary "Contented Boy" courageously stopped a runaway horse. Though poor, he refused to accept a reward until the horseman promised to buy schoolbooks for him during the coming year.[26]

Exhortations to persevere, to labor on, to press toward the mark were legion. The *Fifth Reader* contained an essay by William Wirt in which he observed that "there is no excellence without great labor," and that "genius, unexerted, is like the poor moth that flutters around a candle till it scorches itself to death."[27] Few items in the nose-to-the-grindstone category, however, wielded the influence of the rhyme that began

> 'Tis a lesson you should heed,
> Try, try again;
> If at first you don't succeed
> Try, try again;
> Then your courage should appear
> For, if you will persevere,
> You will conquer, never fear;
> Try, try again.[28]

If McGuffey stressed ideals to be lived up to, he also stressed pitfalls to be avoided. Greed, revenge, and selfishness toward others were castigated, as were procrastination and laziness. "The Quarrel" was the tale of two small boys who, finding a nut, fought over its possession. A young man, called in to adjudicate the dispute, split the shell, giving half to each boy. "The kernel of the nut," he said, "I shall keep as my pay for settling the quarrel." And McGuffey has him add laughingly, "This is the way in which quarrels are very apt to end." [29]

Condemned along with the quarrelsome nutpickers was "Lazy Ned," who owned a fine new sled and dearly loved to beat his fellows in coasting. Because he was too lazy and indolent to climb back up the hill, however, he was compelled to remain a spectator.

> Thus, he would never take the pains
> To seek the prize that labor gains,
>   Until the time had passed;
> For, all his life, he dreaded still
> The silly bugbear of *up hill*
>   And died a dunce at last.[30]

In "The Money Amy Didn't Earn" McGuffey emphasized the disastrous results of wasting time when there was a job to be done. Amy received an offer of thirteen cents a quart for all the blackberries she could pick. Unfortunately, she became so enthralled with the pecuniary possibilities of blackberry picking that she spent the morning estimating how much money she would make. When she finally went out with her pail, she found that someone had already picked the ripe berries. As Amy returned sadly home, she thought of what her teacher had often told her: "Do your task at once; then think about it, for one doer is worth a hundred dreamers." [31]

The most sinister pitfalls were those associated with drinking, dancing, and gambling. McGuffey was here, as in other areas, expressing ideas that formed an important part of the code of the dominant midwestern middle class in the latter part of the nineteenth century. The *Third Reader* contained the tragic story of Tom Smith, who went to the city where he attended the theatre and fancy balls, learned to play cards and "take strong drink." It was the drinking that got the better of Tom, and drove his poor mother and lovely wife to their graves. The climax to this tale of degradation was the arrival of news that Tom had been sentenced to ten years in the state prison for larceny.[32] "How often," deplored an essayist of the *Fifth Reader*, "does the hand of the intoxicated man, lifted against his dearest friend, perhaps the wife of his bosom,

> In one rash hour,
> Perform a deed that haunts him to the grave!"

There was hope for the future, however, for as a result of the temperance movement the day would come when jails and penitentiaries would "stand only as so many monuments of the vices of an age gone by." On that halcyon day, the parent could gratefully say, "My child will not be a drunkard!" [33]

McGuffey looked to the church, the school, and the home as the three great conservators of the ideals and values he considered so important. Churches, as they were regarded by McGuffey and by many others, were not the exclusive guardians of a faith, for they shared with others the responsibility of upholding moral standards. Like the earlier churches of the frontier, those of the McGuffey era were highly regarded, not for their dogmas, but for their social utility in the American setting. Christianity, particularly Protestant Christianity, helped bring about national prosperity because it promoted good order and harmony. And the Bible was "the best of the classics," for among other things, "humility and resignation, purity, order, and peace, faith, hope, and charity are its blessing upon earth." [34]

McGuffey vigorously stressed the need for public schools, but he was convinced that the heart as well as the head needed nurture and training. "Knowledge is only an increase of power," commented an old man in a *Fourth Reader* essay, "and power may be a bad, as well as a good thing." The sea provided him with a convenient analogy: when a ship is steered correctly, hoisting sail enables her to reach port all the sooner, but if she is steered in the wrong direction, she is blown further out of her course as she carries more sail. The moral is that "God's grace in the heart will render the knowledge of the head a blessing; but without this, it may prove to us no better than a curse." [35]

The third essential preservative of McGuffey's high ideals was family solidarity. The most sentimental and maudlin pieces in the Readers—"Somebody's Darling," "A Mother's Gift—The Bible," "My Mother's Hands"—were those relating to the home.

Again, however, the home was an institution that had social utility; in training the young to obedience (children who had McGuffey's blessing always obeyed their parents) and in teaching them good manners, parents were contributing to an orderly society. In the fable of "The Seven Sticks" the importance of family solidarity was clearly demonstrated. A father of seven quarrelsome sons called them to him one day, and handing them each in turn a bundle of seven sticks, he challenged them to break it. Try though he might, each of the sons failed. The father then untied the bundle, and broke the sticks one at a time. If they held fast together and aided each other, he commented, they would certainly prosper. But if they became separated, they were doomed to failure. The tale ends with a couplet:

> Home, city, country, all are prosperous found,
> When by the powerful link of union bound.[36]

McGuffey never left the moral of a lesson in doubt; he drove home his points with the certainty of one who is convinced that he is dealing in eternal verities. This certainty may have stemmed from one of the most fundamental of his teachings: that of an omnipotent and omniscient God who was personally active in the world he planned and created. When virtue was rewarded, as it almost invariably was in the Readers, the inevitable conclusion seemed to be that the Lord had so ordered it. God was also important to McGuffey in his treatment of perplexing problems associated with death and immortality. The *Fourth Reader,* for example, contained a dialogue in verse between a little girl whose brother had just died, and her mother. In answering her daughter's questions, the mother points to a chrysalis from which a butterfly has just emerged. The child responds immediately:

> O mother! now I know full well,
> If God that worm can change,
> And draw it from this broken cell,
> On golden wings to range;
> How beautiful will brother be
> When God shall give him wings,
> Above this dying world to flee,
> And live with heavenly things.[37]

Very closely related to the idea of an immanent God who fed the birds of the air, clothed the grass of the field, and cared for his own was McGuffey's concept of patriotism. God watched over the nation as he did his children, and love of country and of God seemed inseparable. Patriotic sentiments were inculcated in countless maxims, legends, and hero tales, which, as Henry Steele Commager has observed, gave "unity to a people threatened by sectional differences, and tradition to a people without a common past." [38] They also tended to reinforce the concept of mission in the minds of Americans. The treatment of history in the Readers, like that in most religious works, was highly inaccurate. War was regarded as evil, but international conflicts sometimes found "good" nations opposing "bad" nations in contests of freedom against tyranny.[39] In her wars America had fought only for liberty, and it was taken for granted that the United States would never become involved in an armed conflict in the future unless the stars and stripes were unfurled in behalf of some righteous cause.

> Flag of the free heart's hope and home,
>   By angel hands to valor given,
> Thy stars have lit the welkin dome,
>   And all thy hues were born in heaven.
> Forever float that standard sheet!
>   Where breathes the foe but falls before us,
> With Freedom's soil beneath our feet,
>   And Freedom's banner streaming o'er us? [40]

In such paeans did the McGuffey Readers extol the cause of freedom which it was the American mission to promulgate.

Circuit Chautauqua

While the preachments of McGuffey may not have gained universal acceptance, there can be little doubt that his Readers were an accurate reflection of ideas widely accepted by respectable people such as the Bryans. The Middle West produced more than its share of realistic writing in the early twentieth century, but one of the most striking characteristics of its popular thought was a lack of realism. Middle western communities believed in progress and in the improvement of society even though they continually fell short of their ideals. The code which supposedly governed their conduct was violated openly by some and surreptitiously by others. Not only did they fail to practice what McGuffey preached, but they often became unctuous in their refusal to recognize their failure. When a reluctance to face facts became hypocrisy, it repelled men such as Edgar Lee Masters and Sinclair Lewis.

Yet dissimulation could have an important function. In the frontier period the gulf between the actual and the ideal could be passed only by spectacular flights of the imagination. Later an artless optimism gave direction, purpose, and meaning to life on the Middle Border. If there was, in fact, little progress in some areas, there was almost invariably a striving for progress. Kansans adopted a state motto that perfectly expressed this impulse: *Ad astra per aspera.* In their eagerness to reach the stars, moreover, midwesterners grasped at every means of uplift. Educational programs—inasmuch as improvement of the mind was associated with progress—were designed for mass participation and popular appeal. The Grange, the Alliances, and Populism all had their didactic functions, but from an adult educational standpoint Chautauqua was the most important of those agencies that brought enlightenment to the prairies and the plains.

The Chautauqua movement combined the idea of cultural progress with the methods of the religious camp meeting. The lake which gave its name to the institution had long been a popular spot for such gatherings. As the years passed, however, the programs of the Chautauqua Lake Assembly were broadened to include lectures, music, and readings. Boating, bathing, and supervised games were also added to encourage healthful recreation. This combination of evangelism, education, and exercise proved to have magnetic appeal, and thousands were soon making annual summer pilgrimages to the Assembly grounds.[41] Before long several independent Chautauquas were scattered throughout the country, each of them obtaining its summer talent (to distinguish them from actors, who were not considered respectable, performers in Chautauqua were always referred to as "talent") by direct negotiations with speakers' bureaus or with individuals. In 1904 the circuit or tent Chautauqua made its first appearance.

It differed from the "Independents" in that tents and performers moved along a previously arranged circuit, stopping every fifty miles or so for "Chautauqua Week." [42] The circuit Chautauqua was born in the Middle West and it was there that it reached its highest point of concentration, for it was admirably suited to the geography as well as the wants and needs of that section.[43]

The underlying assumption of the Chautauqua movement was that life was real and earnest, and that entertainment was of secondary importance compared with instruction and edification. Not satisfied with merely an educational function, however, those associated with the circuit Chautauqua also regarded it as the purveyor of clean, wholesome entertainment. With the passage of time, the balance between education and entertainment began to shift in favor of the latter, but even when the Chautauqua movement was gasping its last, it was still regarded as the bearer of facts, inspiration, and guidance to small midwestern communities.[44] So impregnated was Chautauqua with the roseate perspectives and moralistic convictions of the Middle Border that any program failing to conform to them was sure to be rejected. "The essential of any Chautauqua programme was its 'message,' " remarked Gay MacLaren, one of the talent who later wrote of her experiences. "A platform performance might be excellent from an artistic or informative point of view, but it wasn't up to Chautauqua standards unless it taught a moral lesson." [45] A similar comment in the *American Mercury* was more sardonic: "The lecturer must be more than merely informative or entertaining; he must also have a message. The Messianic delusion of the lecturer plus the self-improvement complex of the audience—there is your Chautauqua equation." [46]

A message of high moral value was essential to every feature appearing on the Chautauqua platform because Chautauqua audiences always insisted on taking something "worth while" home with them. From New Zealand came the Rawei family to tell of the road "From Cannibalism to Culture," and from South Africa came the Kaffir boys in native dress singing folk songs and telling stories. Such groups were represented as examples of the work that missionaries were doing in remote parts of the world. The Doctors Sadler, William and Lena, might give first-aid demonstrations, pointing out the relationship between health and clean living. Or Dr. William might lecture on worry and self-mastery while his wife discussed the care of infants and children. Lorado Taft, the sculptor, molded the clay head of a woman, and during the course of his demonstration he would change the expression of her face. The burden of his remarks was that if people did not "keep right on the inside" it would certainly show on the outside.[47] Chautauqua audiences demanded such moralistic observations, but Gay MacLaren found their attitude rather disconcerting when she began her career:

> A tall mournful man in long black coat and white tie walked back to the hotel with me. He said he wanted to talk to me. "You should be very proud that God has chosen you for this great work," he said solemnly. By this time I was completely bewildered. These people all seemed to think I was some sort of missionary. No one had said a word about my acting, my pantomime, or my character delineations—all they talked about was my "great mission" and the good I was doing.[48]

Although special features might be of great value in the promulgation of a message, the backbone of the Chautauqua program was the lecture. In general there were two types of lecture, the inspirational and the informative. While all speakers might hope to inspire, there was a group of orators who were specialists in inspiration. These masters of sentimentalism were usually known to their colleagues in the trade as "Mother, Home, and Heaveners." Only rarely did their lectures include facts or figures; but morals, success stories, and homilies abounded. Informative lecturers were much more numerous, yet it was the inspirers who were best remembered. Those associated with Chautauqua in professional capacities were inclined to be critical of the "Mother, Home, and Heavener," but his presence was probably necessary for the successful acceptance of any program.

According to Moreland Brown, operator of White and Brown Chautauqua, the reaction of the audience to the inspirational lecture was closely related to the sensations experienced by participants in revival meetings: "The feeling of exaltation which a member of the audience carried away with him was linked in his mind with Chautauqua, and he loved Chautauqua because of it." [49] A list of titles given to lectures by the buoyant prophets of hope and morality reads like the table of contents for a collection of contemporary sermons: "Tragedies of the Unprepared," "The Man Who Can," "Human Guide Posts," "Cash, Conscience, and Country," "Grit, Grip, and Gumption," "Go Givers and Go Getters," "The High Cost of Low Living." [50] Doubtless the psychological effect of those rhetorical exploits was, as Moreland Brown believed, roughly parallel to the effect of the revival meeting. Both were emotional in their appeal to the heart rather than the mind, and both stressed the importance of the individual man.

There was, however, a difference: the revivalist concentrated on the sinfulness of man and his need for conversion, while the Chautauqua orator often hoped to stimulate self-confidence and therefore emphasized the capabilities of his listeners together with their fundamental goodness. William Rainey Bennett, described by the Redpath Bureau as "optimistic, enthusiastic, sympathetic," was one of the most successful of inspirational lecturers. "A Bennett lecture remains long in the minds of the hearers," promised his advance publicity. "It helps to instil confidence, and causes both young people and older ones to make their own opportunities, and to take advantage of their natural abilities." [51] Typical of the Chautauqua approach were the exhortations of C. W. Wassum in his lecture on "The Secret of Power." Billed as "The Moral Cyclone," Wassum told his audiences:

> Every man has some weak spot in his makeup. Some have more than others. In order to be fit for a command of great power, which is the heritage of man, those weak places must be discovered and made strong. In the battle of life the other fellow is searching for your weaknesses. Remedy them in order that they do not crack under the strain. . . .
> One great trouble with us today is the fact that we are trying to live too many days in one. Have faith in yourself. Live one day at a time. . . .
> In seeking for that control of power, above all you must have optimism. Forget henceforth to repeat in your conversation that times are bad or that business is rotten, you can't make it any better by wearing a long face and I know you can get better results than by looking rotten yourself. [52]

Lou Beauchamp also tapped the rich veins of optimism and progress in his lecture "Take the Sunny Side," which became a Chautauqua classic. So popular was the theme that a school of "sunshine" orators developed.[53] One of the most celebrated members of the group was "Sunshine" Bates whose supreme effort was "The Silver Lining." "Happiness," he said, "is the joy of overcoming. It is the delight of expanding consciousness. It is the cry of the eagle mounting upward. It is the proof that we are progressing." And in his peroration, Bates urged his listeners to "go on up to the mountain top where you can look down into the clouds and see their silver lining." [54]

Even more famous than the sunshine lectures was Ralph Parlette's "University of Hard Knocks," which he delivered more than four thousand times, and which sold more than fifty thousand copies in book form. An essential prop for this chef-d'oeuvre was a jar filled with navy beans and a few walnuts. This was the "jar of life," Parlette explained, and the beans and the walnuts were people. By shaking the jar, he would demonstrate that the walnuts constantly remained on top. "See this poor bean down there at the bottom?" Parlette would ask. "He whines, 'I ain't never had no chance—you just help me up where them big fellows are and I'll show 'em.'" Then with appropriate grimace and gesture, Parlette would put the bean on top, rattle the jar, and show that it invariably returned to the bottom. The lesson was clear: if any would get to the top, he must "change his size and grow greater." [55]

The messages of the Parlettes, the Sunshines, and the Moral Cyclones were, in the jaundiced view of the *American Mercury,* "the poetry of the American peasant, religious poetry, tribal poetry," which explored "his mores, his taboos, his bewilderment at the mystery of the universe, his brute aspiration toward the stars." [56] If its snobbishness can be disregarded, an element of truth emerges from this comment, for like the McGuffey Reader and the camp meeting of an earlier day, Chautauqua was most successful in the agrarian West. And its talent voiced all the self-evident truths, the high-minded sentiments, the earnest hopes and convictions of an emergent folk religion. When tents of the circuit Chautauqua dotted the prairies, the faith of the Middle Border reached fruition. Its articles were not complex; it was not, after all, the creation of a school of theologians or metaphysicians. Growing out of frontier conditions and the separation of church and state, it was flexible, not orthodox; emotional, not rational; moralistic, not dogmatic; optimistic, not hopeless; patriotic, not sectarian. It was the faith by which William Jennings Bryan was sustained, and he became, if not its last, certainly one of its greatest prophets.

II

*

*　*　*

*

A SON OF THE MIDDLE BORDER

CHAUTAUQUA HAD ITS dedicated entertainers, informative lecturers, and inspiring home-and-heaveners, but none of them had the power of William Jennings Bryan to captivate an audience and hold it spellbound. Fortunate indeed was the community that could announce a "Bryan Day" as part of its Chautauqua week. When that day came, farmers traveled for miles the dusty roads that led to the big brown tent. Side flaps were rolled up so that after the tent had filled to capacity the multitude still outside could hear the most celebrated public speaker of the age. How can the magnetism of the man be explained? Charles F. Horner, manager of the Redpath-Horner system, suggested three reasons for the "undoubted perfection of the greatest orator" he had ever heard. First, people who listened to him sensed intuitively his greatness of spirit. Second, he expressed for them their own thoughts and aspirations. And finally, he reciprocated their frequently demonstrated affection for him. Bryan was a son of the Middle Border. He became the prophet of its faith. To some, particularly eastern businessmen and industrialists, he may have appeared as the agent of Lucifer. Whatever Bryan may have been to his contemporaries—devil, saint, or simply a product

21

of the Middle West—his ethical and religious ideas together with their social, economic, and political implications do much to account for his prominence and his power. Horner observed that when Bryan spoke to Chautauqua audiences "there was one quality which seemed never to be absent, and that was reverence." [1] A prophet may have honor in his own country after all.

The Training of a Christian Statesman

The future Commoner was born in 1860 in Salem, Illinois, a section where pro-Southern sentiment was strong during the Civil War. His father, Silas Bryan, was a staunch Democrat who found the circuit court bench a safe port in the storms that were rocking the nation.[2] What influence the war may have had upon young William Jennings is debatable, but that of his parents is more easily discovered. Silas Bryan, for all his reluctance to become involved in sectional arguments, was nevertheless a man of strong convictions. A Jacksonian in politics and a Baptist in religion, he buttressed his views with biblical props. Accustomed to praying thrice daily, Judge Bryan took seriously his relationship with his God. He was equally serious in his acceptance of responsibility for the training of his son.

A visitor to the Bryan home during the seventies conveys an impression of the Judge as an austere yet kindly parent who "discussed on religious subjects and other high topics laying great stress on the importance of education and urging every young man to spend years if necessary to secure the best that colleges could give." William listened attentively to his father's views, as one might expect of any well-bred young man in the late nineteenth century. And it may be assumed that he was equally responsive when "before retiring the old gentleman took down the great Bible and like the Cotter's Saturday Night 'waled a portion with judicious care' and offered up a simple, earnest prayer." [3] For all his earnestness the Judge was no bigot. When William told him of his desire to join the Cumberland Presbyterian Church, his reply was, "You children will have to form opinions of your own. I hope they will be right." [4]

Mariah Jennings Bryan, William's mother, was, her neighbors agreed, an uncommonly strong-minded, sensible Christian woman. It was she who gave her son his first instruction in reading and writing, and it was therefore she who introduced him to William Holmes McGuffey. It was Mariah who sang sentimental lyrics to a wide-eyed Willy—tunes like "Just Before the Battle, Mother." [5] It was Bryan's mother who tempered the austerity of the Judge's home with a flickering emotional flame and bequeathed to her son what William Allen White called his "fine Fourth Reader views of the relations of life." [6]

Important though the influence of his parents was, other forces did much to shape his thinking. It may be true that "intellectually, Bryan was a boy who never left home" and that his college years "did nothing to awaken his mind." [7] But such an interpretation may underestimate the intellectual climate of Jacksonville, where he attended Whipple Academy and Illinois College, and it does little to explain the evolution of William Jennings Bryan the valedictorian and prize-winning orator from timid Willy Bryan who went hopefully off to college carrying the two largest books in his father's library, a Greek and a Latin lexicon. Judge Bryan was determined "that all my sons and daughters shall receive the highest physical, intellectual and moral education to be had in our generation." [8] Fortunately such education was to be obtained close at hand where William could live with a distant relative, Dr. Hiram K. Jones, and his wife.

Jacksonville, Illinois, was one of the most remarkable of midwestern communities, and Dr. Jones was one of its most illustrious citizens. What set Jacksonville apart from other towns was its intellectual atmosphere, and what made Hiram K. Jones illustrious was the leadership he gave to philosophical investigations. Jacksonville was not only the location of Whipple Academy, Illinois College, Illinois Women's College, Jacksonville Female Academy, and state schools for the deaf and the blind; it was also the home of clubs and discussion groups organized primarily for purposes of intellectual stimulation. The most important of those groups were the two in which Dr. Jones took a particular interest: the Plato Club and its successor, the American Akademe. The societies were not so much interested in philosophical research for its own sake as they were in encouraging a type of creative thought which would lead to a "solution of essentially human problems" and give "those solutions metaphysical undergirding." [9] Most of the members were amateur philosophers, but Jones achieved the status of a professional when he taught for four summers in the Concord, Massachusetts, School of Philosophy. Hiram K. Jones, the friend of Emerson, of Bronson Alcott, and of William Torrey Harris, had much to offer young William Jennings Bryan.[10]

Bryan's detractors have subjected his college career to some investigation and considerable ridicule, not to say calumny. That the faculty of Illinois College consisted of only eight men, that its curriculum carried no subject except mathematics and classics beyond an introductory course, that during his years in attendance Bryan withdrew only eighteen books from the College library has often been pointed out.[11] Unquestionably Illinois College had limitations, most of them resulting from inadequate funds, and few would hail it as the Athens of the West. Intimately associated with the missionary thrust of the middle period, the College was in large part a creation of the "Yale Band." Members of that altruistic student association, "believing that evangelical religion and education must go hand in hand," pledged themselves "to go to the state of Illinois for the purpose of establishing a seminary of learning such as shall be best adapted to the exigencies of that country." [12] On January 4, 1830, with one instructor, a trustee, and nine students on hand for the occasion, the College opened its doors.[13] Keeping them open was a continuous struggle, yet the achievements of "Old Illinois" were as notable as hardships were numerous. Richard Yates, later Civil War Governor of Illinois, was one of two men in the first graduating class. And the brilliant record compiled by other alumni suggests a stimulating academic background.

When Bryan matriculated the College may have been understaffed, but the dedication of its faculty was consistent with its missionary past. Furthermore, the achievements of several faculty members helped to compensate for lack of numbers. Chief among them was Julian Monson Sturtevant, who in 1829 had come to Illinois fresh from Yale to assist in opening the College. He had served as president for thirty-two years, and when Bryan was a senior it was an ancient but still active Sturtevant who directed his studies in the social sciences. The author of a textbook in economics, an advocate of free trade, liberal and independent in religion and politics, he was the most stimulating of Bryan's instructors. But there were others: Henry E. Storrs, graduate of Amherst who had studied chemistry, geology, and mineralogy at the University of Gottingen and had received the degree of doctor of philosophy there; Edward Allan Tanner, Professor of Latin whose enthusiasm and learning produced such noteworthy classicists as Edward Capps, Edward Bull Clapp, and Harold Whetstone Johnson.[14]

The backbone of the college curriculum was the classics; three years of Latin and four of Greek were graduation requirements. The study of Greek and Latin literature included the writings of Thucydides, Demosthenes, Livy, Horace, and Tacitus. In addition there were selected tragedies and the *Iliad* in Greek and the *Tusculan Disputations* in Latin. A twelve-week course in rhetoric and a year of German completed the linguistic training of Illinois students, who were evidently expected to have command of the English language before they went to college. In mathematics, trigonometry and college algebra were required and calculus was an elective (one that Bryan did not take). As sophomores and juniors, students were given twelve-week courses in mechanics, physics, astronomy, chemistry, and geology. The senior year, the year of Bryan's most notable academic achievements, was devoted to the social sciences: economics, history, mental philosophy, moral philosophy, and political science.[15]

Perhaps the most important phase of Bryan's college career was his association with his literary society. In the 1840's two literary societies, Sigma Pi and Phi Alpha, were founded. Jacksonville, like a solicitous mother, nurtured such organizations and, deriving sustenance from her, they flourished.[16] When Bryan entered Whipple Academy, he became a member of Sigma Pi, the older of the two societies. Members were expected to entertain and edify their fellows with declamations, oratory, and essays. Bryan took part in all activities of Sigma Pi and seems to have enjoyed an enviable reputation as a performer, for he was always on the program at the opening meetings when the society was trying to impress prospective members.[17] That these societies were not an unqualified blessing may be true. They were involved in campus politics and doubtless helped to encourage personal animosities and rivalries. Bryan did not emerge un-scathed from intrasociety and intramural political battles. He was subjected to the kind of vitriolic attack that was to become commonplace later in his career, and perhaps as a result he failed to win election to the presidency of Sigma Pi.[18] Here it was, then, that Bryan first experienced the sting of political defeat, but it was also here that he began to acquire the experience that made him the most compelling speaker of his time.

Viewing the academic environment of Bryan's college days and attempting to strike a balance, one must grant that there were shortcomings. Instruction was authoritarian and based upon certain textbooks. Original research was virtually unheard of, and the college library was available to students only one hour a day. The literary societies maintained their own libraries, but the average student used these rather sparingly.[19] On the other side of the ledger it must be said that while Illinois College did not break with the prevailing educational philosophy of the time, it cultivated much that was good in it. The fact that the principal social organizations on the campus were literary societies is in itself a favorable commentary on its extracurricular activities. Furthermore, although the curriculum did not contain specialized professional courses, it did put students in contact with the ideas of a few great thinkers and writers. If Benjamin P. Thomas, the biographer of Abraham Lincoln, another Illinois youth who read well but not widely, is to be believed, "more benefit may be derived from assimilation of a few worth-while works of literature than from gorging a full fare of trash and mediocrity." [20]

So much for the intellectual regimen of Illinois College. To what extent did Bryan take advantage of its offerings? If grades are any indication of academic interest and endeavor—and higher education then as now was predicated upon the assumption that they are—then Bryan must be given credit for diligent application to his studies and noteworthy if not brilliant achievements in them. There were eleven members in Bryan's class, and at the end of the four-year course he stood first. The records indicate that he did his poorest work in German, where he ranked fourth, and his best in political science and ethics. One of his finest hours as an undergraduate came when the school paper, the *College*

Rambler, praised him as "the acknowledged hero of his class" for having received one hundred in moral philosophy.[21] In later years he was remembered, not for the quickness of his mind, but for the diligence with which he pursued his studies. Henry E. Storrs said of Bryan the student, "He never shirked a task and never seemed to think that if he could 'get by' that was enough." [22] There can be little doubt that he merited Storrs' accolade.

Bryan's Ethical and Religious Views

Church, school, and home—these according to William Holmes McGuffey were the three great guardians of virtue and preceptors of morality. Bryan was down to the last detail the personification of many a McGuffey hero; he worked hard, he was thrifty, he did not "use" tobacco or alcohol, he did not question the truth of what he was told by older and wiser persons. And church, school, and home were for him the great influences of his formative years. Imbued as it was with the moralism expounded by his parents, McGuffey, the professors of Illinois College, and residents of Jacksonville, the faith of William Jennings Bryan was as simple—and as complex—as the folk religion of the Middle Border. To write him off as a mere "fundamentalist," as though it were perfectly clear what fundamentalism implies, is to lose the key to his thought and life.

From the time of his early "conversion" at a revival meeting, Bryan was nominally a member of the Presbyterian Church. His decision to join that fellowship rather than the little Baptist congregation to which his father belonged was not, however, based solely on his conversion experience. Most of his friends were Presbyterians, and he preferred their company to that of the Salem Baptists. Later in life after his move to "Fairview," the home he built just outside Lincoln, he attended regularly a nearby Methodist church in order to become acquainted with his neighbors.[23] A certain lack of concern for dogmatic distinctions marked Bryan's conception of the church. He could argue that its doctrinal position was a matter to be decided by a majority of its members and that if some disagreed they could leave one church and join another.[24] As a Presbyterian he wore the mantle of Calvinism lightly. He became reconciled to the doctrine of election, he told the Alumni Association of Syracuse University, only after hearing the story of two sincere but unsophisticated Georgia preachers:

> The Presbyterian brother was trying to persuade the Methodist, and the Methodist hung back on the doctrine of election. The Presbyterian brother said: "It's just this way—the voting is going on all the time; the Lord is voting for you and the devil is voting against you, and whichever way you vote, that's the way the election goes." [25]

A flinty fundamentalist would not be inclined to joke about doctrinal matters, nor would he suggest that their observance be established by majority rule. To Bryan such issues not only were of secondary importance, but they were also anachronistic. It was ethics and morality that interested him, not theology. Theological debate belonged to another age; the live issues of the modern world were ethical issues. "Sometimes religion has occupied itself mainly with the contemplation of the unknown future life," he wrote in 1905; "it is today busying itself more with the life that now is; the emphasis is being placed upon the here rather than upon the hereafter." [26]

In the 1920's, of course, Bryan became the champion of fundamentalism. Yet during the opposition years his concentration upon morality for a modern society placed him among the leaders of an ethically conscious Protestantism; and in the same company were followers of the Social Gospel.[27] Walter Rauschenbusch or Washington Gladden might have said that the Christian was now "beginning to see that he can follow in the footsteps of the Nazarene when he goes about doing good and renders 'unto the least of these,' his brethren, the service that the Master was anxious to render unto all." [28] But the observation was also characteristic of the Commoner.

Bryan believed that the foundations of the moral law lay in the ethical teachings of Jesus. Materialism certainly could not furnish a basis for morals, and even reason was not to be trusted completely as a guide to conduct.[29] Philosophical systems were as unnecessary as theological structures, however, for when "the Nazarene . . . condensed into one commandment those of the ten which relate of man's duty toward his fellows and enjoined upon us the rule Thou shalt love thy neighbor as thyself, He presented a plan for the solution of all the problems that now vex society or may hereafter arise." [30] Fundamental in Bryan's thinking was the idea that politics, ethics, and religion were one in truth and that it was his mission as well as the mission of every good citizen to make them a trinity in fact.[31]

This, then, was the first characteristic of his faith: it was primarily an ethical religion. The second characteristic, its emotional rather than rational emphasis, followed from the first. The Commoner was a man of warm impulses and was always reluctant to follow reason into the sterile wastelands of pure thought. He did not have to be either a theologian or a logician to accept the moral teachings of Jesus, and religion was for Bryan a simple, heart-warming experience. The soul, he wrote, was superior to the mind because the soul could "take the mind and purge it of its vanity and egotism, fill it with humility and make it the servant of mankind." [32] He was critical of those whose concern for their fellow men was negligible, those who held themselves "aloof from the struggling masses." "It is better to trust your fellow men and be occasionally deceived," he observed, "than to be distrustful and live alone." And he went on to add, "I fear the plutocracy of wealth; I respect the plutocracy of learning; I thank God for the democracy of the heart." [33] Bryan the politician, as well as Bryan the inspirational lecturer of the Chautauqua circuit, almost invariably made his appeal to the heart.

That he could help bring about a better world by implanting Christian ethics in the hearts of his fellow citizens was to him a comforting thought. And the certainty that the Lord would watch over his own, one of the principal teachings of the McGuffey Readers, was equally cheering. Again and again during the course of strenuous political struggles, Bryan turned to William Cullen Bryant's "To a Waterfowl" for the assurance that

> He, who, from zone to zone
> Guides through the boundless sky thy certain flight,
> In the long way that I must tread alone
> Will lead my steps aright.

Armed with this guarantee Bryan went about attacking evil wherever it might appear: in a currency system that worked an injustice upon farmers, in a policy of imperialism that resulted in a denial of human rights, in gigantic business combinations that corrupted American institutions.

Bryan, Tolstoy, and Jefferson

The quintessence of a religion may often lie in its hagiology; such was the case with the faith of William Jennings Bryan. He had, or professed to have, great respect for the traditional American heroes of war and politics. To minimize the achievements of Washington and Lincoln would have seemed sacrilegious, and their portraits were dutifully hung as icons in his study. There were other giants from the past that Bryan often cited with approval—Andrew Jackson, for example. And among his contemporaries there was no dearth of high-minded and capable men: Mayor Tom L. Johnson of Cleveland; General James B. Weaver, standard-bearer of the Populists; Governor Joseph W. Folk of Missouri; Josephus Daniels, who labored faithfully for the cause during Bryan's campaigns; Thomas P. Gore, the blind senator from Oklahoma; Henry George, whose enthusiastic following gave its support to Bryan; and John Peter Altgeld, to mention only a few. The Commoner regarded such men with affection and sometimes with profound admiration. When he contemplated Leo Tolstoy and Thomas Jefferson, however, it was with the veneration usually accorded to saints.

During the course of one of his trips to Europe, Bryan made a pilgrimage to see Tolstoy, as he later wrote, "not so much to learn his views . . . but it was rather to see the man and ascertain if I could, from personal contact learn the secret of the tremendous influence that he is exerting upon the thought of the world." Characteristically, he came away from his visit to the Count "satisfied that notwithstanding his great intellect, his colossal strength lies in his heart more than in his mind." [34] It was as the Apostle of Love that Tolstoy appealed to the Commoner, and he cheerfully embraced the idea that the "power of love, not the power of the sword" is one of the forces that make for peace. The life of Tolstoy was, he thought, proof of that truth:

He is not only a believer in the doctrine of love, but he is a believer in the doctrine of non-resistance, and there he stands proclaiming to the world that he believes that love is a better protection than force; that he thinks a man will suffer less by refusing to use violence than if he used it. And what is the result? He is the only man in Russia that the czar with all his army dare not lay his hand on.[35]

The life and ideas of Tolstoy had yet another significance for Bryan: they taught him that there is a relationship between the law of love and the idea of progress. He believed they gave the lie to the view that "religious sentiment is an indication of intellectual weakness or belongs to the lower stages of man's development."[36] Those of the "cultured crowd" who regarded "religion as a superstition, pardonable in the ignorant but unworthy of the educated—a mental state which one can and should outgrow" were given a "severe rebuke" by Tolstoy himself when he said that "religious sentiment rests not upon a superstitious fear of the invisible forces of nature, but upon man's consciousness of his finiteness amid an infinite universe and of his sinfulness." The Democracy's Peerless Leader made those concepts the basis of much of his political program. Tolstoy's religion, with its doctrine of love, was uplifting; it would bring about moral improvement and therefore political, social, and economic betterment. That man could make progress, that he could have reached his present stage of civilization by the operation of a law of hate was inconceivable to Bryan. "How can hatred be the law of development," he asked, "when nations have advanced in proportion as they have departed from that law and adopted the law of love?"[37] Tolstoy, he felt, was much closer to the truth than were the Darwinists.

To translate the law of love into practice, Americans would have to adhere to certain fundamental propositions. Bryan found in the Declaration of Independence an exposition of the "basic truths upon which a republic must rest."[38] Authorship of this document that he called the rock upon which the nation was founded would in itself have qualified Jefferson for an important place in the Commoner's scheme of things. But the Sage of Monticello set an example in traits of character which he never tired of contemplating and commending to others. "His culture connected him with the educated and the refined," wrote Bryan, "and yet his creed and principles made him the comrade and work fellow of the people." And why, asked the Commoner in his best *acta sanctorum* rhetoric, was Jefferson a comrade of the people?

> Because he believed in inalienable human rights; because he recognized that all were made in the image of the same God whose likeness he bore; because he wanted nothing for himself that he was not willing that they should also have. He had not one dollar in his purse that had been secured by doing injustice to another man, and, therefore, he was not afraid to trust all he had to laws made by the people.[39]

The inference of this passage is that political and social equality could be achieved in the face of economic and intellectual disparity. According to Bryan's interpretation of Jefferson's thought, men were not "created equal in physical strength, in mental ability, in moral character or in worldly possessions," but they were "created equal in their natural rights" and these could "neither be acquired nor annihilated."[40]

Like Jefferson before him, however, Bryan pictured the good society as a rural society where extremes of "worldly possessions" were rare. The agrarianism of Thomas Jefferson is understandable; in his day urban industrialism had not yet imposed its peculiar stratification on the society of the United States. Bryan's agrarianism, on the other hand, was rooted in his conviction that rural America was being exploited by predatory interests of the industrial East. This difference in approach in no way prevented Bryan's adoption of Jefferson's self-evident truths. Those truths were not conceived in the shadow of the factory or on the littered sidewalks of the urban slum, and the Commoner did not carry them there.

Yet the use he made of the truths of the Declaration of Independence did not assume a static society. "Progress," he wrote, "is measured not so much by the discovery of new principles as by the more perfect application of the old principles." As the "upright man" learns to apply more perfectly the moral principles which he has adopted, he becomes that much better. Bryan, with his penchant for Scriptural quotations, used Solomon to support his position: "The path of the just is as the shining light that shineth more and more unto the perfect day." He granted that Jeffersonian principles had never been perfectly applied and even admitted the possibility that they never would be perfectly applied. But he insisted that this did not relieve Americans from the necessity of applying them as far as possible. "In proportion as the self-evident truths contained in the Declaration of Independence are applied to our government," he concluded, "our people will be happy and our progress will be permanent; in so far as those principles are exemplified in our national life our nation will be a light to the world and a blessing to mankind." [41] Thus did he relate the Declaration of Independence to that concept of mission which was basic to middle western thought.

Implications of a Commoner's Faith

The agricultural discontent that rocked the nation in the late nineteenth century precipitated specific social, economic, and political commitments from the mixture of ideas that composed the faith of William Jennings Bryan. Those commitments took the form of planks in his political platforms, and the specific proposals he suggested for the resolution of issues are to be dealt with in subsequent chapters. It is nevertheless important at this point to examine further the thought that lay behind programs he presented to voters.

Perhaps the most obvious feature of Bryan's character was his sympathy for the underprivileged; the poor and the downtrodden, the sufferer and the social outcast could all be assured that their fortunes were the concern of the Commoner. This sympathy made him the supporter and champion of the farmer and the urban laborer as opposed to the captain of industry. Possibly because he sympathized with "common people," he tended to associate virtue with physical labor. "There are some who regard it as a discreditable thing to engage in productive labor," he wrote. "There are places where they count with pride the number of generations between themselves and honest toil." He felt that the nation was suffering from a "demoralization of its ideals" because of a tendency to measure the worth of an individual by the amount of wealth he controlled: "Instead of asking 'Is it right?' we are tempted to ask 'Will it pay?' and 'Will it win?'" This kind of thinking had its origins, he believed, not in the agricultural sections of the country, but in its market places and financial centers.[42]

"Burn down your cities," thundered the Boy Orator at the Democratic convention of 1896, "and leave our farms, and your cities will spring up again as if by magic; but destroy our farms and the grass will grow in the streets of every city in the country." [43] The agricultural areas were not only the principal producers of economic wealth; they were also the principal protectors of morality. Bryan's "first battle" was fought for a holy cause, "the cause of humanity," and at the height of the fray it was natural for him to refer to the urban sections of the East as "the enemy's country." The McGuffey Readers had never questioned the essential purity of the heart that beat within the bucolic bosom, and neither did the Commoner. But the Readers had suggested a relationship between sin and the city, and again he saw no reason for believing otherwise. Such prejudices were prevalent among those for whom he spoke. As William Allen White observed, "The poor understood his language and believed in him. He could not have talked over their heads if he had tried to do so." [44]

Bryan's concern for the "common people," which he proclaimed with such enthusiasm, seemed to impart a certain demagogic quality to many of his utterances. And yet he was not a demagogue—he was too honest, too sincere, too willing to risk losing an election by sticking to his guns to be accurately described as a demagogue. The inadequacy of that epithet is also borne out by his attitude toward education. Unfortunately the issues of the Scopes trial, which cast him in the role of an enemy to educational progress, have obscured some of his services in this area. While some American demagogues have supported universities, it is probable that none has exhibited his admiration for learning or so stressed the importance of intellectual preparation.

Bryan did not only lend his famous voice to the cause of education; he actively sought out ways and means of raising the level of understanding of "the people." One of the first things he did when he moved to Lincoln was to join a discussion group similar to those that met in the home of Hiram K. Jones.[45] He regarded Chautauqua as an effective means of adult education. Although he did not deny that he was attracted by its monetary rewards, he also believed that he was helping to popularize an institution that had cultural contributions to make.[46] Bryan gave money as well as time to institutions of higher learning. Booker T. Washington's Tuskegee Institute, for example, was the recipient of gifts from him.[47] Students in colleges were also given financial aid through his efforts. When Philo S. Bennett, a wealthy New England merchant, expressed a desire to remember the Nebraskan in his will, Bryan persuaded him to make arrangements for distribution of the money in the form of scholarships for needy students.[48] In 1903 he ran a notice in *The Commoner* offering the services of the paper in securing summer employment for young men and women who wished to earn money for a college education.[49]

The educational philosophy that prompted these efforts was in harmony with Jeffersonian principles and with progressive middle western thought. Bryan, McGuffey, Horatio Alger, and devotees of the Gospel of Wealth all shared a belief in hard work and perseverance. But on the value of intellectual training Bryan and McGuffey left Alger with his hard-working little newsboys. The Peerless Leader ridiculed the idea that working one's way up through the ranks was the best way to reach the top: "Those who are foolish enough to exchange the permanent advantage of an education for the temporary gain of remunerative employment have, as a rule, a protracted season of repentance." Just as the workman increases his efficiency by taking the time to sharpen his tools, so the results more than compensate for the time spent in intellectual preparation.[50]

Because "no one is wise enough to decide in advance which child ought to be educated," Bryan was convinced that universal education was the direction in which the United States would have to move.[51] Whether an individual intended to "dig ditches, follow the plow, lay brick upon brick, join timber to timber, devote himself to merchandising, enter a profession, engage in teaching, expound the Scriptures, or in some other honorable way make his contribution to society," he wanted every citizen to have "all the education that our schools can furnish." [52] He pointed out in a rather crude illustration that a father who cut off his son's arm would be punished criminally in every state in the Union. "And yet in this age the father who would deliberately deny to his boy the advantages of an education and send him out half educated would really be more cruel to his son than the father who cut off an arm." [53] Equal educational opportunity was consistent with democratic principles, and he believed that "the American college is the most powerful ally of American democracy." [54] In his view the "best hope of society" did not depend upon an increase in the number of millionaires, but on an increase in opportunities for men to find work which would bring them "just and equitable recompense." And he added that this meant "not only recompense sufficient to give the family bread, but recompense with that margin which will make it possible to give the children of the family the education and training essential to the rearing of good citizens." [55]

With all its advantages, universal education was no panacea for Bryan. He was too much a moralist to trust only in training of the mind; ethical as well as intellectual sensitivity had to be encouraged and developed. Unless this were the case, an increase in learning would be dangerous. "An athlete bent on mischief can do more harm than a dwarf or an invalid," he said, "and so a well-disciplined mind, misdirected, is capable of doing more serious damage than an ignorant mind." [56] It was precisely at this point that the Commoner was most critical of American intellectuals. The "severest indictment" that could be brought against them was not that they had "a contempt for the rights of the masses" or that they distrusted them. He believed that "the severest indictment today is that they stand idle in the vineyard and do not employ in helpful service the power that they possess." Too many educated persons were "satisfied to simply enjoy life"; too many regarded their education as a private possession which they could use as they pleased. Relying upon the Parable of the Talents, Bryan insisted that "God requires much of those to whom He gives much and if our education has made us stronger, we hold that strength as trustees for those who are weaker. If our shoulders are broader, we must put those shoulders under heavier loads." [57]

This doctrine of service was an extension of the law of love; the sacrifice of self for the sake of others was the means by which the law of love became operative in a concrete world. Bryan felt that every step society had taken in advancing along the road of progress had been made possible by those who had been willing to neglect their own interests for the good of all: "Freedom of speech, freedom of the press, freedom of conscience and free government have all been won for the world by those who were willing to make sacrifices for their fellows." Because he believed that progress was the result of self-sacrifice, he also believed that such sacrifice was the real test of greatness. The paradoxical teaching of Jesus—"He that saveth his life shall lose it and he that loseth his life for my sake shall find it"—was an "epitome of history." The life devoted to self-interest was insignificant no matter what power or influence might accrue to it, but a larger life could be attained by giving one's self to great causes. Bryan quoted Wendell Phillips with approval: "How prudently most men sink into nameless graves, while now and then a few forget themselves into immortality." [58]

There were economic implications in the idea that sacrifice and service were responsible for progress. Such a view was at odds with the dominant philosophy of nineteenth-century captains of industry who agreed with the classical economists that as each pursued his own interests, society as a whole would benefit. But if advancement depended upon sacrifice, as Bryan suggested, then every citizen should "draw from society a reward proportionate to the service that he renders to society." The prophet of middle western moralism seems to have been aware of the obvious difficulties in this "divine measure of rewards." At any rate, he did not make proposals which would guarantee its establishment. He could only say that "in proportion as we approximate to the right solution . . . we place progress upon a sure and permanent foundation." [59] One thing, however, was certain: the best way to achieve an ideal society was to establish a form of government in which "the people" should be masters of the nation's destinies.[60] In the perfect society each individual would find his greatest security in "the intelligence and happiness of his fellows" and the welfare of each would be the concern of all.[61]

The Democratic platform of 1908, drawn up by a Bryan-dominated convention, declared that the overshadowing issue of the campaign was "Shall the People Rule?" [62] That question begged another: How shall the people rule? The Commoner's views on this crucial problem provide a touchstone to his activities as a politician, for he believed that only through political parties could citizens secure the enactment of laws or effect reforms. As long as organizations of a party were in "good working order and properly governed," its members could, through them, "initiate policies and select candidates." "Every voter ought to belong to some party," thought Bryan, "and in choosing a party he ought to select that party which, all things considered, offers the best opportunity of securing the application to government of the political principles in which he believes and the adoption of the policies he believes to be best for the country." Party members alone could help to frame the platform and choose candidates, but the enjoyment of those privileges carried with it corresponding obligations. Chief among these was the obligation "to act with the party so long as the party is true to its principles and avowed purposes." [63] It was not to be expected that all party members should have identical opinions on any given issue, but support should be given to parties and candidates that *most nearly* agree with us." [64]

Bryan believed as did Jefferson that it was natural for two parties, one democratic and the other aristocratic, to dominate the political life of any country. "The democratic party would naturally draw to itself those who believe in the people and trust in them, while an aristocratic party would naturally draw to itself those who do not believe or trust the people." [65] While he took little pains to mask a prejudice in favor of his own party, he admitted that both radical and conservative parties were necessary in a progressive state. Where there is no dispute, no discussion, no conflict of thought, there is more death than life. "The moving waters are the pure waters," he said; "the stagnant waters soon become poisonous." [66] It was the responsibility of voters to choose in free elections which party they would have in power. But once the election was over the party rejected at the polls had duties as important as those of the victorious party. "Jefferson declares that free government exists in jealousy rather than in confidence," observed Bryan, "and it is certainly true that public servants are most faithful when their acts are under constant scrutiny." [67]

It was the special task of the party out of power to suggest changes of a radical nature. Parties tended to become conservative when in power, and responsibility discouraged precipitate action. Therefore if any progress was to be made, according to Bryan's view, it would have to be initiated by the party out of power rather than the party in power. He agreed that the conservative was necessary "to keep the radical from going too far," but at the same time the radical was necessary "to make the conservative go at all." [68] Bryan's function, and the function of the Democratic party so long as it remained out of power, was to keep issues alive and to agitate for change. Not any kind of change would do, of course, for change would have to be consistent with the melioristic ideology of the Middle Border. That is to say, it would have to be progressive, not reactionary change.

Once the issues had been clearly presented, or rather once the advocates of both sides to a question had stated their arguments, Bryan would have the voters decide between the two. The principle of majority rule was an axiom of democratic society. He recognized that the majority might make mistakes, but he insisted on looking at the alternatives: "The only escape from the rule of the majority is to be found in the rule of the minority, but if the majority make mistakes, would not a minority also?" [69] Majority rule, instead of encouraging error, more often than not reduced error. A single individual, subject to bias and prejudice, might be wrong on any given question, but among masses of men those biases and prejudices tended to cancel each other out. Bryan's commitment to majority rule, coming as it did in a period before American individualism had been threatened by the perfection of various techniques in the manipulation of public opinion, rested upon a belief in the innate wisdom of "the people." Jefferson, Jackson, and Lincoln had had confidence in the people "both as to their right to a voice in government and as to their capacity for self-government." [70] Bryan could not think of questioning the virtue and abilities of hard-working men and women who listened to him so attentively on the Chautauqua circuit, men and women who were, after all, a good cross section of "the people." To do so would be to question an article of the faith that was his heritage.

The Commoner's theory of representation followed from his ideas on majority rule. The duties of representatives were subject to two different interpretations. The first alternative, that they were elected to think for the people, Bryan rejected in favor of the second, "that the people think for themselves and elect representatives not to think for them but to act for them." [71] He thought it dangerous for the holder of an elective office to "put his own interests above the rights of the many." He was aware of the argument that a representative might conscientiously disagree with the voters, but he dismissed it: "A conscience that hibernates during the campaign and only comes forth when the people are helpless to recall their suffrages,—such a conscience usually reaches the maximum of its sensitiveness when some vested wrong is about to be overthrown." [72] In pleading for the direct election of senators Bryan summed up his position: "There is more virtue in the masses than ever finds expression through their representatives, because representatives are influenced, to a greater or lesser degree, by their personal interest." [73]

Service was the measure of greatness for the representative of the people no less than for others; and the best service he could render was to carry out the wishes of his constituency in all things. That he should be free of personal interest was particularly important because it was his responsibility to pass legislation that would correct abuses, eliminate corruption, and guarantee political honesty. Acquiescence in the idea that legislation is a nostrum against which the gates of hell can never prevail may be an occupational disease among reformers in politics. Bryan had almost unlimited confidence in the efficacy of legislation. He often acted on the assumption that a nation can legislate morality, that if evils existed laws would eradicate them. Yet he did not fail to see that society is made up of two sides, an external side consisting of institutions and an internal side or temper which makes the useful existence of those institutions possible. "Just as more evil is restrained today by conscience than by legislation," he wrote in 1905, "so in the awakening to which we look forward the application of moral principles to industry and to commerce will have a more potent influence than any written regulations that may be prescribed by state or national authority." [74]

Bryan believed earnestly if ingenuously that an awakening would come, that operation of the law of love, respect for the equality of all men, sympathy for the masses, establishment of universal education, acceptance of the ideal of service to others, and government by majority rule would bring about a society in which justice and virtue would reign supreme. His belief in the idea of progress is the thread running through most of his speeches and writings; it is the link between the message he preached and his conception of the mission of America. It is also a clue to much of his political appeal. So George F. Rinehart, editor of the Helena, Montana, *Daily Independent,* could write during the campaign of 1908:

> Mr. Bryan is an optimist. He believes the world is getting better all the time, and it is impossible to be around him a great deal without sharing his hopeful view of things. I confess that I have caught the infection and believe firmly in the triumph of righteousness over every form of wrong. That accounts for my unfaltering faith in Bryan.[75]

The Commoner did indeed feel that the world was getting better. "Aristocracy is passing away and democracy is coming to her own," he observed with satisfaction in 1912. "There is not a land upon God's footstool in which the power of the people is not growing; not a country on this earth where the forces of privilege are not retreating." [76] No force, regardless of its power, could prevent the emergence of an ideal; armies and navies, however strong, were impotent against it. "Thought inspired by love" would yet "rule the world." [77] But no matter how far Americans might progress, there would still be room for improvement, for "the larger the area of our vision . . . the more we see that needs to be done." To Bryan this meant that although there were still improvements to be made, the time for rendering services to humanity was at hand. "If we are ever going to be helpful," he said, "we must be helpful while we are still imperfect. The command is not, 'Let him that is perfect help the imperfect,' but rather, 'Let him that is strong help the weak.' " [78] The American people, if true to their destiny, could help the weak of all races and creeds. Stimulated by "civil and religious liberty, universal education and the right to participate . . . in all the affairs of government," they could teach individuals to respect the rights of others, proclaim equality before the law, "excite in other races a desire for self-government and a determination to secure it," and imprint the American flag "upon the hearts of all who long for freedom." American civilization could truly become "Time's noblest offspring." [79]

III

*

* * *

*

THE CROSS OF GOLD

Taking a page from Emerson, Professor Ralph Gabriel suggests that a *volksglaube* thrives best if it has "a fallacy to expose, a blunder to pillory." [1] The acute distress that hovered darkly over the plains in the last years of the nineteenth century provided a setting well suited to the elaboration of a middle western faith. An agricultural revolution had gradually replaced diversified farming with a highly specialized, technologically complex, capitalistic form of business enterprise. [2] Finding himself a part of the cash-market economy, dependent on railroads, middlemen, and other distributive facilities, in constant need of capital, and compelled to assume greater risks than ever before, many a prairie farmer failed to achieve the prosperity he had thought would be his in the Garden of the World. Whatever the causes of his suffering, real or imagined, he had his own way of looking at economic realities. He did not question the beliefs that were his inheritance; he sought instead the defect, the sin, in American life that thwarted his progress and suppressed his optimism. He seized upon a hero created in his own image and a devil created in the image of his oppressors, and he breathed into them the breath of that life which legendary figures enjoy.

43

It was after contemplation of those mythical beings that the yeoman of the Middle Border found fallacies to expose and blunders to pillory. It was then too that he found a spokesman in William Jennings Bryan, prophet of the faith that made his reasoning plausible.

Agrarian Unrest

Preachers and poets, essayists and editors, advertisers and orators, seers and statesmen had taught the farmer to regard himself as the "bone and sinew of the nation." He had been taught that the contented yeoman, garnering the products of the land God had given him, was a figure of noble proportions, the ideal man and the ideal citizen. Living in close and harmonious communion with a bountiful nature, he was led to believe that he had acquired an integrity and in mid-America enjoyed a salubrity incomprehensible to the depraved populations of urban centers.[3] The Middle West had clearly justified even the high hopes of missionary planners; it had become "a land of churches, and schools, and charities, of pious homes, and great religious enterprises."

Furthermore, the yeoman who achieved those results was to be rewarded materially as well as spiritually. The tiller of prairie sod had been told that the Platte Valley was a "flowery meadow of great fertility clothed in nutritious grasses, and watered by numerous streams"; he had been told to follow prairie dogs and Mormons if he wished to find good land; he had been told that in the West the yield was often thirty bushels of wheat per acre, and seventy of corn.[4] The weather, so often intemperate on the plains, roguishly lent its support to western propagandists. An unusual amount of rainfall in Colorado and on the high plains of Kansas and Nebraska during the eight years before 1887 seemed to substantiate the optimistic theory that settlement, tree planting, plowing, and irrigation would make such precipitation permanent.[5] Surely the Middle Border would continue to prosper. Happy and honest, the source of civic virtue, the sturdy yeoman of the western agrarian tradition would tap the potential of the plains and transform the Great American Desert of the past into the Garden of Eden of the future. But in the decade of the nineties the dream of the prairie farmer vanished, leaving only chimerical vapors to remind him of its existence—and to increase his bitterness.

In a famous editorial, written in 1896 at the height of rural unrest, William Allen White asked a rhetorical question: "What's the matter with Kansas?" [6] The answer suggested by the staunchly Republican Emporia editor was not intended to please long-suffering farmers, but the question was crucial. What was the matter with Kansas? What, indeed, was the matter with agrarian sections of the entire West?

By the late nineteenth century farm mechanization had wrought agricultural wonders of deep significance. The invention of soil-working implements, seed planters, cultivators, and hay-making and harvesting machines resulted in fantastic savings in man-hours of labor. A one-acre crop of wheat which had required over sixty-one hours of hand labor could be harvested in less than three hours, twenty minutes by machine. Thirty-eight hours, forty-five minutes on one acre of corn was cut to fifteen hours, eight minutes. [7] Farmers invested heavily in new farm implements, often going into debt on the assumption that they could pay for them later out of what they could earn. With the new implements the farmer could till more land, and he not infrequently mort-gaged his holdings and made other sacrifices in order to expand his operations. Mechanization encouraged product specialization, and cash crop cultivation became commonplace. Urban indus-trialization also influenced the lives of farmers and their families; spinning and weaving were unprofitable when the real cost of store clothes was less than that of homemade garments. As Pro-fessor John D. Hicks has suggested, the independence of the farmer began to disappear when he, "like the manufacturer, came to produce a commodity for sale, and to live, not directly upon the fruits of the soil, but upon the profits of his factory farm." [8]

Farm commodities, however, were not the only source of profit. The rapid expansion of the agricultural frontier in the nine-teenth century led to phenomenal rises in land values, and this in turn created a boom psychology. Farmers often tended to rely on this process of appreciation for their margin of profit, and to capitalize more and more on it. When its real attachment was to land values and not to land itself, the agrarian society of the

United States developed a peculiar mobility.[9] The interplay among various forces at work on American agriculture thus becomes apparent: mechanization aided rapid expansion, expansion resulted in appreciation of land values, the appreciation of land values induced speculators to encourage further expansion, and increased expansion (particularly in the subhumid areas of the plains region) was a challenge to mechanical genius.[10] The product of these influences was a rootless and harried farmer-businessman who gambled with his land when he was not competing with carriers, middlemen, and manufacturers for a share of the consumer's dollar.

Insecure as his position was, the prairie farmer was made sharply aware of other problems facing him. In marketing his cash crop he learned gloomy facts about railroads and railroad rates. From specializing in one kind of grain he discovered the middleman and was startled by the disparity between the prices of what he sold and the prices of what he bought. These difficulties were more in evidence in some sections of the West than in others. The eastern portions of the Middle West managed to remain relatively prosperous as compared with the trans-Missouri West (and with the South), and the reason for this prosperity lay in greater diversification. The corn-livestock belt, which extended from Ohio westward through Iowa, experienced fewer economic pressures from railroads and middlemen than did wheat-growing areas.[11] But out on the plains, far from his market and with little choice of carrier, the wheat farmer found that the costs of marketing his product often resulted in losses.

In spite of great expectations, then, and in part because of them, farmers of the Dakotas, Nebraska, and Kansas suffered reverses in the late eighties and throughout the nineties. And for somewhat different reasons hard times prevailed in the cotton South as well. Because of wide variation and inadequate data, farm prices have been an enigma.[12] Nevertheless, it has been clearly established that markets for corn, wheat, and cotton were unfavorable and transactions frequently ruinous. The base-price index plummeted from 132 in 1865 to 46.5 in 1896, and agricultural prices were considerably below the average for all commodities.[13] When the price of Kansas corn dropped to ten cents a bushel, it was apparently burned as fuel, a move hardly likely to warm the cockles of the rural heart whatever its effects on room temperature may have been. "Many a time," recalled Vernon L. Parrington, "have I warmed myself by the kitchen stove in which ears were burning briskly, popping and crackling in the jolliest fashion. And if while we sat around such a fire watching the year's crop go up the chimney, the talk sometimes became bitter . . . who will wonder?" [14]

Freight rates charged by railroads worked an additional hardship upon many farmers, particularly those in the trans-Mississippi West. Ton-mile rates on western and southern railroads were often twice to three times as high as rates between Chicago and New York. In 1877 rates charged by the Burlington were four times as high west of the Missouri River as they were east of it. Rate wars, long-and-short haul discrimination, rebating, pooling arrangements, and traffic associations consistently worked to the disadvantage of the farmer. Charged higher rates, shippers at noncompetitive points were forced to help the railroads make up losses incurred in rate wars. The long-and-short haul incubus was particularly exasperating. The cost of shipping grain from Chicago to Liverpool was less than from some Dakota farms to Minneapolis.[15]

The railroads insisted that the rates were not unreasonable, and they could point to the fact that in 1895, thirteen of the twenty-four roads operating in Kansas were in the hands of receivers. In the same year, railroads in the Dakotas earned $228,000 less than enough to pay taxes after operating expenses were deducted.[16] The farmer, of course, was not impressed by official statements from railroad statisticians; he was much more inclined to listen to Jerry Simpson, who blamed the rate squeeze on stock watering. According to his estimates, the construction costs of 8,000 miles of Kansas railroad had been $100,000,000, whereas they were capitalized at $300,000,000 and bonded for an equal amount. "We who use the roads," he concluded, "are really paying interest on $600,000,000 instead of on $100,000,000 as we ought to." [17]

The problems of the farmer, serious though they were, could be met as long as eastern and foreign capital continued to flow into the agricultural areas and harvests remained good. Adequate moisture on the plains resulted in the favorable seasons of 1883-1884. And the availability of money for loans led to widespread if not extravagant speculation prior to 1887. In Kansas and North Dakota there was one mortgage for every two people, and in Nebraska, South Dakota, and Minnesota there was one for every three.[18] The rates at which money was loaned varied greatly from county to county. In general, the older areas were more successful in securing lower interest rates than were the newly settled regions. Proximity to railroads, acceptability of land titles, and quality of soil also helped to determine the rate charged. These considerations, which were certainly justifiable from the investor's viewpoint, nevertheless meant that those who were least able to pay were charged highest interest rates.[19] Whatever the rate, many farmers had done little toward paying off their mortgages when the land boom collapsed, and the 11,000 foreclosures in Kansas between 1889 and 1893 were indicative of what took place in most of the wheat-growing areas.[20]

At this point when the money needs of the western farmer were greater than ever before, he found himself beset by insistent demands for more funds. He was faced not only with the problem of paying installments on mortgages and farm machinery, but also with the necessity of paying his taxes and maintaining his credit with merchants from whom he obtained his supplies. The farmer in this predicament, debt-ridden and finding money hard to come by, reduced his economic hardship to simple terms. The shortage of money, he thought, was the root of all evil.[21] He had seen the population of the United States doubled since the Civil War; he had seen the volume of business expanded. Yet in spite of those developments, the number of dollars in circulation had actually declined so that the value of the dollar in 1895 was three times what it had been in 1865.[22] For the mortgagor of the West, the appreciating dollar meant paying back far more (in terms of volume of commodities) than had been borrowed.

What, then, was the matter with Kansas? In 1893, in response to a questionnaire sent out by the state bureau of labor and industry, farmers ticked off the items: low prices, drought, money scarcity, high interest rates, high railroad rates, high taxes, middlemen.[23] In analyzing the causes of their grievances, however, they found it difficult if not impossible to recognize harsh economic facts. The myth of the virtuous yeoman was too deeply ingrained. For generations the United States had been primarily a nation of farmers, and even after trade's unfeeling train had usurped the land, the farmer was identified with democracy and with the only kind of nobility possible in a democracy—nobility of character. He was a special creature, peculiarly blessed by God. If this was generally true of the American farmer, it was particularly true of those who braved drought, prairie fires, grasshopper plagues, blizzards, and chinch bugs, and who survived the yet more terrible isolation of the wind-swept plains in the West. Lot had chosen the well-watered valley of the Jordan, but God made his covenant with Abraham, who had been left with the land of Canaan. The prairie farmer was therefore incapable of seeing himself as an organic part of the national economy. Special creature that he was, he nevertheless had to account for his plight. And so he adopted an explanation: he was the victim of a vast conspiracy emanating from urban financial centers.[24] Eastern and foreign capitalists, reasoned the farmer, had deliberately brought about his misery.

One of the most popular themes in American folklore of an earlier day is that of the sophisticated sharper who finds himself outwitted by those he considers gullible bumpkins. Yet the farmer during the period of agrarian unrest could not fit this theme to his own experience. He was obviously losing the game. Why? Mere wit and cleverness he could match, but his antagonists seemed to be aided by something more: the occult powers of the Evil One. Apparently in league with Satan, these men had invested in mortgages and bonds and railroad stocks; they fixed the prices on grain and cotton; through their corrupting influence over state governments, they benefitted from the taxes he paid. Railroad rates were high that they might receive dividends, and farm prices were low that they might accumulate profits. The farmer, Richard Hofstadter has remarked, wove "a vast fabric of social explanation out of nothing but skeins of evil plots." [25]

In this analysis, western and southern farmers were joined by residents of other sections. In Colorado, for example, there was widespread recognition that the development of the mineral empire was dependent upon outside capital. To many it seemed that eastern and foreign investors had made the Rocky Mountain West, with all its resources, a fief of Wall Street.[26] With such support, the farmer refused to admit that improved communications had gone far toward making the world an economic unit, and that the low prices he received were indicative of an international price decline brought about, in part, by the extensive cultivation of hitherto untapped agricultural areas. He refused to admit that he had embarked on his current operations with insufficient capital, or that vast tracts of land in subhumid regions should never have been subjected to his plow. But he could readily believe the assertions of the Wichita *Courier:*

> All this gigantic loaning on western real estate represents millions of English capital wrung from the poor of India by British brutality and shrewdness. Having invested their money they proceed to reduce the volume of our money by bribery and that masterly policy which they know well how to use. It is well known that the mortgage holder in most cases wants to get the property . . . and secure the owner as a tenant. When the foreclosures are finished up the proper measures will be taken to increase the volume of money . . . and hold our population as English tenants.[27]

This and similar allegations made a significant impression on William Jennings Bryan and his supporters. For the prophet of midwestern moralism to agree with the farmer's conception of social sin was easy and natural. "You may go to New York or Boston and find financiers who doubt the greatness of this country and proclaim the necessity for foreign aid," he said in a typical observation during the campaign of 1896, "but the men who do that know more about Europe than they do about the United States." Those true patriots who were willing to cast their lot with the Republic had the right and the power to take the reins of government into their own hands and "administer the law, not for foreign syndicates, but for the people of the United States." The "money trust" had made puppets of public servants in the past, and there was no reason to believe that it would abandon its efforts to control policy in the future. Responsible officials had "no more right to betray the people into the hands of financiers of London than Benedict Arnold had to betray the American colonies into the hands of the British," yet that is precisely what would happen if the people did not foil the devil and restore justice to American life.[28]

Populists and Democrats

At the turn of the century, Flavius J. VanVorhis, chairman of the Indiana Silver Republican Committee, wrote a letter providing a link in the chain of recrimination against financial houses which was a dominant theme of Bryan's correspondence:

> I do not see how any one can fail to realize that combinations beginning in New York of which the New York Association of Banks was the first organization, have been the foundation upon which has been builded all the subsequent combinations that now threaten the abandonment of the principles upon which our government was founded. For years the influences that organized and controlled this combination of banks, have controlled the organizations and machinery of both parties and kept them in a condition that it was a matter of no consequence to the financial interests which party succeeded in an election.[29]

Long before VanVorhis penned this indictment, the farmers had attempted to secure redress of grievances and alleviation of suffering by political means. In trying politics, however, they had found political parties wanting. "The parties lie to us and political speakers mislead us," said Mary E. Lease bitterly.[30] John Peter Altgeld was not a western farmer, but he agreed. "To be an eligible candidate now," he said in 1895, "often means to stand for nothing in particular and to represent no definite principle, but to be all things to all men and, in the end, be contemptible." Corruption resulting from the concentration of capital, he thought, had tainted everything it touched, including politics, with "moral leprosy." [31]

Political disillusionment born of economic disillusionment resulted in the launching of a full-scale attack upon the methods and forms of American politics. Pathetically aware of the indifference of major parties, and repelled by the activities of spoilsmen in both Republican and Democratic ranks, many farmers and agrarian sympathizers in the West and South saw a third party as the only way out of their distress. If both of the major parties refused to recognize agricultural problems or deal adequately with them, then dissatisfied farmers would have nothing to lose by forming a party of their own.

And so the People's party was born. For several years in the nineties Populist hopes ran high; it seemed to them not inconceivable that they could do what the Republican party had done earlier—become one of the governing parties. During those years leaders of the new party patiently developed a program embracing a multitude of reforms designed to meet the fundamental problems of land, transportation, and finance. It was a program that included, among other things, the free coinage of silver at a ratio of sixteen to one; a circulating medium of at least $50 per capita as opposed to the $20 per capita then operative; a graduated income tax; postal savings banks; government ownership and operation of all railroads and telegraph and telephone systems; reclamation of all alien landholdings; the initiative and referendum; the direct election of senators; and one term only for the President and Vice President.[32] Populists were not content merely to mouth the hackneyed phrases of old-line politicians, or to prop up dead political horses. They wished to hear discussions on "the living questions of financial and other reforms." [33]

Populists, however, predicated their hopes for success upon an assumption that was delusive in its simplicity. They believed that there was a natural bond of interest among the producing classes, among farmers, workers, small businessmen, and toilers everywhere. And they hoped for a working alliance among those groups that constituted the "producing masses." As one Populist manifesto proclaimed:

> There are but two sides in the conflict that is being waged in this country today. On the one side are the allied hosts of monopolies, the money power, great trusts and railroad corporations who seek the enactment of laws to benefit them and impoverish the people. On the other are the farmers, laborers, merchants, and all other people who produce wealth and bear the burdens of taxation. . . . Between these two there is no middle group.[34]

Concentrating on a kind of social dualism that pitted the common people against the hosts of wickedness, party leaders tended to ignore the heterogeneous character of American society. They had to learn from experience that small businessmen and farmers did not always agree, or that eastern laborers might have their own peculiar interests, or that southern farmers could be as concerned with racial as they were with economic questions.

There were other chinks in the Populist armor. There was, for example, the problem of leadership. Farmers had seldom elevated men of the soil to political office; they had depended, for the most part, upon country lawyers, small-town editors, and other professional men to serve as their spokesmen. Disappointed in the achievements of such persons, they had finally turned to their own ranks, only to be disappointed again. "If the farmer went to the capital fresh from the plow, among a crowd of lobbyists," observed one writer, "he was as clay in the hands of a potter. If his constituents kept him there year after year, until he learned the ways of legislation, then he ceased to be a farmer and became a member of some other class." [35] It was this failure to secure adequate representation that had been a major impetus behind the formation of a third political party. Yet the new party still did not attract many leaders who could speak for agrarian interests and at the same time win elections. It is a matter of no small significance that while Populist leadership included men who had a genuine devotion to agrarian principles, it also included men who had experienced the monotony of years of political failure and who had an overweening passion for success at the polls. The desire for victory left them open to temptation; they were willing to barter part of their program in exchange for public office.[36] This willingness accounts, in part, for two developments that sounded the death knell of the Populist party; one was the rise of the free silver issue to monolithic proportions, and the other was fusion with the Democracy.

Populist speakers had learned during the campaign of 1892 that free silver had a wider appeal than any other plank in the platform. If, as the farmer had been led to believe, the "money power" had organized a great conspiracy to rob him of his birthright, then currency reform was the one proposal that laid an axe to the root of his difficulties. In the meantime, other influences tended to focus the nation's attention on the money question. A severe depression followed in the wake of the panic of 1893, and Grover Cleveland secured repeal of the Sherman Silver Purchase Act, which he insisted had brought on the economic crisis. Little was accomplished by repeal, however, for other problems emerged. Secretary of the Treasury Carlisle had to work frantically to maintain the gold reserve through bond issues.[37] Even though the gold standard was preserved, hard times persisted. All the labors of the Cleveland administration served merely to underscore the Populist belief that greedy financiers were playing fast and loose with the people's welfare in order to multiply ill-gotten gains.

Free silver, therefore, became the symbol not only of reform of the currency, but of a righteous revolt against plutocratic government as well. And to think of the silver issue in isolation apart from the social and economic conditions that contributed to its appeal is, as James A. Barnes has suggested, "not merely to leave Hamlet out of the play; it is to omit the play altogether." [38] Yet silver inflation did have an allurement separate from its symbolic significance; in the view of the prairie farmer, inflation of any kind was a panacea worth trying. He wanted an elastic currency that could be expanded as the needs of agrarian debtors dictated. Many Populists were committed not to silver but to what they considered an honest dollar. "If gold and silver cannot be issued in sufficient volume," said Ignatius Donnelly, "by all means let us have paper money." [39] In the nineties, however, the free coinage of silver seemed to promise the kind and quantity of currency the farmers sought. Finally, there was a further advantage in the adoption of the silver cause. Those Populists who favored it fondly hoped that it would unite the mineral West, the agricultural prairies, and the cotton South under the People's party banner, and that it would also prevent the formation of a separate silver party. "It seems to me that at no time since our party was organized have the prospects for a great victory been so flattering as today," wrote national chairman H. E. Taubeneck just before the political conventions of 1896.[40]

While the silver issue had a certain utility, dangers were inherent in the sacrifices Populists made for its sake. Campaigning on free silver without reference to any of the other planks in the Populist platform (a policy advocated by General Weaver, Taubeneck, and others) meant tailoring the agrarian program to suit the tastes of those who had little sympathy with other reforms. A western silver mine owner or an eastern merchant could support silver vigorously but at the same time oppose the farmers' solution to problems of land and transportation.[41] Organizational changes as well as compromises on principle could develop from emphasis on free silver. Republicans and Democrats both counted silverites among their number. Instead of joining the People's party as its leaders hoped, outsiders might effect a fusion in which Populists would lose their identity.

Yet if both major parties came out in opposition to silver inflation during the campaign of 1896, it was just possible that Populists would be able to establish their authority over dissident Republicans and Democrats.[42] Taubeneck was less certain of a split in the Democratic party than he was of a Silver Republican bolt; yet he believed that "the Administration and the gold-bugs" would control the Democratic convention.[43] Bryan himself had urged Populist leaders to delay meeting until after the two major parties had committed themselves to platforms and candidates. The Populist convention could then "take advantage of the errors of the old parties" and with greater ease "bring about a consolidation of all the silver forces." [44] But at Chicago, Democrats repudiated the only President they had elected in forty years, nailed a silver plank securely to the platform, and nominated the Nebraskan who told administration men that they could not "crucify mankind upon a cross of gold."

The Populists, who had staked everything on the possibility that the party of Grover Cleveland would never deny him, were thrown into confusion. Ignatius Donnelly posed for himself the vital question: "Shall we or shall we not endorse Bryan for president?" He clearly saw what such endorsement might mean. "I like Bryan," he wrote, "but I do not feel that we can safely adopt the Dem. candidates. I fear it will be the end of our party."[45] The middle-of-the-road or orthodox element was inclined to ignore the action of the Democrats. As one loyal member of that faction put it, "Let the old Rotten Democrat machine with its camp followers, gold bugs, place hunters, straddle bugs, humbugs, demagogues etc. etc. go to the devil." [46] On the other hand there were proponents of compromise, particularly in the West, who favored acceptance of the Democratic slate. William V. Allen, Senator from Nebraska, was a strong Bryan man, and Governor

Davis H. "Bloody Bridles" Waite of Colorado wrote that "the silver crowd *must* support him." [47]

In the end Populists saw no alternative to Bryan, and he was duly nominated at their St. Louis convention. They did, however, see an alternative to Arthur Sewall, the Democracy's nominee for Vice President. Over strenuous objections from Democrats, Tom Watson, self-styled Jeffersonian radical from Georgia, became vice-presidential candidate of the People's party. The compromise at St. Louis complicated matters, for it gave Bryan two running mates and completely satisfied no one. (The Democratic idea of fusion, said Watson, was "that we play Jonah while they play whale." [48]) Most Populists nevertheless displayed a marked willingness to cooperate with Democrats in the common cause. Even middle-of-the-road Ignatius Donnelly campaigned for Bryan and entertained the hope that he would receive a cabinet appointment for his efforts. As the campaign wore on, he persuaded himself that his candidate had been "raised up by Providence to save the country from sinking into old world conditions." [49]

Bryan undoubtedly had a remarkable capacity to engender devotion and confidence. "I do not believe he can be beaten," James Manahan wrote his wife from Lincoln where he was in the thick of the fight. "I firmly believe that God is on his side and helping him for the sake of the poor all over the world. He is right and right must win over evil and injustice." [50] Whether or not Bryan was on the side of the angels is beside the point: his campaign was far more attractive to western farmers than to the urban poor. Mark Hanna, Republican campaign manager, shrewdly observed, "He's talking Silver all the time, and that's where we've got him." [51] The G.O.P., with a campaign fund at least ten times that of the Democracy, hired 1400 speakers to counter Bryan's thrusts. The burden of their message was essentially the theme of McKinley's letter of acceptance:

> It is not an increase in the volume of money which is the need of the time, but an increase in the volume of business. Not an increase of coin, but an increase of confidence. Not more coinage, but a more active use of the money coined. Not open mints for the unlimited coinage of the silver of the world, but open mills for the full and unrestricted labor of American workingmen. [52]

That coercion was used by employers has been clearly established. Yet a significant segment of the labor vote went to McKinley because it was believed that labor had nothing to gain from the free coinage of silver. After listening to Republican orators, urban workmen were not sure that they wanted the world's silver poured into United States mints. And many were certain that they did not want to be paid in fifty-three-cent dollars.[53]

Election day came and went. Bryan polled more votes than any candidate had ever received before—and lost. He had carried on a strenuous campaign in the Middle West and the Northeast, but every state east of the Mississippi and north of the Ohio went to McKinley. The Nebraskan's strength in urban areas was remarkable (fully two-thirds of his popular vote came from McKinley states), yet it was not enough.[54] Up at Nininger, Minnesota, Ignatius Donnelly read with mounting dismay the telegraphic reports that brought the news of Bryan's defeat. He opened his diary and poured out his feelings: "Will the long lane never have a turning? Will the sun of triumph never rise? I fear not."[55] If his fears were for the People's party, they were justified.

Bryan and Silver after 1896

Populists never recovered from the disastrous campaign of 1896. To make matters worse, many feared that their carefully constructed reform program had been annihilated along with the party organization. "Free silver is the cowbird of the reform movement," complained Henry Demarest Lloyd. "It waited until the nest had been built by the sacrifices and labour of others, and then it laid its eggs in it, pushing out the others which lie smashed on the ground."[56] Some historians have tended to disagree with this assessment. They have suggested that the eggs were not smashed at all; on the contrary, it has been argued, they hatched peeping chicks that contributed to a grand crowing chorus of reform as they sprouted their wings. On the other hand, recent students of twentieth-century progressivism have demonstrated that much of its impetus was urban rather than rural in origin, and that progressive legislation was not a direct result of agrarian agitation. The difficulty with the view that Populism brought about the progressive movement is that it is superficial.

It fails to take into account the differences in economic outlook and motivation which distinguished the two waves of reform. One inadequacy of the urban interpretation is that it ignores William Jennings Bryan and his following.[57]

It is true that Bryan was bound to the People's party with silver chains, but he by no means rejected all other reforms it proposed. He insisted throughout the period from 1896 to 1912 that "conditions make issues; parties must meet issues as they arise." [58] In 1896 the silver question was paramount because of economic conditions then prevailing, but the Democratic platform also contained planks demanding arbitration of labor disputes, trial by jury in contempt proceedings arising out of the issuance of injunctions, maintenance of a tariff for revenue only, an income tax, enlargement of the powers of the Interstate Commerce Commission, and extension of the Civil Service.[59] While Bryan did not emphasize those planks during his first campaign, he later built up a program embodying a variety of reforms, many of which had been urged by the Populists. His continuous agitation for reform served as a stimulus to his victorious Republican opponents. He commanded considerable support and they could ill afford to deal cavalierly with his demands. Perhaps Bryan was right when he said that the radical was necessary to make the conservative move forward. In any case his opposition leadership was a link between the agrarian crusade of the nineteenth century and the progressive movement of the twentieth.

In 1925 H. L. Mencken listed what he considered to be the contradictions of Bryan's life and concluded that "if the fellow was sincere, then so was P. T. Barnum." [60] From time to time Bryan did vary the stress he placed upon issues, adopt reforms to meet new needs, or develop new remedies for old abuses. But to infer from this that his course was a vacillating one, or to suggest that he was protean in his espousal of any new issue that might capture votes, is to overlook the extraordinary consistency with which he attempted to translate his fundamental convictions into social, economic, and political realities. His consistency was one of the reasons for his effectiveness as an opposition leader, and nowhere was it more evident than in his pronouncements on free silver after his defeat in 1896.

The silver tumult gradually died down after McKinley entered the White House. The cyanide process for reducing gold from ore and the discovery of new deposits in Alaska, Australia, and South Africa increased world output of the precious metal from an average of five or six million ounces annually to 22,000,000 ounces by 1910. Both drought and floods damaged European crops in 1897, and American wheat exports almost doubled. As a result of those developments gold began to come into the country in significant volume for the first time since 1891, and the inflation that farmers had demanded came about even though their advocate had lost the election. Then too for various reasons the business cycle took an upward turn, signalling a recovery that would bring more credit to farmers and bolster higher prices for agricultural commodities.[61] Republicans, of course, suavely accepted the thanks of a nation grateful for its new prosperity, and many a Democrat wondered why his party had listened to the siren song of silver.

Bryan refused to believe that the Democracy had been deluded. Principles that were true in 1896 would also be true in 1900, or 1996 for that matter. "We have only to stand firm," he wrote Governor Altgeld, "and we shall yet be able to drive the gold monopoly, the trusts and the syndicates from the national capitol." [62] It was not easy to stand firm when prosperity returned. Friends and supporters tried to persuade him that inclusion of a silver plank in the platform of 1900 would be a political mistake and that the Chicago platform should be reaffirmed in general terms only. "We cannot, cannot, cannot and will not, will not, take up '16 to 1' in the East," wrote newspaperman James Creelman from New York.[63] William Randolph Hearst wired "that the people don't want free silver and that we can't make them want free silver and that if we try we will lose the opportunity to do great good in other directions." [64] Bryan men in the West too thought specific restatement of the silver plank unnecessary. "We did declare our position on that subject very clearly in 1896," noted Governor William J. Stone of Missouri, "and if we now say that we reaffirm and reindorse that declaration, how does it strengthen us with silver men to specifically restate the proposition?" A silver plank in 1900 he thought would be superfluous.[65]

Trenchant though such arguments may have been, Bryan could not be budged from his position. If the party still believed what it had said in 1896, he wrote Stone, "there ought to be no backwardness about so stating it that it cannot be misunderstood or misconstrued." [66] He refused to dodge or straddle, and in a letter to national chairman James K. Jones he made his views unmistakably clear: "I believe that a reaffirmation of the Chicago platform, no matter how explicit, would be regarded as evasive of the money question if we reiterate other things in the platform and fail to reiterate the silver plank." [67] The Kansas City convention yielded to Bryan's wishes; after some delay and the threat of a fight on the floor, it once more wrote free silver into the campaign. While its action may have been a tactical error, the Democratic nominee had no regrets when he was making his second race for the presidency, nor did he have any later. He told Carter Harrison that a general reaffirmation of the Chicago platform would have lost more votes than it might have gained. And this was the opinion he held until the day he died.[68]

Bryan was not ready to admit in 1900 that sufficient gold had been released to make bimetalism unnecessary. "The thing to be desired is a stable dollar," he told the Bryan Traveling Men's Club in St. Louis after his second defeat, "and that can only be secured by legislation which will furnish a volume of standard money sufficient to keep pace with the demand for money." The nation had as yet been given no assurance that gold alone could satisfy that demand.[69] Not until 1907 did he concede that free silver had become a dead letter. And even then he maintained that it was no longer an issue because the principle he represented had been vindicated:

In 1896 the republican speakers were talking about the possibilities of a flood of silver, and yet, today, the annual production of gold is greater than the annual production of both gold and silver in 1896. This increase in the world's supply of money has been felt the world over and the "period of the Roosevelt administration" has been marked by improved conditions in Europe as well as in America.[70]

Meanwhile, changing times had created new issues to claim Bryan's attention.

IV

*

  *   *   *

*

PARTY POLITICS AND IMPERIALISM

WILLIAM JENNINGS BRYAN and the Populists had many things in common, for they shared the moralistic heritage of the Middle West. Both were agrarian in background and sympathy, both believed that government should be controlled by the "common people," both would place restrictions upon the greed of those who exploited the poor and the underprivileged, both had implicit faith in the destiny of a reformed America. Similar though their ends were, however, Bryan and the Populists differed markedly as to means. The Populists worked hard to form a new party devoted to certain principles; Bryan labored for similar causes within the Democratic party. The Peerless Leader thus chose to follow a course which Populists eschewed, even though major parties did respond to their demands. They prepared the way for overthrow of the most iniquitous spoilsmen; their agitation roused the nation from apathy and taught politicians to respect righteous political indignation.[1] Bryan carried the movement a step further by insisting that the Democracy write into its platforms the principles for which he stood. Yet he did not stop at this point. Because he was never elected to the presidency, he could not use his platforms as a foundation for administrative action, but as leader of the minority party he measured Republican administrations by the plumb line of his principles. The Spanish-American War with its militaristic and imperialistic implications provided the first real test of his opposition leadership.

Political Parties and American Democracy

The significance of Bryan's activities in opposition to the Republican majority can best be seen in relationship to the structure of American politics and to criticisms of American parties made by some of his contemporaries. The United States is democratic, but democracy is a word with many definitions: "government by the people"; "government by consent of the governed"; "government by discussion among free men"; "government based upon political equality and majority rule." Such definitions, moreover, suggest merely the location of ultimate power; they do little to indicate how power is to be made effective. It is as agencies through which power may be exercised that political parties have a place in democratic societies.[2] Parties of a democracy may vary in number and in composition, but national politics—if not state politics—in the United States have usually been carried on under the direction of two major parties. This is not to say that the two parties have always functioned efficiently, or that, as Professor Hicks has put it, "thanks to the Republican cloud of righteousness by day and the Democratic pillar of fire by night, the nation has somehow never lacked for wise leadership." [3] On the contrary, a persistent criticism is that major parties have not made any notable contribution toward framing issues or carrying out programs to which voters have given approval.

In the Bryan era a number of political scientists came to believe that a thorough transformation was essential if parties were to be of any real service. Woodrow Wilson, A. Lawrence Lowell, Henry Jones Ford, Frank J. Goodnow, and others argued for "responsible party government." [4] When two major parties are distinguished by the principles which they adopt, their argument runs, conflicts of opinion and program result. Yet a stalemate is avoided by granting temporary power to the majority organization and giving the minority an opportunity to criticize those who must initiate and carry out policies. Through such criticism limitations are placed upon the use of power, new ideas and reforms are suggested, and the electorate is kept informed on issues. Responsible parties are necessarily disciplined, i.e., members vote together and are in other ways unified. Citizens can associate legislation and policy with a party rather than with individuals, and at the polls the majority party can be called to account for how the government has been run. Thus the electorate controls government even though it does not participate in its day-to-day activities.

Advocates of responsible two-party government demonstrated that in no sense could the parties of the United States be described as "responsible." In 1885 Woodrow Wilson pointed to the difference between their behavior outside and their behavior inside Congress:

> Outside of Congress the organization of the national parties is exceedingly well-defined and tangible; no one could wish it, and few could imagine it, more so; but within Congress it is obscure and intangible. Our parties marshal their adherents with the strictest possible discipline for the purpose of carrying elections, but their discipline is very slack and indefinite in dealing with legislation. At least there is within Congress no *visible*, and therefore no controllable party organization. The only bond of cohesion is the caucus, which occasionally whips a party together for cooperative action against the time for casting its vote upon some critical question.[5]

Until the schizophrenia of political parties—their unity outside the formal government as opposed to their decentralization inside it—could be resolved, Wilson believed that the power of spoilsmen could never be broken and responsible party government could never be established. He therefore found it necessary to consider the question of why parties operated as they did, and his analysis furnishes a provocative insight into workings of the political machinery of his day.[6]

Wilson accepted the view that the real leaders of parties were not the ostensible leaders; the real ones were the local political bosses concerned more with private gain than with public policy. He did not, however, agree with some contemporary analysts that the causes of bossism lay in the reluctance of honest and upright citizens to enter the political arena. He thought that boss rule and party irresponsibility resulted from something more fundamental: the basic structure of American politics itself. From writings published prior to his election as President, the Wilson argument can be reconstructed.

In the first place, he believed that a consistent line of policy could be produced only by effective leadership, and that when men in positions of power constantly worked against one another leadership could not be effective. In 1885 he asserted that rivalry among the three branches of government had resulted in the conquest of executive and judiciary by Congress. Unhappily, that body was so organized into standing committees working in jealous independence of one another that it was incapable of real leadership even within itself.[7] The President could not be expected to reassert his authority because, as Lord Bryce also suggested, the "great men" were not usually elected to the presidency.[8] Almost twenty-five years later, when a growth in the power of the executive caused Wilson to modify his views, he still maintained that "you cannot compound a successful government out of antagonisms."[9]

Another contention, which Wilson expressed most clearly in 1908 when he published *Constitutional Government in the United States,* was that the only alternative to chaos was domination by someone. Inasmuch as there was no provision for leadership within the framework of the official or formal government, outside agencies had to provide it. If the organs of government were to be united, in other words, they would have to be united by political parties. It was through their caucuses and their conventions that the "indispensable means of agreement and cooperation" was brought about; it was the party system that directed the government of the United States, "both in its policy and in its personnel."[10]

Finally, Wilson observed that if the parties were to carry out the tasks which had devolved upon them they could not risk being as leaderless as was the formal government. It was this need, he felt, which gave rise to political bosses who devoted all their energies to running the party and who put puppets into office with the power they controlled. The worst consequence of boss rule was the secrecy with which it operated. "I would a great deal rather live under a king whom I should at least know," he said during the campaign of 1912, "than under a boss whom I don't know." [11] Working in secrecy, bosses were able to concentrate upon the spoils of party management—patronage and graft —because voters could not hold them responsible for carrying out public policies.[12]

Unquestionably, much of the criticism that developed out of the age of spoilsmen was justified. After the Reconstruction period the two major parties had come to hold entrenched positions. On matters of principle they stood for little or nothing; their platforms were composed of generalities designed to catch votes, not to serve as a blueprint for legislation. Torchlight processions, waving of the bloody shirt of the Rebellion, and other "hurrah" methods employed during political campaigns obscured the fact that their programs were virtually indistinguishable. Party leaders, bosses and officeholders alike, had concern for the popular will only to the extent that they could exploit it. Nor did some of them care much for fame or glory. Lord Bryce agreed with Wilson that plunder and spoils provided the most compelling political force in the United States. Politics, he observed, had become "a gainful profession, like advocacy, stockbroking, or the getting up of companies." Its attractions consisted in salaries and "the opportunities it affords of making incidental and sometimes illegitimate gains." [13] Such opportunities were plentiful when cynical and domineering captains of industry considered the bribing of politicians a justifiable business expense. Until the agrarian revolt focused attention on political evils, and the urban response to industrialism found expression in the progressive movement, parties were more interested in plunder and patronage than in platforms and principles; they differed on the division of political loaves and fishes, not on issues.[14]

William Jennings Bryan readily sympathized with criticism of American politics that attributed undue influence to the money power. Like Wilson, he was an advocate of two-party government because he thought it the only system capable of providing majority rule. With the proponents of responsible party government, he believed that parties should not hesitate to take unequivocal positions on controversial issues. His ideas were apparent in his attitude toward platforms, which he thought were entirely consistent with democratic representation: "A platform announces the party's position on the questions which are at issue; and an official is not at liberty to use the authority vested in him to urge personal views which have not been submitted to the voters for their approval." [15]

Refusing to consider frequent suggestions that he lead a third party movement, Bryan elaborated on his conception of what parties should be and how they should function. In 1901 he urged an Ohio follower not to "carry the idea of a separate party any farther," but rather "to support the ticket . . . and then commence at the primaries next year and obtain possession of the party." [16] Again in 1910 when Louis F. Post, disciple of Henry George and editor of *The Public,* suggested a conference of progressives from both parties, Bryan replied that little good could come of it. "No men prominent in either party would attend it," he argued, "because it would impair their standing in their own parties." Furthermore, he pointed out that if Republican insurgents or radical Democrats started talking about a new party they could only injure their chances in the fight they were waging in their respective organizations.[17] This position, which Bryan maintained consistently throughout his career after 1896, was more fully explained when he wrote:

Reforms are secured through representatives, and representatives must be elected before they can act officially. A united and compact minority may, as it often has, defeat a divided majority. The Kansas City platform [of 1900] placed a large body of men and a national organization behind a number of important reforms. While the party stands true to its position it affords the best hope that the masses have of obtaining relief, and new parties, however well-intended will retard rather than accelerate progress. Several parties composed of honest and earnest men who hold some principles in common, but differ about other questions, may by co-operation secure the things upon which they agree. But when they war among themselves, they prevent the securing of those things which they all want, without advancing the reforms about the merits of which they differ.[18]

Bryan's fealty to his party was as unswerving as the staunchest

Democrat could ask, but to independents and insurgents it was incomprehensible. "History will never be able to harmonize his courageous conduct in exposing wrong and evil and advocating righteous government, with his weak and unreasonable advocacy of the election of men to office simply because they were Democrats," wrote George Norris shortly after the Peerless Leader's death in 1925.[19] The two aspects of his career are not as irreconcilable as Senator Norris thought. The primary concern of reformers, Bryan held, should be to gain control of the party to which they belonged. If unable to nominate reform candidates, they should at least try to secure a reform platform, for candidates would be committed to the principles it contained. Failing in one or both of their objectives, they should still remain loyal to the party in order to work more effectively for acceptance of the principles in which they believed.[20] Such intense devotion to his party, right or wrong, may have contributed to Democratic unity in elections without adding to unity in Congress. Bryan may actually have helped to foster some of the evils deplored by advocates of a responsible two-party system. Yet he did believe that the majority should rule, that parties should become identified with basic principles, and that party members were bound by the discipline of their platform.

Willis Abbot, a laborer in the Commoner's vineyard, has left a story which well illustrates Bryan's allegiance to his platform and his relationships with party bosses. As the campaign of 1900 approached, Richard Croker of Tammany Hall sent for Abbot and asked him to tell Bryan that if the Nebraskan ignored the silver issue, Tammany would carry New York State for the Democratic ticket. Whether or not Bryan was aware of comic possibilities in quoting Scripture to the hard-bitten Croker, that is nevertheless what he did in his reply. "Please say to Mr. Croker," he wrote, "that I say to the Chicago platform, to every plank in it, including the silver plank, as Ruth said to Naomi: 'And Ruth said, Intreat me not to leave thee, or to return from following after thee, for whither thou goest, I will go; and where thou lodgest, I will lodge; thy people shall be my people, and thy God my God.'" Abbot recalled that when he read this passage to Croker, the powerful chieftain grew impatient. With a wave of his hand he angrily signalled Abbot to stop reading, and as he stalked off he growled, "I didn't think Bryant [sic] was that kind of a feller. You can tell him from me that I'm through." [21]

Croker later reversed himself and supported Bryan; he apparently had no other choice, so great was the Commoner's prestige in 1900.[22] But in his interview with Abbot he had unwittingly composed what might have been used as an epitaph for an age, an age in which private interests predominated over the general good. The new era saw neither the development of broad, fundamental differences between the two major parties nor the emergence of responsible party government. What it did see was an increased concern for political principles, political morality, and the public welfare.

Making Way for Liberty

In 1898 the United States threw down the gauntlet to a faded and threadbare Spanish government and for 113 days successfully fought what John Hay thought was a "splendid little war." [23] The Spanish-American War marked a turning point in American foreign policy and signalled the arrival of the United States as one of the great powers; never again was the country to enjoy the sense of security that accompanied nineteenth-century isolation. Nevertheless, most Americans appeared to welcome new responsibilities that military victory over Spain presented to them. Few citizens were, like President McKinley, in a position to see some of the incredible complexities of American involvement in affairs at remote corners of the earth. Aware of several possible courses of action and the limitations of each, McKinley had difficulty in deciding which one to take after an armistice had been signed. He paced the floor of the White House. He prayed. He finally chose to follow the popular will and the path of empire.[24]

Down in Florida Colonel William Jennings Bryan of the Third Nebraska Volunteers also pondered the nation's fate and arrived at different conclusions despite his usual confidence in the views of "the people." At the outset of war Bryan had patriotically offered his services, but unlike Theodore Roosevelt and the

Rough Riders he had seen no action. His battles were political ones, and as he awaited his release from the Army he prepared for a major engagement.[25] That he should make mistakes in the conflict over imperialism was perhaps inevitable, but the mistakes he made were tactical errors. Far better than most of his contemporaries, he understood the implications of imperialistic expansion.

If Bryan later saw the dangers of imperialism so clearly, why did he not raise his voice against going to war with Spain in the first place? One explanation may be that for all his efforts in behalf of a movement of protest, he had not yet become accustomed to criticizing the party in power from the vantage point of an opposition leader. When opportunities to attack the McKinley administration presented themselves, Bryan forbore.[26] But more important reasons for his support of the war may be added. Students of the Spanish-American conflict have shown that Bryan sections of the country were strongly in favor of military action. Hatred of oppression characteristic of the Populist revolt and silver crusade was no doubt easily transferred from the "gold ring" to Spanish tyrants in Cuba. It may well be that the frustrations of their defeat in 1896 made underdog elements in American society peculiarly susceptible to belligerent suggestions. Perhaps they looked forward to capturing the citadel of the presidency with the battle of cry of "Free Silver and Free Cuba."[27]

Whatever influence the social unrest of the nineties or political ambitions (together with nonagrarian pressures such as those emanating from the yellow journals) may have had in precipitating the conflict, it is clear that the Spanish-American War was not inconsistent with moralistic beliefs of the Middle Border. Bryan and his followers were not pacifists, however much they might respect Tolstoy and men of his convictions. William Holmes McGuffey had emphasized that wars might be good or bad, just or unjust. His Readers had taught schoolchildren to respect those patriots who had died glorious deaths for the sake of some noble cause. Arnold Winkelried was a McGuffey idol because in offering his body as a target for Austrian spears he helped to save Swiss freedom:

> "Make way for Liberty!" he cried:
> Then ran with arms extended wide,
> As if his dearest friends to clasp;
> Ten spears he swept within his grasp:
> "Make way for Liberty!" he cried,
> Their keen points met from side to side;
> He bowed among them like a tree,
> And thus made way for Liberty.[28]

This was the spirit in which William Jennings Bryan supported the declaration of war against Spain, and it was the spirit in which he enlisted in that struggle. Sacrifice in war as well as in peace was the measure of greatness. The function of the soldier was not to kill, but to be killed.[29] Bryan and many of his fellow countrymen would make way for liberty in the territories held by degenerate Spanish oppressors.

The view that Bryan countenanced the Spanish-American War out of sympathy for the Cubans is given added weight by the position he took with respect to other areas subject to imperialistic activities. Bryan thought, for example, that British rule in India was "as arbitrary and despotic as the Government of Russia ever was," and he deplored England's refusal to give the Indians any form of representative government.[30] He enthusiastically adopted the cause of the Boers during the campaign of 1900, and he wished to commit the United States to a policy of intervention little short of direct military aid. "Three quarters of a century ago, when our nation was small, the struggles of Greece aroused our people," he said in his notification speech. "In 1896, all parties manifested a lively interest in the success of the Cubans," and yet, he lamented, the advocates of imperialism could not be persuaded to say anything in behalf of the Boers when they were engaged in a struggle that "must result in the extension of the monarchical idea, or in the triumph of a republic." He warned Americans: "If this nation surrenders its belief in the universal application of the principles set forth in the Declaration of Independence, it will lose the prestige and influence which it has enjoyed among the nations as an exponent of popular government." [31] Bryan believed that the Boer War was "one of the greatest, if not the greatest, among all the heroic struggles in the world's history." It was one in which the United

States had a direct interest, for "every monarchy that is transformed into a republic strengthens the United States." [32]

When Bryan and his followers entertained such sentiments, they were easily convinced that a war for the liberation of Cuba was justifiable. Deplorable though the use of force might be, it was sometimes necessary. "Until the right has triumphed in every land and love reigns in every heart," observed the Commoner, "government must, as a last resort, appeal to force." In 1898 he could declare that "the time for intervention has arrived. Humanity demands that we shall act." [33] Yet to fight for humanitarian objectives was one thing; to accept the consequences of the American victory over Spain was quite another. Curiously enough, some individuals among the groups that had opposed the war—the conservative, big-business, management alignment—became ardent supporters of the imperialism that grew out of it. On the other hand, Bryan and some others who had favored war as a means of freeing Cuba rejected the idea that the United States should take over the Philippines and other territories released from the clutches of the defeated Spaniard.

Those who favored the acquisition of territories did so for many reasons. Expansionists often frankly admitted that they were interested in new markets and commercial possibilities. They contended that withdrawal from the Philippines would create a power vacuum certain to be filled by rival nations, possibly at the cost of another war. Many of them, influenced by Darwinism, considered colonies essential to the struggle for national supremacy. At the same time, they argued that the Filipinos were half devil and half child and incapable of self-government; it was therefore an American responsibility to uplift and civilize them. Others believed that, like it or not, the United States was destined to extend its authority.[34] "Fate has written our policy for us," Senator Beveridge could confidently assert; "the trade of the world must and shall be ours." [35] And with equal confidence clergymen such as Charles H. Fowler of Buffalo, New York, could give moral sanction to commercial arguments by proclaiming that the three greatest events since the crucifixion of Jesus were "first, the conversion of St. Paul. This opened the door to the Gentiles; this was our chance. Second, the firing on Fort Sumter. This made the Saxon race fit for evangelical uses.

Third, the blowing up of the *Maine*. This unified the nation and set us about our work." [36]

The problem Bryan faced immediately after his release from the Army was that of making his opposition to such arguments effective; the forces opposed to imperialism had to be formed into a well-disciplined phalanx that could lead a majority of the people to reject the acquisition of new territories. He found that anti-imperialists had already developed a plan to block any treaty coming to the Senate with a colonial empire among its provisions. They were, of course, opposed to the Treaty of Paris, which provided for the cession of Puerto Rico, Guam, and the Philippines to the United States. Andrew Carnegie, who differed from many of his business associates in his vigorous opposition to imperialism, estimated that the McKinley administration lacked two or three votes of controlling the two thirds of the Senate necessary for ratification. He urged Bryan to aid in defeating the treaty, and so help to give the country time to reflect upon what course of action to take.[37]

Bryan, however, did not approve of this plan. It would mean using a minority of the Senate to effect a purpose with which he agreed. But a minority, however wisely its influence was exercised and however just the cause in which it labored, could nevertheless lead to tyranny, and on these grounds the Commoner proposed different tactics. "I am going to keep up the fight," he wrote Carnegie, "until victory is won . . . not by a *minority* of the Senate but by a *majority* of the people." [38] If the voters were to decide the question, Bryan felt that the treaty would have to be ratified; only then would the United States be free to deal with former Spanish subjects according to American principles. It was safer, he argued, "to trust the American people to give independence to the Filipinos rather than to trust the accomplishment of that purpose to diplomacy with an unfriendly nation." [39] When passions aroused by the crisis had cooled, the people would surely do the right thing. In the meantime, ratification of the treaty would end the war and make further military appropriations unnecessary.[40] If the Senate could be persuaded to pass a resolution promising independence to the Filipinos, so much the better.[41]

Bryan was not disappointed that there should be a fight over ratification; he believed that it would draw attention to the subject of imperialism and serve to educate citizens on the issues at stake.[42] But he was mistaken in thinking that voters would be enlightened by the Senate debate. Senators themselves were abysmally ignorant of conditions in the Philippines, and at the last minute, discussion was further complicated by the outbreak of hostilities against American authority in the archipelago. In the end the treaty was ratified, but by the narrowest of margins a declaration favoring Philippine independence was rejected. The cause which Bryan championed won only half a victory, if that.[43]

Critics of the Commoner, many of them attributing far too much influence to his efforts in behalf of the treaty, charged that he was searching for an issue which would arouse voters in 1900 as silver had in 1896.[44] Such charges are difficult to prove. As Paolo Coletta has shown, Bryan might have prevented ratification had he been so inclined, but his support of the treaty had little to do with the final vote. Shrewd leadership by Senators Lodge, Hanna, and Aldrich and effective use of the patronage lever by McKinley were far more influential in bringing about ratification than arguments which Bryan advanced.[45] Furthermore, if he had been thinking of seeking election solely on the strength of his opposition to imperialism, Bryan would not have discouraged support from Andrew Carnegie. And he clearly spelled out his thoughts on their relationship: they could never agree on questions relating to trusts and currency and would therefore find any close political alliance unworkable. "I believe that the gold standard is a conspiracy against the human race," he told the steel magnate. "I am against the trusts. I am against bank currency." [46] He pleaded that Carnegie withhold any pledge of support, conditional or unconditional:

I am making this fight in my own way and hope to see the question disposed of before 1900 so that the fight for silver and against trusts and bank notes may be continued. You and I agree in opposing militarism and imperialism, but when these questions are settled we may find ourselves upon opposite sides as heretofore. Let us fight together when we can, and against each other when we must, exercising charity at all times.[47]

Because the McKinley administration refused to entertain any suggestion of independence for the Philippines, the issue of imperialism was not disposed of before 1900. When the Democratic convention in Kansas City declared it to be the "paramount issue," Bryan acquiesced. Yet he had given Carnegie fair warning —"you need not delude yourself with the idea that silver is dead" —and he was true to his word.[48] He refused to abandon silver and so lost much of the strength (and financial support) he might have gained by appealing exclusively to anti-imperialists. The evidence seems to indicate, therefore, that the Commoner was not motivated by a selfish and unscrupulous desire for the presidency. "It was Bryan's persistent faith in both the spirit and wisdom of the American people, never destroyed," concluded Josephus Daniels, "that led him into the error, if error it was, of favoring ratification and appealing to the people rather than to diplomacy." [49]

Who Is Going to Contract?

Irrespective of the worth of Bryan's analysis from a theoretical standpoint, he appears to have made a serious tactical miscalculation. Americans were presented with a *fait accompli* after ratification of the Treaty of Paris. "It is no longer a question of expansion with us; we have expanded," said President McKinley. "If there is any question at all it is a question of contraction; and who is going to contract?" [50] Certainly not the United States. The gaudy bandwagon of commercial opportunities drawn by the handsome chargers "Duty" and "Destiny" made Bryan's arguments seem pedestrian. The issue of imperialism was not, in the minds of most voters, a live issue in 1900. Then too, acceptance of the treaty had left anti-imperialists divided. David Starr Jordan hoped "that we can make a better fight against Imperialism now that we have ratified the Spanish treaty and slain a hundred thousand Filipinos under the cover of its sanction." [51] Many others, however, entertained the doubts that Grover Cleveland expressed to Judson Harmon: "How certain can you be that he [Bryan] would save you from imperialism? What did he do towards that end when the treaty of peace was before the Senate;

and how do you know what such an acrobat would do on that question if his personal ambition was in the balance?" [52]

Even though the issue of imperialism failed to stir voters in the campaign of 1900, Bryan was, ironically, never more cogent than when discussing the subject. In the first place, he distinguished between imperialism and expansion; expansion, he said, "is the taking in of territory which can be created into states," whereas imperialism involved "the conversion of a republic into an empire, wherein part of the people govern themselves and also govern the colonies." He was not opposed to expansion, but he was convinced that the United States would endanger the doctrine of self-government at home if it embarked upon a colonial policy abroad.[53] Moving from the assumption that the establishment of an American empire would be a disastrous policy, Bryan questioned the legal right of the United States to assume control over the Philippines. He argued that when we made common cause with the Filipinos and armed them to fight against Spain, our action was tantamount to disputing Spain's title to the islands. If we bought the Philippines with the payment of $20,000,000 provided by the Treaty of Paris, we secured a title which we ourselves had refused to recognize as valid. And because we could not logically defend our ownership, our only alternative was to turn the property over to the occupants—to the Filipinos. "History furnishes no example of turpitude baser than ours," Bryan remarked, "if we now substitute our yoke for the Spanish yoke." [54]

The Commoner vigorously attacked what he considered the principal imperialist arguments: (1) that the acquisition of colonies would make the United States a world power; (2) that commercial interests made an empire desirable; (3) that American control over far-flung territories would facilitate the spread of Christianity; (4) that there was "no honorable retreat" from the position the United States had taken. He answered the first contention of the imperialists by saying that the United States had been a world power since 1776, and that the essence of this power lay in the universal attraction of the American experiment. The emergence of the principle of self-government had been, he thought, the "overshadowing political fact of the nineteenth century," and it was this that had made the United States conspicuous among the nations of the earth.

In discussing the commercial argument, Bryan conceded that retention of the Philippines would be profitable to army contractors, ship owners ("who would carry live soldiers to the Philippines and bring dead soldiers back"), and to those officials sent to the islands as overseers. But to farmers, laborers, and the vast majority of American citizens, colonies would bring only "expenditure without return and risk without reward." When force is used to establish trade, said Bryan, the profits are never large enough to cover expenses, and no one would defend such a policy "but for the fact that the expense is borne by all the people, while the profits are enjoyed by a few." He also suggested that laboring groups would suffer if oriental workers were employed at low wages either in this country or in the Philippines.

Bryan felt even more sure of his ground in meeting religious arguments for a colonial empire. He invited those who employed them to compare "the swaggering, bullying, brutal doctrine of imperialism with the golden rule." He could find no warrant for imperialism in the Bible; the command "Go ye into all the world and preach the gospel to every creature" had, he observed, "no gatling gun attachment." [55] W. G. Eggleston, of the Helena, Montana, *Daily Independent,* clearly caught the spirit of Bryan's message when he wrote a new battle hymn for the Republic:

> In the beauty of the lilies
>   Christ was born across the waves,
> As he died to make men holy
>   We will fight to make men slaves;
> When weak nations cry for freedom
>   We will crucify the knaves—
>   "Plain Duty" marches on.
>
>   *   *   *   *   *
>
> The jingle of the dollar
>   Is the only rule of right,
> And we care not for the justice
>   If we only have the might;
> For the strenuous life is calling
>   Us to put out freedom's light.
>   Plain duty marches on.[56]

Bryan declared that an honorable retreat from the Philippines was possible and that there was an honest solution to the problem. The solution, embodied in the Democratic platform, would grant independence and would protect the islands from encroachment by any other power. He thought it "better a thousand times that our flag in the Orient give way to a flag representing the idea of self-government than that the flag of this Republic should become the flag of an empire." Of all contentions advanced by imperialists, the declaration that the nation's destiny demanded retention of the Philippines most aroused Bryan's ire. This complacent philosophy was, he said in an idiom that would have done credit to Theodore Roosevelt at his vituperative best, "the subterfuge of the invertebrate, who, lacking the courage to oppose error, seeks some plausible excuse for supporting it." The prophet of midwestern moralism had definite ideas on the American destiny, and it seemed to him that the imperialist interpretation smacked of false doctrine.

By an historical definition, Bryan was right. Until the decade of the nineties, Americans had understood that their destiny was a product of the national will—that none could resist their expansion when they chose to extend the boundaries of the United States. As the nineteenth century drew to a close, this idea underwent a metamorphosis. Our destiny, men came to believe, was in the coils of fate; they accepted the proposition that an American empire could not be resisted.[57] Bryan sensed this change and attempted to reorient American thought along traditional lines. "Destiny is not a matter of chance; it is a matter of choice," he said. "It is not a thing to be waited for; it is a thing to be achieved." [58] He agreed with George Washington that it bore an intimate relationship not to the acquisition of territories, but to American progress in working out a republican form of government. "Immeasurable responsibility!" warned the Commoner. "The destiny of this republic is in the hands of its own people, and upon the success of the experiment here rests the hope of humanity." [59]

The election of 1900 should not have been considered a mandate on imperialism; "Bryanism," which suggested monetary jugglery and economic radicalism, was as much an issue as imperialism.[60] Even though the issue was not clear-cut, however, the policy of the McKinley administration in the Philippines was to be continued. A conscientious leader of the opposition could not let the question die, nor capitulate to the administration's point of view, even though he had failed to win majority support for his own program. In the pages of *The Commoner* and in speeches, Bryan continued to agitate for the right of the Filipinos to govern themselves. "The President is an emperor, and will remain so until the republican party reverses its policy or until the people retire that party from power," he asserted as McKinley began his second term.[61] He was highly critical of the Supreme Court when it declared, in effect, that the Constitution did not follow the flag and that civil rights precedents did not apply in the island possessions:

> It will be interesting to American patriots to learn that rights for more than a century considered inalienable are now divided into "general" rights and "local" rights; that some belong to everyone, while others belong only to some, and that some who enjoy all rights are to decide what rights are safe in the keeping of others.[62]

When McKinley was killed by a demented assassin in Buffalo, Theodore Roosevelt became the youngest President to take the oath of office. The tempo of life in the White House quickened, but for the time being policy in the islands remained the same. Not that Roosevelt and the Republicans had no doubts about it. The Philippine insurrection was an ugly affair from beginning to end, and the administration began to question the value of its oriental commitments.[63] In 1905, when Secretary of War William Howard Taft appeared before the House Ways and Means Committee, he said he expected the United States to grant independence to the Filipinos ultimately, adding only that their present status would be maintained until they had learned to govern themselves.

Yet Bryan was not satisfied. Taft had made no promises and given the Filipinos no assurances; he had shown himself antagonistic to the basic principles of the Declaration of Independence by denying their present capacity for self-government. There was a vital difference between a commitment to grant independence as soon as a stable government had been established and a "vague prophecy" that independence would come provided political capacities could be developed. But if we would be true to our faith, the former alternative demanded acceptance:

> If we are going to deal with the Filipinos according to American principles we must begin by recognizing that the Filipinos have both the right to self government and the capacity for it and then promising independence proceed to assist them to establish a republican form of government, which, when established, shall be turned over to the elected representatives of the people, just as the Cuban government, when formed was turned over to the Cuban people.[64]

Bryan's position on imperialism throws into high relief both his weakness and his strength as a politician. In one sense he failed his first test as an opposition leader. His actions during the ratification debate were confusing and subject to misinterpretation. He contributed nothing to party discipline in supporting a treaty which the President also wanted the Senate to ratify. In the election of 1900 voters did not decide the question of expansion, even though Bryan labeled it the paramount issue; he only gave his critics an opportunity to suggest that he was following expediency rather than principle. And in the years following he was unable to persuade a majority of his fellow countrymen to adopt his point of view. It is true that by 1907 Roosevelt was ready to admit that "the Philippines form our heel of Achilles," and that "we shall have to be prepared for giving the islands independence of a more or less complete type." [65] But Bryan's arguments were not responsible for the President's change of heart; the emergence of Japan as a great power in the Orient and the possibility of a Japanese war in 1907 were far more important considerations.[66] It was not until July 4, 1946, long after most people had forgotten he ever discussed it, that the Commoner's hope of independence for the Philippines was realized. Although there may have been rejoicing in heaven, Bryan could not claim the credit.

In another sense, however, he did not fail. He was largely instrumental in having his ideas on imperialism written into the

Democratic platform not only in 1900 and 1908 when he was his party's nominee, but also in 1904 and 1912. Indeed, Woodrow Wilson enunciated the Bryan doctrine during the campaign of 1912 in words but little changed: "We are not the owners of the Philippine Islands. We hold them in trust for the people who live in them. They are theirs, for the uses of their life." [67] This was Bryan's real victory and the essence of his most outstanding contribution to American political life. He was successful, to a remarkable degree, in controlling his party and securing its commitment to the principles in which he so ardently believed.

V

*

*   *   *

*

SHALL THE PEOPLE RULE?

BRYAN WAS NOT so preoccupied with the silver issue and the problem of imperialism that he could not devote attention to other questions. "Shall the people rule?" rhetorically demanded the Democratic platform of 1908. The query was meant to suggest the need for economic and political reforms supported by the Nebraskan throughout the opposition years. The questions on which he ventured observations were many, and the problems for which he offered solutions were various. During the period from 1896 to 1912 his basic position remained a consistent one, and if this does not reveal the kind of growth so evident in the career of Woodrow Wilson, it does speak well for Bryan's fidelity to principle. Moreover, his fidelity and consistency indicate that he did not spend all his time in a single-minded search for new issues with which to attract votes. Again and again he could call attention to the fact that he had long been an advocate of this or that proposition. Granted he did waver on two important questions and have difficulty in justifying his views on a third. Nevertheless he at no time doubted that the people should rule. The issues Bryan discussed after his second defeat may be considered minor when each is compared separately to silver, with which he is most commonly associated. But taken together they assume far greater significance, even when it is recalled that silver had symbolic as well as intrinsic importance. They were the bricks out of which Bryan, using the moralism of the Middle Border as mortar, constructed a program of opposition.

Economic Reform

Because economic developments were of such overwhelming significance and made such a profound impression upon American life, it followed that the most important reforms Bryan advocated in the opposition years should be economic ones. The first of these, the tariff, was the issue which figured most prominently in his first congressional campaign in 1890. He won election to the House largely on the strength of some eighty speeches on the subject.[1] He not only talked about it; he also studied it from various points of view. Prepared as he was, his appointment to the Ways and Means Committee was logical as well as fortunate. It was as a member of this committee that Bryan made his first major speech in Congress on March 16, 1892.[2] And a major speech it was; it catapulted the Nebraskan to a position of importance rarely achieved by a freshman congressman. Questioned and challenged (one might almost say cross-examined), he displayed not only understanding of the issue, but exceptional skill in debate as well. The speech is important to this study, however, not because of its immediate impact upon the nation or the influence that its reception had upon Bryan's political fortunes. It is important because during the opposition years the Commoner did not retreat from the position he had taken as a young and relatively unknown congressman from the plains.

Bryan was never a free trader; tariff reform, or tariff reduction, was the policy he advocated. "In going from a vicious to a correct system the most rapid progress can be made by degrees," he said in 1892, adding that all legislation "must be practical rather than ideal." [3] In 1908 he suggested a plan for the gradual reduction, not the elimination, of tariff duties.[4] When Louis F. Post commented upon Bryan's position with respect to the tariff in 1909, he used the phrase "free trade." Bryan suggested that "tariff reduction" more accurately expressed his views. Republicans, he felt, were incapable of understanding the term "free trade" as it was used by tariff reformers; to them it meant only opposition to all tariffs. "If one says that he is a free trader, he has to spend a good deal of his time explaining what he means by free trade," Bryan observed, "whereas if he says he is for tariff reduction, he puts the republicans on the defensive." [5] It was the principle of protection, therefore, not a tariff for revenue, that incurred his opposition.

Bryan indicted the protective tariff on several counts. He pointed out repeatedly that it was immoral and unjust because it worked a hardship on many while benefitting only a few. It was, as he saw it, merely a "device by which one man is authorized to collect money from his fellow men." [6] In a speech given in 1904 he said that if he were forcibly to collect one dollar from each person in the audience and give the money to some man upon the speakers' platform, it would be larceny; yet he believed that "a protective tariff that makes it impossible for you to buy abroad without paying a certain amount as a fine embodies the same principle." [7] Bryan argued that raising the tariff must of necessity put pressures upon the common man. Employing an analogy reminiscent of Lincoln, he said that back in Illinois, when the corner of a rail fence had settled too low to the ground, it was customary to repair it rather than to build a new fence.

How did we do it? We took a rail, put one end of it under the fence corner, then laid a ground chunk for a fulcrum. Then we would go off to the end of the rail and bear down; up would go the fence corner—but does anybody suppose there was no pressure on that fulcrum? That, my friends, illustrates just the operation, as I conceive it, of a protective tariff. You want to raise an infant industry, for instance; what do you do? You take a protective tariff for a lever, and put one end of it under the infant industry that is to be raised. You look around for some good, fat, hearty consumer and lay him down for a ground chunk; you bear down on the rail and up goes the infant industry, but down goes the ground chunk into the ground. [8]

It was the manufacturer, not the consumers, the organizer of trusts, not wage-earners, who benefitted from the protective tariff. And all the expressions of concern for the common man voiced by protectionists were just so much window dressing to catch his eye and his vote. The protective tariff would, argued some, provide jobs for working men by making it possible for industries to produce at full capacity. Ridiculous, answered the Commoner. Those who held this position were "fit companions for the people who are supposed by Bastiat to have petitioned the French legislature to find some way of preventing the sun from shining, because it interfered with the business of the candlemakers." [9]

To contend, further, that high wages were a concomitant of high tariffs was to mask the real purposes of protectionist groups. For twenty-five years, Bryan said in 1908, American workers had been told that they had much to gain from a protective tariff, yet it was manufacturers who contributed most heavily to the Republican campaign chest. "Is it not significant," he asked, "that the manufacturers, who furnish the funds, are so little advertised as beneficiaries?" It was by no means certain, moreover, that high tariffs did result in high wages. That American laborers received higher wages than English workmen who were not protected by tariffs proved nothing, because English workmen received higher wages than did workers in Germany where high tariffs were in force. If the United States had better wages, then, they were the result of the greater intelligence and skill of American workers, the hopes which free institutions inspired in them, improved machinery, better working conditions, and the effectiveness of labor organizations.[10]

Bryan had little but contempt for the manner in which Theodore Roosevelt dealt with the tariff. After reading the President's annual message in 1902, he concluded that T.R. had "gone over bag and baggage into the ultra-protectionist camp and will henceforth be 'persona grata' with the great corporate interests." [11] There was some justification for such a conclusion. Earlier in the year Roosevelt had recognized a "strong general feeling for tariff reduction." The difficulty lay in "an equally strong local feeling in each locality against tariff reduction on what concerns that locality." The problem was complex. Besides, wrote the President, "I do not think a reduction of duties would be of any substantial benefit." [12]

The tariff never did receive much attention from the Roosevelt administration, but during the campaign of 1908 Republicans promised revision. In fulfillment of that pledge, President Taft labored to push the Payne-Aldrich tariff through Congress in 1909. Taft thought it "really a good bill." In fact, he became increasingly enthusiastic and later characterized it as "the best bill that the party has ever passed." [13] The new law did contain some downward revisions, but tariff reformers insisted that the revisions upward were more significant. Bryan charged the administration with bad faith: "The bargain with the tariff barons has been fulfilled; 'the goods have been delivered' in return for campaign funds furnished by the protected interests." The President, he thought, had concluded "an alliance, offensive and defensive," with conservative leaders in Congress to enact a legislative program contrary to the interests of the people.[14] Two years later, after the congressional election of 1910 had brought disaster to Taft forces, Congress passed a bill providing reductions in the woolens schedule. But Taft vetoed it on grounds that a scientific study of the tariff was needed before further action could be taken. Substituting Taft's name, Bryan rephrased his earlier comment on Roosevelt: "He has gone over bag and baggage into the protectionist camp. Revision was but a fitful dream; he sleeps soundly now." [15]

Bryan did not merely criticize Republicans; he suggested an alternate program. His proposals embodied the idea that placing necessities of life upon the free list was an essential first step in tariff reform. Inasmuch as all taxes, he said, must come out of incomes, regardless of the method or system used to collect them, they are all essentially income taxes. The tariff was a tax upon consumption because the price of an article included the tariff on it. But "people do not eat in proportion to their income; they do not wear clothing in proportion to their income; they do not use taxed goods in proportion to their income." The tariff, therefore, like any tax on consumers' goods, was really a graduated income tax, "the largest per cent being collected from those with the smallest income and the smallest per cent from those with the largest income." [16] And admitting the necessities of life duty-free would help to equalize the tax burden.

In the campaign of 1900 and again in 1908, Bryan suggested a further reform which grew out of his conviction that the protective tariff encouraged the organization of trusts. While he did not offer it to the Treasury Department as a lodestone for obtaining revenue painlessly, he did think of it as a stone that might kill two birds of prey—trusts and inequitable tariffs. His plan (incorporated by Governor Albert B. Cummins into his "Iowa Idea" in 1901) was to place on the free list all articles coming into competition with those controlled by a trust. He did not work out the details of this proposal; he only suggested that Congress fix a deadline for the dissolution of trusts. Any trust in operation after that date would have to compete with foreign products admitted duty-free.[17]

To make up for shortages in revenue resulting from tariff reforms, Bryan urged the passage of an income tax law. In 1894 he spoke in favor of a tariff bill which contained provisions for a tax of two per cent upon all corporate income and upon all individual incomes in excess of $4,000.[18] This bill, which came to be known as the Wilson-Gorman tariff, passed both houses of Congress and became law without President Cleveland's signature. The efforts of Bryan and others who worked for inclusion of the income tax in the act were to no avail, however, for the Supreme Court declared the measure unconstitutional in 1895.[19] Bryan thereafter labored to secure an amendment to the constitution. In 1906 he observed that the income tax was working well in many of the countries he had visited, and he thought it disgraceful that the United States had been unable to "compel wealth to bear its share of the expenses of the Government which protects it."[20] The Democratic platforms of 1908 and 1912 contained planks favoring a graduated income tax, and ratification of the sixteenth amendment in 1913 was as much a victory for the Commoner as for any single person.[21]

Bryan did not believe that modifications in the tariff laws would alone be sufficient to prevent the evils of large business combinations, and the trust question was another major issue of the opposition years. He applied the term "trust" freely to describe "any agreement made among independent corporations for joint action in the restriction of trade, the division of territory, or the fixing of price or terms." The aim of the trust, he felt, was to establish a monopoly, and the essence of a trust was to be found "in its ability to eliminate competition and control the market." In creating a monopoly, trust organizers could lower prices of raw materials, cut labor costs, and raise prices of articles produced. A trust, according to Bryan's definition then, was "a corporation which by itself or in conjunction with other corporations controls a sufficient proportion of the article produced or handled to enable it approximately to determine the terms and conditions of sale or purchase." [22]

A number of circumstances, he thought, had made possible the rise of trusts in the United States. The first was not peculiar to this country; it was that cupidity which was a part of human nature and therefore universal. The God-given instinct for self-preservation was easily perverted into selfishness, and if trusts were to be controlled, this fact of life would have to be recognized. A second cause of trust development was, as has been indicated, the protective tariff. A third was the policy of rate discriminations and rebates followed by the railroads. And finally, Bryan believed that the federal system of government had encouraged trust organization. When trusts were prosecuted in United States courts, he said, they hid behind state sovereignty, and when they were prosecuted in state courts, they found cover under federal jurisdiction.[23] At a White House conference on the conservation of natural resources in 1908, he expressed the view that "most—not all, but most—of the contentions over the line between the Nation and the State are traceable to predatory corporations which are trying to shield themselves from deserved punishment, or endeavoring to prevent needed restraining legislation." And to the tune of great applause, Bryan contributed a felicitous sentence to the reform movement: "There is no twilight zone between the Nation and the State, in which exploiting interests can take refuge from both." [24]

Thriving under these conditions, trusts had had a pernicious influence on American life. A campaign song of 1900 reiterated the old Populist antagonism to powerful business combinations:

> Trusts and monopolies,
> Curse, where'er they stand
> Now endanger everything,
> In this glorious land.[25]

Bryan was convinced that they did endanger not only the national economy but the national character as well. When competition disappeared, the necessity for skill and brains would disappear with it. Nepotism would infect the business world, for "when there is no competition anybody can sit in the office and receive letters and answer them because everybody has to write to the same house for anything he wants." Economic power, wealth, political influence would be passed on from generation to generation without regard to individual merits.[26] The phrase "economic royalist" was stirring in the womb.

Bryan feared that the corporate man would deprive the natural man of his dignity. "God made man and placed him upon his footstool to carry out a divine decree," declared the Commoner, but "man created the corporation as a money making machine." Could anyone doubt the deleterious results of man's folly? He made the corporation "a hundred, a thousand, ten thousand, a million times stronger than the God-made man"; unlike God, who set a limit to the life of his creation, laws made possible the indefinite projection of corporate existence; the "God-made man" had a soul and would be "held accountable for the deeds done in the flesh," but the soulless corporation need have no fear of the judgment. Bryan was willing to concede that corporations had been created in good faith and that they could serve valuable economic purposes, but he believed that "we can never become so enthusiastic over the corporation, over its usefulness, over its possibilities, as to forget the God-made man who was here first." [27] And when the trust raised the prices of its products, reduced to an unwarranted degree the prices of raw materials it used, arbitrarily fixed terms and conditions of labor so as to take advantage of the worker, produced inferior articles, squeezed out small stockholders and competitors, and discouraged the man with independent inclinations, it was taking American society down the road which led to the destruction of American individualism. The trust was "a menace to the political welfare of the country, for political independence can not long exist with industrial servitude." [28]

What was to be done about the evils resulting from trusts and monopolies? Although President Roosevelt gained a reputation for trust-busting, he was never willing to commit himself to unequivocal policy. The antitrust prosecutions for which he was famous indicate his readiness to assume responsibility for the regulation of business, but they were not undertaken because trusts had violated fixed rules. T.R. avoided the rigidity of clear-cut policy; he himself would determine when trusts should be prosecuted. His early pronouncements on the trusts drew sharp criticism from Bryan. The President's "fatal mistake" in his first annual message, wrote the Commoner, was his failure "to recognize that a private monopoly is always, and under every circumstance, a menace to the public." [29] Even after Attorney General Philander C. Knox announced that the government would ask dissolution of the Northern Securities Company (the first of forty-four actions begun by the Roosevelt administration), Bryan was not satisfied that anything would come of it. Knox had brought suit under the Sherman Act, but he had not once mentioned its criminal clause.[30] Civil action alone would not prevent the growth of monopoly:

> Strange doings there'll be in the sweet by and by,
>> When Philander busts up a trust.
> The east will be west and the wet will be dry
>> When Philander busts up a trust.
> The pigs will be flying on wings of pure white,
> The sun will be shining through hours of night,
> And machine politicians will strive to do right
>> When Philander busts up a trust.[31]

Trusts were broken up, of course, and Bryan was pleased that some progress was being made. Yet his own plan, advanced tentatively at the Chicago Anti-Trust Conference in September 1899, would be more effective in preventing monopoly. Implied in the Democratic platform of 1900 and stated specifically in 1908, the plan called for a system of licensing big business. Any corporation engaging in interstate commerce would be required to take out a federal license before being "permitted to control as much as twenty-five per cent of the product in which it deals, the license to protect the public from watered stock and to prohibit the control by such corporation of more than fifty per cent of the total amount of any product consumed in the United States." [32] Not many corporations—possibly not even one per cent of them—would be required to secure a license because only a few controlled 25 per cent of the product consumed. But that small number controlling from 25 to 50 per cent could, under a licensing system, be prevented from engaging in those practices which Bryan found so objectionable.

His percentages were established arbitrarily, and while Bryan did not insist upon the figures given in the platform of 1908, he did feel that specific percentages were necessary for effective enforcement of such a law.[33] When a corporation controlled as much as 25 per cent of any product, it could certainly exert an influence in establishing the price of that product and the terms of sale. It would therefore bear watching. Its license could be revoked if it watered its stock or gave evidence of trying to monopolize any branch of business. The system would not inhibit the growth of a corporation up to a certain point, the point where it controlled 50 per cent of the business in which it was engaged. Here Bryan thought the line should be drawn and the corporation prevented from engaging in interstate commerce until it had curtailed or limited its operations.

Bryan's plan for controlling the trusts aroused some spirited opposition. His friend Louis F. Post thought it "undemocratic in political principle, unsound in economics, of disputed constitutionality, and unwise in practical politics." The national licensing agency would accelerate the trend toward centralization and threaten the autonomy of the states in regulating business. Bryan had assumed that trusts made monopolies, whereas the real problem was that monopolies made trusts. His plan would therefore "no more check the development of evil trusts than a sparrow could check the progress of a locomotive."[34] On the other hand, Theodore Roosevelt was attracted to the idea. "I have always been inclined to Bryan's view on the license matter," he wrote William Dudley Foulke. "About half of Bryan's views are right."[35]

The Commoner defended his plan against Post's criticism. Congress, he noted, had the power to regulate interstate commerce. Under that power he contemplated using the license program to supplement state control, not supplant it: "The license would not enable a corporation to do business in a state except according to the laws of the state." [36] In 1907 he opposed Roosevelt's scheme for national incorporation, just as Post had opposed his own plan, precisely because it disregarded the rights of states. "The president's Hamiltonian ideas" made him "an easy victim" of railroads and other big businesses.[37] When a bill embodying the Roosevelt proposal was introduced in the Senate, the Judiciary Committee agreed with Bryan in reporting that the process for securing incorporation left too much to administrative discretion.[38] A similar proposal by the Taft administration received the same cold reception both in Congress and from the Commoner.[39]

Still Bryan continued to urge his licensing program. Looking toward the extirpation of monopoly, he once more anticipated the position taken by Woodrow Wilson in 1912. "We think it is better to prevent monopolies," Bryan argued, "than to first authorize them to prey upon the public and then try to punish them for doing so." He observed that Mr. Taft, like Mr. Roosevelt, favored control of the trusts rather than their extermination, "but after years of experience the people have learned that the trusts control the government." [40]

Bryan believed that other measures would also contribute to the effectiveness of the crusade against the trusts. He strongly urged, for example, legislation against interlocking directorates and penitentiary punishment for heads of corporations found guilty of violating antitrust laws.[41] But he believed that no remedy for trusts could possibly be effective until the public conscience recognized them as morally wrong. "Just as long as respectable people can conspire to rob their fellows through trust methods without losing caste," he said, "it will be difficult to do anything." Churches and other agencies influential in shaping public opinion should take a more active part in educating the people on their ethical responsibilities. They should boldly proclaim the idea "that grand larceny is as wrong as petit larceny—that the rich man who bankrupts his rival through monopoly methods is as much an offender as the burglar—that the lawyer who sells his brains to those who conspire against the public is as guilty as one who helps to plan a hold-up." Only when this truth became apparent and the people obtained full understanding of trust evils could regulatory laws be enforced and trust magnates prosecuted like horse thieves and housebreakers.[42]

If ethical principles were important to trust regulation, they were equally necessary in the area of money and banking. Here too "conscience is a better guide than self-interest which ignores the rights of others." Even after the silver issue had declined in importance, Bryan continued to insist that self-interest ought not to take precedence over justice, that "whether a rising dollar is better for the man with money and fixed investments, or whether a falling dollar is good for the debtor" was at best a secondary consideration. He believed that another question was more fundamental: "What system will best preserve the parity between money and property, and reduce to a minimum the fluctuations, not merely of the metals as compared to each other, but of the measure of value as compared with that which it is to measure." [43] During the years of opposition, Bryan was wary of any monetary reform that would give more powers to "the money trust," or enable it to make money scarce or plentiful "by the mere pushing of a button." [44] He was almost Jacksonian in his fear of banks. Such elasticity as was necessary, he said in 1907, should be controlled not by bankers, but by the government through the issuance of treasury notes and the regulation of government deposits. He went on to add, however, that what was needed at the moment was not an emergency currency; in this year of the banker's panic he thought that greater security for depositors was more crucial.[45]

Bryan's device for providing such security was one of the issues of the campaign of 1908, although he had suggested it fifteen years earlier. Basically the proposal was to establish a guarantee fund by a tax on deposits, and this fund was to be used to alleviate distress in any area and prevent losses to depositors. Bryan would require that all national banks subscribe to the plan, and he would make it available to any state banks wishing to use it.[46]

Unlike many of his proposals, guaranteed banks had actually been tried, and he could therefore speak with the assurance of one whose conclusions were based on experimentation. In December 1907 the Oklahoma legislature had enacted a guarantee law in line with Bryan's suggestions, and its success was regarded by the Commoner as a vindication of his views. According to this law, all state banks and as many national banks as desired were taxed one per cent on their deposits and the money put in a guarantee fund. A banking board was established and authorized to make assessments and administer the fund. When a bank failed, the board was responsible for taking possession, paying the depositors in full, and reimbursing the fund from collected assets of the insolvent bank. During the first six months of the law's operation deposits in unsecured banks decreased by more than one million dollars, while deposits in guaranteed banks increased by more than four million. "No amount of criticism of the timid depositor can change the facts," said Bryan; "the people who deposit money want more security than the laws at present give them." [47]

So convincing were his arguments here that President Roosevelt was, as he confessed to Taft during the campaign of 1908, "a little puzzled how to furnish you a complete and slashing answer to Bryan's proposal." [48] Was there an answer? A few Republicans were never able to find one and were inclined to support the deposits guarantee. Others thought Bryan had not been clear in making his suggestions and advocated postal savings banks instead. Most probably agreed with the remark of William B. Ridgely, president of the National Bank of Commerce in Kansas City: "I have no doubt in the world that the Oklahoma Bank Guaranty statute has increased the number of banks started by irresponsible and inexperienced people." [49] Bryan viewed the issue from another angle. In providing for the guarantee fund he was "simply looking at the banking question from the standpoint of the depositor, and compelling the banks to make good the promise of security by which they draw deposits to the banks," and he found this point of view "entirely in harmony with the party position on other questions." [50]

Bryan's views on one of those questions, the issue he called "government by injunction," rounds out his analysis of the American economy and completes the list of economic reforms for which he consistently campaigned. The Commoner had a strong pro-labor strain in his makeup; he could not have presented himself as a champion of the people without it. Among all agencies improving conditions and protecting the rights of the laboring man, labor unions, in his estimation, stood first. Labor organizations had protected workers in contests with management and had encouraged the arbitration of labor disputes.[51] Nevertheless they were handicapped by the tendency of courts to yoke them up with combinations organized in restraint of trade. As a result, antitrust laws had been used more effectively against unions than in breaking up trusts. Bryan, the spokesman for toilers everywhere, insisted upon drawing a distinction between trust and labor organizations: the trust was a "combination of dollars," but the labor union was "an association of human beings"; in a trust, a few men at the top controlled the articles produced by others, but in a labor organization "the members unite for the protection of that which is their own, namely, their own labor"; the trust dealt with "dead matter," while the concern of the labor organization was with "life and with intellectual and moral forces." If labor organizations had to be regulated, therefore, they should be regulated "by a law which deals with man as man, and not by a law that was aimed to prevent the cornering of a commodity or the forestalling of the market." [52]

The Democratic platforms of the opposition years declared against "government by injunction" and supported the use of a jury in cases of indirect contempt arising out of labor disputes.[53] Bryan argued that a labor dispute should not, in itself, be regarded as sufficient cause for an injunction, and if one were issued, "it must be based upon acts which would justify an injunction if there were no industrial dispute involved." If an injunction were violated, Bryan and the Democracy demanded the substitution of trial by jury for trial by the judge. They had no quarrel with the right of the judge to decide cases of direct contempt, i.e., contempt committed in the presence of the court, or with the right of the judge to determine punishment for indirect contempt. But when violation of the court's decree had to be established by evidence, they believed that a jury would be more impartial than a judge and therefore better able to decide each case upon its merits. In thus cutting away legal shackles the Commoner and his cohorts would grant labor unions the freedom effectively to assert their demands for a fair share of industrial profits.[54]

Roosevelt too believed that labor should have its proper reward. In the anthracite strike of 1902 he saw to it that miners received fair treatment. Yet he seldom took an uncompromising stand, and Bryan soon spotted what he thought was a basic weakness in the President's position: "He enters into an elaborate argument to show that there is no difference between a combination of capital and a combination of labor, and he thus injures labor." [55] To straddle the labor question was bad enough; to indicate hostility toward labor was worse. And in the campaign of 1908 candidate Taft seemed hostile. He grudgingly admitted that labor could legitimately organize and even strike, but he confided to Roosevelt that Bryan's proposals would result in "clogging of the wheels of justice." [56]

The Commoner used a different metaphor. He thought that in many respects American industry could be compared to military organizations: some individuals were commanders and others were responsible for carrying out orders. One of the problems of the national economy was "to divide the results fairly between the captains of industry and the privates in the ranks." Not unnaturally the captains, who had customarily made the division, had overestimated their own importance and kept too large a share for themselves. The labor question therefore reduced itself to a question of distribution, and Bryan believed that to secure justice in this, as in other economic areas, was a proper function of government.[57]

Political Reform

The Commoner considered economic reform most essential to the welfare of the state, but he believed that such reform could best be achieved through political means. Abuses existed in politics itself, however, and he was led to propose measures to remove them. If his remedies seemed superficial, it was because he had confidence in the fundamental soundness of the American system of government. "We have the best government on earth," he said. "It gives the largest liberty, the greatest hope and the most encouragement to its citizens." [58] Bryan was not one to question the wisdom of the Founding Fathers. His mission was not to bring about a revolution; it was, rather, to work toward the perfection of American political life in the tradition of Jefferson, Jackson, and Lincoln.[59]

That tradition was democratic, and the Commoner believed that "the nearer the government is brought to the voters the better it is for both the government and the people." [60] If a few men of power controlled policy at the moment, a little political tinkering would release the popular will. A most important adjustment, in Bryan's opinion, was the direct election of senators, a measure described by the Democratic platform of 1908 as "the gateway to other national reforms." [61] He had not been the first to suggest it, of course, but Bryan had favored the idea since his first congressional campaign in 1890. He had seen corruption and wirepulling in state legislatures when a senator was to be elected, he had seen the will of the people thwarted, and he had declared, "We favor an amendment to the Federal Constitution which will take the election of U. S. Senators from the State Legislatures and place it in the hands of the people where it belongs." [62] In 1892 the Nebraskan had voted for a resolution in the House redeeming that campaign pledge. When the measure failed in Congress, he had helped to secure its adoption by the Democratic party in 1900, 1904, and 1908, and he and his party were to reaffirm this position in 1912.[63]

In *The Commoner* Bryan urged readers to write their senators requesting support of the reform, and he invited all newspaper editors to do the same. One million postal cards sent to the senators would, he thought, insure passage of the resolution.[64] Either he failed to get the cooperation he sought, or the power of the press was not as great as he believed; little came of his writing campaign. Still he persevered, and when he returned from his trip around the world in 1906, he was "more strongly convinced than before." He had seen agitation for a native congress in India, he had noted the establishment of a Duma in Russia, and in other areas he had detected an increasing desire for democracy in its broadest sense. If the United States were to share in this movement, and if other reforms were to pass both houses of Congress, it was essential that the Senate be "brought into harmony with the people." [65] So assiduous was he in pleading this cause that Josephus Daniels believed him chiefly responsible for the ultimate adoption of the seventeenth amendment.[66]

Changing the rules of the national House of Representatives so as to limit the powers of the Speaker was a measure for which others, particularly George Norris, deserve a larger share of credit. Yet Bryan had, in his first campaign, supported this reform also.[67] In 1908 the issue played an even more important part. The Commoner acknowledged that a considerable element of the Republican party favored remedial legislation. Nevertheless a few Republican leaders had been successful in controlling the party organization and suppressing the progressive wing. In so doing they had "forced a real majority in the House to submit to a well-organized minority." Instead of condemning this action, the Republican convention had "eulogized Congress" and added insult to injury by nominating one of the ringleaders of the "well-organized minority," James S. Sherman, for Vice President. Bryan could only conclude that the Republican party was committed to such tyrannical activities. But there was hope in the Democracy. It had pledged itself "to such a revision of the rules as will bring the popular branch of the Federal Government into harmony with the ideas of those who framed our constitution and founded our Government." [68]

Bryan was sympathetic to any measure that would tend to bring policies of the government into closer alignment with the will of the people. This was the reason he gave his support to women's suffrage, direct primaries, agitation against lame-duck congresses, a single term for the President, and the initiative, referendum, and recall. He could not claim to have originated these reforms, but in view of his basic assumptions failure to support them would have been preposterous. "Shall the people rule?" The 1908 platform did not include planks on any of the political reforms Bryan was known to favor except for the popular election of senators and reform of the House rules. Yet this platform, tailor-made to suit the Commoner, cannot be considered as evidence of inconsistency or shiftiness. He was, after all, pledged to the two corrective measures he considered essential if other reforms were to be enacted into law; and by suggesting that they were gateways to other reforms, Bryan and his party virtually promised continued reform. "Shall we open the gate," he asked, or should the Speaker be permitted to bar the way in the House, and "exploiting interests" allowed to control the Senate? "Shall the people rule?" Certainly, Bryan felt, this was the paramount question:

No matter which way we turn; no matter to what subject we address ourselves, the same question confronts us: Shall the people control their own Government and use that Government for the protection of their rights and for the promotion of their welfare? or shall the representatives of predatory wealth prey upon a defenseless public, while the offenders secure immunity from subservient officials whom they raise to power by unscrupulous methods? [69]

Sooner or later Bryan always returned to the "gold ring," to the "money trust," or to "predatory wealth." The agrarian, Populist influence was too strong in him to be kept silent for long. Large business combinations and organized wealth were not only economically unsound; they also had a corruptive influence upon political and social institutions. Bryan regarded the benefactions of millionaire philanthropists as little more than bribes to silence dissidents and secure the support of teachers, clergymen, and other molders of public opinion. When a Minnesota cleric said that he would accept money from the devil if he could use it to build churches to war on the devil and "do him up," the Commoner replied that "those who accept Rockefeller's money are not trying to 'do Rockefeller up.'" On the contrary, they were "as cooing doves in the presence of the oil trust magnate." [70]

Nowhere was the pernicious influence of such philanthropy more apparent than in the field of higher education. Even Illinois College was not immune. Bryan was chairman of the board of trustees when his destitute Alma Mater sought what he thought was tainted money: a gift from Andrew Carnegie. The famous old grad resigned in protest and even went so far as to ask that his name be erased from the roll of the alumni.[71] The action could have been predicted; Bryan had long before stated his position in the first issue of *The Commoner*. The statement was in the form of a dialogue reminiscent of William H. Harvey's *Coin's Financial School*, which had played such an important part in the campaign of 1896:

"Good morning, gentlemen," said Professor Twiggem, mounting the rostrum of the lecture room and facing the multitude of students gathered from all parts of the world. "I am proud to see so many of you this morning."

A ripple of applause swept over the lecture room as Professor Twiggem drew from his pocket a roll of manuscript and adjusted his glasses.

"We are here this morning, gentlemen, for the purpose of discussing the subject of industrial combination," said the Professor. "We are to discuss it with reference to its effect upon free—"

"Pardon me, professor," interrupted the Academic Censor, "but has your manuscript been passed upon by the manager of the Yardstick Oil Company?"

"It has, sir."

"And has the superintendent of the Consolidated Embalmed Beef Promotion Syndicate carefully scrutinized it?"

"He did that last night, sir."

"And has the third vice president of the Amalgamated Steel, Iron, Brass and Copper Company placed his official 'O.K.' upon your remarks?"

"He has, sir."

"Then, sir, may I ask if the Ancient and Accidental Society of Possible University Donors has properly examined your manuscript?"

"It has, sir. All possible interests have been consulted and pacified."

"Then, sir," said the Academic Censor, "here is your ticket which entitles you to proceed with your remarks."

A few moments later Professor Twiggem was reading from his manuscript and the assembled students were paying as little attention as possible.[72]

This satirical piece had probably been called forth by the firing of six Stanford University professors whose opposition to the importation of Japanese labor had offended Mrs. Stanford. "If the young people who attend our universities are to make the most of their opportunities," Bryan said with reference to the incident, "then it is essential that men and women who instruct them shall have the brains to think for themselves and the courage to express their opinions without fear or favor."[73] This statement calls to mind the notorious "monkey trial" at Dayton, where Bryan seemed to depart from the position he took here. The Dayton episode was the last in Bryan's career and therefore lies outside the scope of this study. But a comparison of the two cases, it is worth mentioning, indicates that Bryan actually was not as devoted to the cause of academic freedom as he was to the principle of majority rule. For a wealthy donor to control what was taught in the classroom was to permit an individual to exercise powers that by right rested with the majority of the people who in any way gave support to the institution concerned. For John T. Scopes to teach evolution in a public school was to violate a law passed by a legislature representing the majority of the taxpayers of the state. The difference between the Stanford dismissals and the Scopes case is that in the former, arguments based upon the value of free inquiry suited Bryan's purpose, while in the latter they did not.

There was little doubt in Bryan's mind that the greatest sores on the body politic resulted from policies advocated by a small group of self-seeking and sinister men and imposed on the people through devious means. One of the most effective methods of thwarting the general will, he felt, was through the purchase of candidates for public office, too many of whom were willing to barter principles in return for sizable campaign contributions. These contributions had been so effective in winning elections, however, that the willingness to sell out to organized wealth had given place to extortion. Politicians, particularly those in the Republican party, had been quick to adopt the "fat-frying" process; they had made legislation favorable to predatory interests contingent upon gifts to fill party coffers.

Bryan thought that the remedy for this evil lay in the publication of campaign contributions shortly before the election, and he outlined his plan in 1907. He would not publish all contributions, because small ones were usually made by people patriotically motivated. But he would fix a certain minimum, and a certain deadline—he suggested ten days before the election—at which time all contributions above the minimum would be published along with all expenditures. No contributions were to be accepted after that date, and following the election a final statement of expenditures would be required.[74] The Democratic party in 1908 adopted a plank substantially endorsing this plan. Although the Republicans did not follow suit, Taft pledged full publicity in his acceptance speech delivered after Bryan had suggested that as nominees they agree to publish funds contributed. While Taft would not consent to publicity prior to the election, his course during the campaign was impeccable—painfully so, thought Theodore Roosevelt.[75]

Bryan also won a victory for another idea—international arbitration—but it proved to be a bitter one, for it failed to have the results intended. Most of the Commoner's issues and reforms were domestic in nature. Imperialism was an exception, but even here Bryan had opposed extending American influence into areas not contiguous with the United States itself. Nevertheless, he was not isolationist in his thinking, and the arbitration of international disputes was one of the reforms nearest his heart. It was a proposal ideally suited to the thinking of one who spoke so movingly of the "Prince of Peace." Bryan had long supported arbitration in disputes between management and labor, and at the conclusion of the Russo-Japanese treaty in 1905 he suggested that President Roosevelt follow through on the action he had already taken and make arbitration treaties the next step in his foreign policy.[76] The next year, visiting England, he attended the sessions of the Interparliamentary Union and offered several suggestions on the amicable settlement of international disputes. When he returned to the United States, he launched a crusade for treaties of conciliation with other nations—a crusade that reached its culmination when he became Woodrow Wilson's Secretary of State and signed thirty such treaties.[77]

Bryan's peace plan provided for international agreement to postpone war until after an impartial court had conducted an investigation of questions in dispute and made recommendations. He did not propose that any agency be granted the power to enforce those recommendations. Force was inconsistent with peace; it was also unnecessary. Impartial scrutiny would be sufficient to reveal the facts, give time for calm consideration of the issues, and mobilize public opinion (which would usually be in favor of peace).[78] If the United States took the lead in negotiating peace treaties, it would be "a power in the best sense of the term"; others would follow its example. Those who opposed Bryan's plan argued that disputes involving national honor could not be settled by arbitration. But he observed that "whenever a nation wants to fight, it manufactures a question of honor." And he went on to add that investigation of every controversy not settled by diplomacy would clear up confusion between questions of fact and of honor. Once the facts had been obtained, "we would generally find there was no real question of honor." [79]

After describing his plan to an international conference at Edinburgh in 1910, Bryan wrote Taft pointing out that the British government seemed willing to negotiate just such a treaty as he had outlined. The President was receptive to the suggestion that an agreement be formulated. He yielded to no one in his dedication to world peace. Secretary of State Philander Knox was therefore directed to begin diplomatic discussions, and by the summer of 1911 treaties with England and France were ready for presentation to the Senate.[80] Once again Bryan and Andrew Carnegie exchanged views on the ratification of a treaty, and this time they agreed. The Commoner was in a jubilant mood when he wrote the pacific philanthropist: "I can not conceive of any question arising between civilized nations which can not be adjusted more satisfactorily by reason than by force, and I rejoice that universal peace seems so near." [81]

The Taft treaties went beyond Bryan's proposals; they called for arbitration of all justiciable differences between contracting nations, not merely investigation of disagreements. Yet it seemed to Bryan that they were "such a long step in advance" that he tried to persuade his friends in the Senate to vote ratification.[82] He was not the only private citizen to discuss the matter with senators. Theodore Roosevelt, who by this time had broken with Taft, wrote antitreaty letters to Henry Cabot Lodge and Elihu Root, and his views were in harmony with senatorial opinion.[83] Insisting upon its right to decide whether or not a question should be submitted to arbitration, the Senate quashed the treaties with amendments the President was unable to accept.[84] Although Taft reluctantly withdrew from the contest, both he and Bryan were sanguine when they looked to the future. Earlier the Commoner had asked, "Is it too much to hope that as years go by we will begin to understand that the whole human race is but a larger family?" [85] The answer came in 1914.

Prohibition, Public Ownership, Immigration

To discuss in terms of his fundamental consistency the issues on which Bryan expressed opinions is to run the risk of minimizing inconsistencies and ignoring contradictions. The Commoner modified his position with respect to two questions: prohibition and government ownership of railroads. And on one other issue, immigration, his views seemed to contradict some of the cardinal tenets of his faith. Complete and logical philosophical systems are rare, if indeed they can be said to exist at all. Furthermore, it may be doubted that rigid adherence to such a system in all its ramifications would produce happy results. Bryan reacted to circumstances emotionally and intuitively rather than rationally. He trusted his heart more than his head. He was not logically or rationally consistent in all questions.

On the issue of government ownership Bryan overreached himself and was placed in the embarrassing position of having to qualify, if not retract, some of his statements. He and his followers gazed longingly at proposals for the public ownership of utilities and carriers but for some time were reluctant to advocate them in political campaigns. In 1904, however, he wrote Louis F. Post that while he did not expect the party to support every reform he advocated, he did think that the Democracy would have to face up to the future. He then revealed that he intended to encourage the formation of "municipal ownership clubs" in order to strengthen the movement in that direction and to encourage agitation for state ownership of railroads.[86] During the next year several articles on government ownership appeared in *The Commoner*. One pointed out that there was a difference between "natural monopolies" and enterprises in which competition was possible, and that there was strong sentiment for doing municipal work directly rather than through franchises granted to private corporations. Another typical piece suggested that a precedent for the government ownership of railroads was established when a railroad across Panama was acquired by the Roosevelt administration, and that the only question left open for dispute was the advisability or necessity of such a step. "If the government has a right to own and operate a railroad in Panama connecting the oceans," ran the argument, "it has a right to own and operate a road in the United States, connecting the oceans, and it can proceed to build or buy such a road whenever the people are convinced that public interests can be promoted thereby." Still another article urged municipal ownership of telephone lines.[87]

If Americans were apathetic toward these observations, they reacted violently in 1906 when Bryan, returning triumphantly from abroad, trumpeted his support of government ownership of trunkline railroads:

> I have already reached the conclusion that railroads partake so much of the nature of a monopoly that they must ultimately become public property and be managed by public officials in the interest of the whole community in accordance with the well-defined theory that public ownership is necessary where competition is impossible. I do not know that the country is ready for this change; I do not know that a majority of my own party favor it, but I believe that an increasing number of the members of all parties see in public ownership the only sure remedy for discrimination between persons and places and for extortionate rates for the carrying of freight and passengers.[88]

He thought that only trunk lines should be operated by the national government, and that the states should be left responsible for local lines. But the details of his proposal seemed of minor importance; it soon became apparent that the majority of his party did not favor it. If it was a trial balloon he had launched at his New York reception, it exploded in mid-air. Perhaps the time would come, as the Commoner suggested, when a choice would have to be made between "Government ownership of the roads and railroad ownership of the Government." [89] Few were ready to believe that the time had arrived, and as he listened to the voice of the people, Bryan became convinced that they were right.

He spent much of his time during 1907 explaining that he had not meant to make government ownership an immediate political issue and that he believed there should be more experimentation with rate regulation first. "Mr. Bryan," noted *The Commoner,* "fully agrees with those who believe that it would be unwise to turn attention from regulation, on which the people are ready to act, to government ownership, upon which the people are not ready to act." [90] The New York *World* asked the crucial question: "But does he really believe in government ownership, now that he has found it unpopular?" [91] Bryan took refuge in the doctrine of majority rule. He had no desire, he said, "to force government ownership upon the country," and even if that were his wish he was powerless to do so "against the will of the people." [92] During the Democratic convention of 1908, he wired his brother that any mention of government ownership in the platform would be a mistake. "Those who favor it do not ask for it, and if those who oppose it were to secure such a plank it would be regarded as a deliberate rebuke to me." [93] The withdrawal was thus complete.

Bryan was to reverse his position on one other major issue, prohibition, during the opposition years. Because he commented on that question most extensively before 1896 and after 1912, it does not really fit in with other reforms of the opposition period. Yet the year 1910 was a significant one for both the man and the issue, and Bryan's attitude toward prohibition deserves consideration here. Throughout his life the Commoner was a total abstainer, but until 1910 he refused to join the temperance movement. In 1890 he had even campaigned against prohibition, not because he approved of drinking, to be sure, but because he believed that the question was a moral and not a political one. And although he had not solicited the wet vote, it is probable that his support of the state platform which favored high licenses and local option satisfied the proponents of the saloon and helped to give him his victory at the polls.[94]

By 1910, however, the local option experiment had been tried in Nebraska and had been found unworkable; saloonkeepers of towns declaring themselves dry had simply set up their establishments outside village or city limits. County option was therefore suggested as a more effective solution to the problem, and it became an issue in the state convention at Grand Island. Bryan led the minority favoring county option and was soundly defeated. Nebraska Democrats also nominated for governor James C. Dahlman, who promised free beer on the state house grounds if elected. The wets, as it turned out, did not get their lawn party; the Commoner still had a following among his beloved "people," and without his support Dahlman was defeated.[95]

Given his earlier pronouncements, why did Bryan support prohibition in 1910? In making his explanation, Bryan said that he had been reluctant to take up the issue. He had urged the state legislature to adopt the initiative and referendum as a means of avoiding it, for the question of county option could have been decided by the people directly, and a split within Democratic ranks could have been averted. But the "liquor interests" had exerted pressures and the initiative and referendum had been by-passed. If prohibition had become a political question as well as a moral one, therefore, it was the "favor-seeking corporations" that had forced it into politics. "The fight against evil is always an uphill one," Bryan wrote his old Populist supporter, General Weaver, "and the hill is never steeper than when you fight the liquor interests." And when opponents of prohibition vowed to destroy the Commoner politically, he answered that if they were successful in doing so, "my death will be a warning to the fathers and mothers of the power of this foe to the home and American life." [96]

Eventually, of course, Bryan gave up county option and devoted his energies to the national prohibition movement. It would not be too much to say that the fight in Nebraska over county option was one link in the chain of events that led to the ratification of the eighteenth amendment in 1919. Yet the Commoner's reversal of his earlier position has another and perhaps deeper significance. Even though the temperance crusaders were successful in securing the eighteenth amendment—even though "the people" were still with him—Bryan's espousal of the prohibition cause in 1910 signalled the decline of his influence as a party leader. Too many of his fellow Democrats at that time agreed with the opinion Henry Watterson expressed to Norman E. Mack:

I have a long letter from Mr. Bryan explaining his "attitude" as to the Prohibition question. The real point was and is that he should have no "attitude" at all. As in the matter of Railway Ownership, he should have left the Temperance question severely alone. The moral philosopher may say whatever is uppermost in his mind; but the Statesman—especially the party leader—must have some reserves.[97]

Bryan was a more appealing figure when he entertained no reservations than when he did. He expected other Americans to live up to the values of their heritage and he always tried to do so too. Nevertheless he felt compelled to take at least one position which was difficult to reconcile with the idea of·human dignity and worth that formed a part of his faith. He attempted a reconciliation, certainly, but it failed to ring true. The issue involved was unrestricted Oriental immigration, to which Bryan was unalterably opposed.

He believed that those who favored throwing open the Golden Gate to immigrants from the Orient could be divided into two groups: first, those who believed that "universal brotherhood requires us to welcome to our shores all people of all lands"; and second, a much larger group that favored such a policy "on the ground that it will furnish cheap labor for household and factory work." [98] The validity of the moral argument, said Bryan, depended upon what the purpose of the immigrant happened to be and upon the power of the United States to assimilate these peoples. If they came, as Bryan believed they did, only to accumulate savings and then return to the Far East without having contributed anything to American life, they could not "demand admission on moral grounds." [99] And if their coming was advantageous for employers who wanted to cut labor costs, it was the reverse for American workers driven into the streets by an abundant supply of cheap labor. Moreover, race riots were an inevitable result of such a development.[100]

Bryan thus contrived to see unlimited immigration of Orientals as a work of the devil. "Our own power to help the world by the absorption of surplus population has certain natural and necessary limitations," he said, admitting his reservations. "We have a mission to fulfill and we can not excuse ourselves if we cripple our energies in a mistaken effort to carry a burden heavier than our strength can support." [101] This was a far cry from the noble sentiments the Commoner expressed when he spoke of world peace. His remarks were a reflection of an attitude that brought tension to the West Coast and discussion of war with Japan in 1907.[102]

Consistency, Moralism, and Opposition Leadership

To sum up, Bryan's course with respect to issues of the opposition years warrants two generalizations. The first is that he often acted on his belief that issues were made by circumstances and events. As suggested in Chapter III, conditions existing on the plains in the late nineteenth century created the issue of free silver. Imperialism was the result of events taking place after 1898. Bryan also defended modifications in his program by arguing that they were justified by the dynamics of American life. He did not insist upon making government ownership an issue in 1908 because he was "not sure the people are ready to consider the question." [103] And he told Nebraska Democrats in 1910 that the activities of those opposed to prohibition had brought about a change in conditions which made a reversal of his earlier stand against that reform necessary. Yet the real importance of the idea that events make issues lies in its influence upon Bryan as an opposition leader. Because any development was likely to create an issue, he subjected each new event to searching analysis. He was committed to the idea that the people must rule, and he labored to keep them informed through his newspaper and his lectures. Inasmuch as he wrote and spoke critically rather than impartially, he functioned admirably as a leader of the opposition.

The second generalization to be drawn from Bryan's activities during the period from 1896 to 1912 is that he was remarkably consistent. His program revealed few internal contradictions, and it was, for the most part, a logical extension of the moralism of the Middle Border. Furthermore, once having taken up a position on any question, he was extremely reluctant to surrender it. This reluctance was perhaps most in evidence during the campaign of 1900 when he refused to leave a free silver plank out of the Democratic platform. In spite of the combined efforts of friends and politicians—in spite of their arguments that silver was dead—Bryan remained "perplexingly indifferent" to their appeals.[104] The same obstinacy or adherence to principles manifested itself again and again during the opposition years. Occasions when he stated his position in equivocal terms were rare. Having such a man as leader of the opposition was of incomparable benefit to voters of the United States. His criticism of the party in power was always based upon premises that were well known, and the Commoner therefore served not only as a critic, but also as a kind of yardstick of reform.

VI

*

*   *   *

*

BRYAN AND THE PROGRESSIVE

MOVEMENT

THE YEARS BETWEEN the turn of the century and 1917 have come to be known in American history as the progressive era. This was a period when the nation seemed to awaken from slumber as a new dawn chased away shadows of venality and selfishness from political and economic life. He who does what is true, reasoned Americans, comes to the light, and they were ready to believe that the rosy tints sweeping over the landscape emanated from the light that shone more and more unto the perfect day. The dawn symbolized progress, for progress was as pervading and as inevitable as the dawn. Progressivism was not peculiar to any single element of American society. It was a mass movement encompassing Populistic agrarianism and urban humanitarianism, rural radicalism and respectable middle-class reform. Its philosophy could not be expressed in neat, consistent, logical formulae; it was without dogmatic structure, if not without dogma.

Admittedly the progressive impulse was so complex as to defy generalization. For purposes of analysis, however, the classification proposed by Richard Hofstadter is helpful. There were, he suggests, two broad influences in progressive thought, one formed out of the agrarian tradition, and the other shaped by what were primarily urban developments.[1] Never really becoming identical, the two influences often overlapped and appeared to merge. To contrast the disciples of Bryan with the apostles of Roosevelt is to contrast one type of progressivism with the other, and one of the supreme ironies of the Commoner's political career is that he found himself in opposition to men whose feelings at many points matched his.

The identification of urban with rural progressive thought was made easier by the agrarian bias of most reformers and their tendency to shape programs with a view toward the West. T.R. wooed and won the heart of middle-class America, both in the cities and on the farms. That a newspaper editor from Emporia, Kansas, should give articulate expression to Roosevelt's opinions is a monument to the universality of their appeal. Yet in spite of similarities between the two strands of progressive thought, differences did exist, and Bryan labored to make them apparent to his compatriots. He was not entirely successful in his opposition to the Roosevelt administration, but his efforts aided the reform movement which was his primary concern.

Progressives—Urban and Rural

The Commoner was perceptive in detecting the apparently unimportant differences in stress and emphasis which were evidence of a significant difference in mentality between the urban progressives and the rural wing of the movement for which he was the spokesman. That he sensed the difference in mentality also seems likely, but he never spelled it out in specific terms. He neither probed deeply into the philosophical assumptions of his opponents, nor felt compelled objectively to ask why they held the views they did. He was not searching for understanding of American urban development; he was far more concerned with meeting arguments than with finding reasons for their existence. He was, furthermore, only remotely connected with the problems of urban life. He had been reared in a rural environment, he established his permanent residence in a state with economic interests that were overwhelmingly agricultural, and the moralism of the Middle Border had profoundly influenced his thought. Although he had great sympathy for the industrial laborer and shaped his platforms to appeal to workers, this sympathy was not the result of firsthand experience, careful observation, or thorough investigation.

Bryan's attitudes were grounded in his emotions rather than in reason. When he followed the dictates of his heart rather than his mind, Bryan was romantic, and his ready acceptance of the farmer's cause in the Populist period indicates a romantic temperament. He did not offer proof that the "gold ring" or the "money power" had deliberately set out to bilk the farmer of his just rewards. He only saw that the stout-hearted pioneer men and women who had braved the elements in establishing homesteads on the plains were suffering, and relying on his intuition, he concluded that much of their suffering was the result of heartless and callous exploitation. The Commoner was sensitive to social wrongs, just as revivalists have been sensitive to sin. The parallel can be extended. The revivalistic solution for evil is conversion, and Bryan sought to convert Americans, particularly those living in the metropolitan centers of the East where Satan was most active.

On the afternoon of August 8, 1896 Bryan boarded the train to begin a journey that would take him to Madison Square Garden for official notification of his nomination. It was a dramatic moment; the Boy Orator brought to mind the youthful David going out to slay Goliath. In response to calls for a speech, he said:

> In ordinary times I would have desired to have the notification take place at my home. But this is not an ordinary campaign, and, feeling that the principles in which we are interested should rise above any personal preferences which we may have, I expressed the desire to be notified in New York, in order that our cause might be presented first in the heart of what now seems to be the enemy's country, but which we hope to be our country before this campaign is over.[2]

Not only would the giants of Wall Street be slain, but conversion would occur on a grand scale. The devil would be defeated, the enemy's country would be won, and the people would be saved. The incident illustrates Bryan's approach to social and economic problems: what the nation needed was not analysis of the causes of injustice but conversion to reforms that would restrain evil.

Progressive leaders of urban mentality were also concerned with placing limitations on wrongdoing; they too spoke in moral terms. Yet their method of dealing with wickedness tended to be realistic rather than romantic or revivalistic. Well-educated and moderate, they encouraged painstaking investigation and fact-finding; unlike Bryan and his agrarian followers, they distrusted emotion and placed their faith in reason. In the preface to his little book *Sin and Society*, which had great appeal for the urban progressive, Edward Alsworth Ross wrote:

> This book deals with sin, but it does not entreat the sinner to mend his ways. It seeks to influence no one in his conduct. It does seek to influence men *in their attitude toward the conduct of others*. Its exhortation is not *Be good*, but *Be rational*. To modify conduct one touches the heart. To modify the judgements on conduct one speaks to the intellect. The latter is the method of this book. Its aim is to enlighten rather than to move.[3]

The Commoner preached a message of love and taught that America would progress to the fulfillment of her mission when conversion permitted love for man to rule in every heart. The urban progressives espoused a scientific humanism. "Your pious leanings are not in accord with the progressive reform and regenerative movement of the age," wrote one of Bryan's correspondents.[4] Such men believed that progress would come through the exercise of man's rational faculties, that if social evils were to be eliminated it would be as the result of scientific investigation.

Bryan and the urban progressives therefore developed differing conceptions of reality. When the latter undertook the investigation of slum conditions, the frauds perpetrated by political machines, the manipulations of financiers, and the widespread vice that flourished in rapidly growing cities, they came to the conclusion that evil-doing was universal. Every class, every interest group, every section was directly or indirectly responsible for failure to realize in full the promise of American life. The urban progressives saw dangers in powerful labor unions as well as in powerful trusts; they condemned passivity to corruption as well as corruption itself. Bryan, with his invincible faith in the common man, believed that wrong-doing was the work of a vicious few. Reality for him included the dignity of those who earned their bread by the sweat of their brow as well as the utter depravity of a few conspirators of great wealth and power who had selfishly appropriated what rightfully belonged to the sons of toil. Repeatedly Bryan drew upon this view of reality, as he did when dashing off his comment on "Frenzied Finance," Thomas Lawson's widely read muckraking series dealing with operations of the stock market:

> Mr. Lawson's phrase, "Frenzied Finance," is too mild. Conscienceless finance is a more accurate description of what goes on in Wall street. "Frenzied" would imply an excitement so intense as to temporarily suspend the operation of the reason, but some of the Wall street transactions are *deliberately contrived schemes* for deception and pillage.[5]

The rapid industrialization of the United States after the Civil War brought a train of abuses deplored by both urban and rural progressives and figuring prominently in their respective conceptions of reality. Just as these views on reality differed, so also did urban and rural reactions to postwar economic developments differ. The nationalizing of business was accompanied by a status revolution in which the old gentry of long-established wealth and social position saw itself being replaced by the new captain of industry as a controlling power in American life. According to Professor Hofstadter, this displacement was the motivating force behind the political activities of urban progressives.[6] What evidence supports his contention? Statistical studies by George Mowry and Alfred D. Chandler, Jr. reveal that with few exceptions progressives belonged to the middle class, that most were college graduates, that they held positions of responsibility in the professions and in business, that many of them came from old and respected families, that the majority belonged to Protes-

Bryan's parents—Judge Silas Bryan, a dedicated Jacksonian Democrat and fervent Baptist, and Mariah Jennings Bryan, a "strong-minded, sensible Christian woman."

W. J. "Willy" Bryan about seven years after his birth March 18, 1860.

All photos and drawings from the Nebraska State Historical Society collections unless otherwise credited.

Bryan's birthplace at Salem, Illinois.

The Bryans' farm home near Salem.

Townsend Studio, Lincoln

Bryan (fourth from left standing) represented Illinois College at an intercollegiate debate contest in 1880. The young woman is Jane Addams.

Bryan wearing the white silk tile, a custom of college juniors in Illinois.

Bryan, the young lawyer of Jacksonville, Ill. (1883-1887), and of Lincoln, Neb. (after October, 1887).

The "Boy Orator of the Platte" campaigning (successfully) in the fall of 1890 for election to Congress from Nebraska's Second District.

Congressman Bryan and Mrs. Bryan (the former Mary Baird) arriving in Washington, D. C., to start his second term, January, 1893.

The Chicago Coliseum during the Democratic Convention, June, 1896.

In the wake of his famous "Cross of Gold" speech, young Bryan is swept to the nomination for the Presidency.

The National Free Silver Party notifies Bryan that he is also its
candidate for President at ceremonies in Lincoln Sept. 8, 1896.

Some of the newsmen assigned to Bryan for the 1896 campaign pose with Bryan, holding daughter Grace, Mrs. Bryan, holding W. J. Bryan, Jr., and daughter Ruth, seated at the feet of her mother.

Eastern newspapers wanted pictures of Bryan the farmer, so photographers obliged with these poses of Lawyer Bryan on his small acreage east of Lincoln.

Bostwick Studio, Omaha

Bostwick Studio, Omaha

Bryan campaigned indefatigably and spoke at hundreds of places, including (above) a whistle stop in Stromsburg, Neb., and (below) a lumber camp in a southern state.

His visit to alma mater, Illinois College, included a serenade by students.

A typical small-town rally for The Great Commoner, this one in St. Peter, Minn.

A campaign photograph widely distributed by the Bryan forces.

"HELL BROTH."

Harper's Weekly bitterly attacked The Great Commoner.

A MIGHTY RISKY EXPERIMENT

Chicago Historical Society

"He keeps talkin' silver all the time and that's where we've got him," said Mark Hanna, McKinley's campaign manager. This GOP broadside held up the spectre of a 53-cent dollar for eastern workingmen.

Although Bryan lost, he received more votes than any previous candidate for the presidency. Victorious McKinley gives his inauguration address.

Library of Congress

Bostwick Studio, Omaha

Bryan volunteered for the war with Spain. Here he rides at the head of his Nebraska regiment at the Trans-Mississippi Exposition in Omaha in the summer of 1898.

Col. Bryan with General Fitzhugh Lee in camp in Florida.

In August, 1900, Bryan and his wife pose for a campaign picture in Lincoln, a few weeks after The Great Commoner was nominated to try a second time to defeat McKinley, this time with Adlai E. Stevenson as his running mate.

Bostwick Studio, Omaha

In "the second battle" Bryan made silver an issue, and the principal GOP broadsides argued that if McKinley was right in 1896, he was right in 1900.

Chicago Historical Society

Bryan's congratulatory note to McKinley.

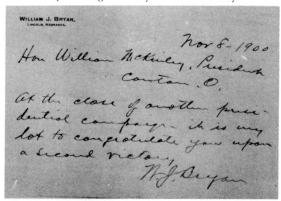

Bostwick Studio, Omaha

Undismayed by defeat, Bryan in January, 1901, founded *The Commoner*, which achieved a small circulation but great influence as a spokesman for the Democracy as he understood its mission. Above, the home of *The Commoner* in Lincoln, Neb., and below, Bryan lending an unfamiliar hand on the press.

Bostwick Studio, Omaha

Editor Bryan at his desk. *Bostwick Studio, Omaha*

When Bryan was absent on extended speaking tours, *The Commoner*'s presses were kept rolling by his younger brother Charles, who was to become a nominee for Vice President in 1924.

Bostwick Studio, Omaha

THE LAND OF THE FREE

INDUSTRIAL FEUDALISM

His Old Friend, John—"Excuse me, Sam, but I cawn't help larfing when I think
ow 'ard you worked to throw off the yoke of British oppression."—New York Journal.

The plight of the farmer, the trusts, and private ownership of utilities
were frequently the subject of cartoons in *The Commoner*.

"ECONOMY OF PRODUCTION"--HOW THE PROCEEDS ARE DIVIDED.

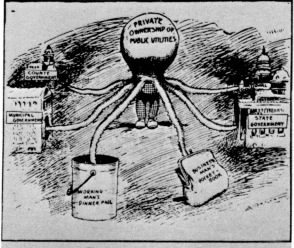

"A head in everything."

The greatest octopus of them all.

Some of the Nebraskans Now in the City to Welcome W. J. Bryan Home

Bostwick Studio, Omaha

When Bryan returned from a year's world cruise in August, 1906, many of the party faithful were in New York City to greet him, among them many Nebraskans, cartooned in the New York *World*.

The *World* joyously proclaims Bryan's return to America.

Bostwick Studio, Omaha

Bostwick Studio, Omaha

The crowd for Bryan's official welcome at the Hotel Victoria in New York City.

Bryan haircuts distinguish the Nebraska delegation.

Bostwick Studio, Omaha

Bryan's triumphal tour westward to his home in Lincoln took on all the appearances of a campaign train. Here he greets a crowd in Iowa.

As the entourage neared Lincoln, Bryan's train was halted for an advance reception by home-town friends.

Bryan was nominated for the presidency a third time in June, 1908. This was the scene at Fairview, his new Lincoln home, following notification ceremonies in August.

"SHALL THE PEOPLE RULE"

A 1908 campaign poster.

A campaign rally at Omaha.

A popular campaign portrait.

"SADOME"
DRAWN BY KEMBLE

Bryan as Salome in *Harper's Weekly*, Sept. 5, 1908.

Before the era of radio and television in American politics, perhaps no candidate for the presidency was seen and heard by more people than Bryan. These pictures of The Silver-Tongued Orator were taken during a speech in Virginia in 1907. The photographer is unknown.

Chautauqua
1911
Banner Program

Art
Oratory
Music
Recreation

Literature
Science
Government
Fellowship

Wm. J. Bryan

Woodbine, Iowa
July 22 to July 28

ATH·VAWTER

A Chautauqua PSALM

The chautauqua is coming soon. Whether or not I shall attend is not a debatable question.

The chautauqua comes but once a year. It affords opportunities I shall surely grasp while they are here.

And there are just seven chautauqua days in a whole year. So I shall be there every one of the seven days.

I am not selfish. So I shall take my folks with me of course. They will enjoy it as much as I.

I want my wife to get the thrill of it all. My boy shall hear the great speeches. My girl will like the music.

The ordinary run of life entails many problems. The chautauqua is built for joy; and joy is a good thing for my family.

My hands have labored long and steadily. I shall give them a little rest at chautauqua. At the same time I shall get the brain tonic of the wholesome enthusiasm there.

All my friends and neighbors will be there. It is a wonderful place for sociability. It is a picnic a week long; and I need the picnic.

I love good music too. The chautauqua brings me the very best in great abundance and variety. I shall fill my soul with it this time.

The geniuses of every community are awakened by the chautauqua. It is a mid-summer God-send to the whole population. I am located in the front booster wagon.

The commonplace experiences of every day incline one to become hidebound and also cultivate ingrowing dispositions. The chautauqua shakes us up and shakes us loose. I want to be so shaken. Shake with me.

I am fairly prosperous. I can well afford the small expense. I can take the time it requires. I can't hope to live forever, so I will get the best the chautauqua has to offer while the opportunity is here.

I shall urge all my friends to get in with me on this chautauqua joy. I would feel mighty lonesome by myself. And they will get in too. They know a thing or two.

The programs are going to be delightful. There are musicians, entertainers and orators galore. And Thaviu, the little Bandmaster, is coming back with a band of forty. Come and sit with me in the front row.

It is my chautauqua. Nobody can enjoy it for me. I shall take pleasure in doing all the enjoying I can, up to my capacity. I shall start in with the Spanish Orchestra, the first day, and stay with it 'till Joy Night.

Bryan was a devoted disciple of the Chautauqua and its mission of bringing culture to the common man. During his active political career, Bryan gave scores of Chautauqua addresses.

Bryan napping in the men's smoking parlor of a train bearing him to another Chautauqua speaking engagement.

In the summer heat of Baltimore in 1912, it was Bryan who helped break a convention deadlock by dramatically announcing his support of Woodrow Wilson.

As Bryan watched the inaugural parade in March, 1913, the presidential carriage bore two smiling men closely linked to his political demise: W. H. Taft, who soundly defeated Bryan in 1908, and Woodrow Wilson, the new leader of the Democratic party whom Bryan had unstintingly supported.

In the spring of 1913, Bryan entered the White House, not as President, but as Wilson's Secretary of State. The Commoner could find solace, however. After sixteen barren years, the Democracy now possessed the great prize of American politics.

tant churches with a New England background, and that a great many opposed Bryan in 1896.[7]

No doubt such substantial and respectable men felt threatened by the parvenu who had acquired great power in industry, and no doubt they were attracted to a movement that promised to control him.[8] At this point the interests of urban and rural progressives coincided; both wished to curb the malefactor of great wealth, albeit for slightly different reasons. The yeoman farmer of the Jeffersonian tradition had disappeared; at least the most powerful and influential population groups were no longer agrarian. The Populist effort was after all an attempt to regain what farmers thought had been lost as a result of the machinations of the money power. If the urban progressives felt the pressure of a status revolution, the rural progressives believed they had already experienced one. While one group appealed to those who had something to lose, the other felt that something had already been lost. This sense of loss—or impending loss—made both wings of the progressive movement susceptible to the virus of nativism.[9]

Immigrants poured into the United States in unprecedented numbers between the turn of the century and the outbreak of World War I, but it was not size alone that distinguished this human tidal wave. It came at a time when western farmers still nursed some of the xenophobia left over from Populism, and when the urban gentry exhibited concern over loss of status. Unlike earlier migrations, this one for the most part was made up of peoples from southern and eastern Europe; by 1907 about 80 per cent came from Italy, Austria-Hungary, Poland, and Russia.[10] Although the wave struck the American coast with prodigious force, it did not have the momentum to carry a majority of these people beyond eastern cities and out to farmlands of the Middle Border. The shock of its impact was felt throughout the country, however, and it seemed all the more severe because in religion most of the immigrants were either Roman Catholic or Jewish.

Religion for the newcomer was a way of life providing continuity with the past. For this reason churches of the "Little Italys" and "Little Polands" and synagogues of the ghettos tended toward conservatism; permanence of form offered security in a world of uncertainty.[11] The rural progressives were so far removed from metropolitan slums that they were not much concerned with the psychological or spiritual needs of those who lived there. They probably could not have seen religion through immigrant eyes anyway, for their own churches were Protestant, their denominational affiliations were tenuous, and theirs was the optimistic and moralistic faith of the Middle West. The nativism that sometimes characterized rural progressive thought was therefore in large measure a reaction to immigrant religion. Like many of the Populists who believed Jewish bankers were a part of the Lombard Street–Wall Street conspiracy against them, rural progressives could be anti-Semitic. They were, however, more likely to be alarmed by what they regarded as the Catholic menace, which was usually in some way or other associated with the money power; nativism among the followers of Bryan was most commonly directed against Rome.[12]

Urban progressives were also troubled by the immigrant, his outlook, and his institutions. They were, of course, much closer to problems resulting from the congestion of various ethnic groups in some of the least desirable sections of large cities. Huddled there in squalor and poverty, immigrants were easy prey for machine politicians. Progressives of the cities, with their yearning for good government, were deeply disturbed, and they enlisted in the effort to facilitate Americanization of newcomers. But the great gulf fixed between immigrants and reform groups in metropolitan areas was difficult to bridge. The immigrant regarded political relationships as fundamentally personal, and he remained indifferent to the abstract appeals of urban progressives. Efficiency, system, order, balanced budgets, improved administration, and lower taxes were rejected by the slum-dweller. He wanted humanity, not balanced budgets; sympathy and assistance, not efficiency and order; mercy without justice, not justice without mercy.[13] And for all the graft and corruption associated with city machines, this much can be said for them: they did understand the immigrant mind and they did provide help when help was needed. "I stick to my friends high and low, do them a good turn whenever I get a chance, and hunt up all the jobs going for my constituents," said George Washington Plunkitt of Tammany Hall.[14] Here was an approach the immigrant could comprehend, and when reformers attacked the boss, they served only to clothe him in the Lincoln green of Sherwood Forest and surround him with the prestige of a Robin Hood.

Disappointed in the results of their efforts, some of the urban progressives accepted nativist myths. Others, with a devotion to duty that commands respect, continued to labor in the slums and in settlement houses. In spite of racism and nonsense in both its branches, the trend of the progressive movement was in the direction of at least a theoretical acceptance of the immigrant. Lincoln Steffens and Frederick Howe pointed out that not all the shame of the cities was attributable to the newcomer. Bryan often meliorated the extreme nativist views of his supporters.[15]

Nevertheless ethnic and religious sensitivities, when aroused, could cause complications. Every political campaign has its secret history, and the secret history of 1908 reveals the political confusion that nativism created among progressives. Earlier in his career Republican candidate Taft had seen service as civil governor of the Philippines. One of the knottiest problems he had faced related to the disposition of lands formerly held by Spanish friars. To negotiate a solution he had visited the Vatican, as Roosevelt put it, "in order to go straight to the headquarters of the business corporation with which he has got to deal in acquiring that business corporation's property." [16] Although Taft's visit to Rome had not produced immediate results, an agreement had finally been reached in November 1903. By its terms the United States had purchased all but 10,000 of the 400,000 acres in question for $7,543,000. Congress had authorized the insular government to raise the cash through a bond issue, and this done, lands were gradually sold in small amounts and on easy terms to Filipinos.[17]

The settlement seemed an equitable one and the problem had been appropriately laid to rest. Yet when Taft received the Republican nomination, the matter was exhumed and displayed as evidence of his friendliness toward Rome. At the same time, illogically, diatribes against his Unitarian convictions were widely circulated. "Think of the United States with a *president* who does not believe that Jesus Christ was the Son of God, but looks upon our immaculate Savior as a . . . low, cunning imposter!" expostulated the *Pentecostal Herald*.[18]

Such assaults caused Roosevelt to write his associate in consolation, "The attacks upon you by a certain type of small Protestant bigots [sic] are so infamous as to make my blood boil." [19] Democratic strategists, however, did not consider them entirely unwelcome. Josephus Daniels complained to his wife that there were "so many cranks to talk to," but the cranks seem to have persuaded the national committee that Taft forces were making political capital out of his mission to the Vatican,[20] Perhaps Democratic leaders reasoned that Republican gains would be countered if Protestant fears could be sufficiently aroused. At any rate little was done to pacify either the nativists or those who had misgivings about Taft's own religious beliefs.[21] "The Republicans are making an effort to reach our Catholic Democrats," Bryan wrote Henry Watterson, "but we are planning to meet this, and will, I think, succeed measurably well, although I would not be surprised if we lost a little in this direction." [22]

When the returns were tabulated, many who had supported Bryan were convinced that he had lost more votes in that direction than anyone had anticipated. Taft himself thought "the tremendous influence of the Catholic vote" one of the decisive factors in swinging New York over to the Republican column.[23] Bryan was puzzled, and for several weeks he printed letters in *The Commoner* under the headline, "Solving the Mystery of 1908." In the Bryan Papers there are nearly a hundred letters (no doubt a small portion of the total he received) which play upon the same monotonous theme—that Taft was the center of a popish plot. Comments such as the following might be multiplied *ad nauseam:*

I am sure you by this time know whence your defeat came from. It was ordered from Rome. You have only to look at the vote in Catholic counties to be convinced.

It was not Taft's strength; it was not your weakness; it was the Pope of Rome who elected Taft as President.

The Catholics and Jews were mainly the cause of the disaster . . . Catholic priests here were running around and frightening Democratic Catholics.

I want to call your attention to the two greatest sources of danger to our country, viz. *catholocism* [*sic*] and *foreign immigration*.

I am satisfied now that we were defeated yesterday by the Catholics. Taft's purchase of the Friar Lands in the Philippine Islands made him solid with the Pope.

Think not you have lost in the *hearts* and *minds* of the True Jeffersonian American People, we are with you; the Negro, Old Soldiers, Foreigners, Socialists, Populists, Catholics et al are the cause of it all.[24]

Bryan himself stood above such prejudices, but the reiteration of charges against the Catholic Church led him to make inquiries of friends in a position to judge their validity. The Reverend J. F. Nugent, one of Bryan's warmest admirers among the Catholic clergy, advised him that "the bishop didn't change a vote *nor couldn't* if he wanted to." James K. McGuire of the Democratic National Committee was certain that there had been no organized opposition to the Commoner within the Catholic Church and that no orders had been issued by Catholic bishops.[25] The election of 1908 remained a mystery to Bryan despite the number of explanations offered. Yet he did believe that defections occurred. "We need to do something to bring back the catholics who voted for Taft in 1908 and who will vote for him this year," he wrote Woodrow Wilson during the campaign of 1912. "*That is the one weak point* in our fight this year. I see, already, evidence of activity along this line." [26]

How many nativists supported Bryan in 1908 can never be known. That there were some who did poses an important question: To what extent was he influenced by them? During his years of opposition he was never fully in accord with nativist views; he hoped to win back Catholic voters, not proscribe them. So long as he held a position of leadership in the Democratic party, his major interest was in using it to bring about the reforms he advocated. This required all the assistance he could secure, and even nativists were not to be despised if they could be made to serve the reform cause. Accomplishment of his principal objectives required unusual political skill; a party composed of many different elements had to be persuaded to take united action. The Commoner was tried during the opposition years and he was not found wanting. Just as city bosses understood the immigrant and won his allegiance, so Bryan understood rural America and commanded its support. Pressing toward liberal reform in many areas, he retained the fealty of those who could hardly be considered liberal in their racial and religious attitudes.

The election of 1908 underscores the difference between urban and rural reactions to the immigrant and his institutions. Although nativism could be found in both progressive types, the xenophobia of the Midwest was religious in emphasis, while in the cities it had other—often racist—characteristics. This phenomenon helps to explain the divergence between the urban and rural mentality. Racism can have a pseudo-scientific rationale, and most of the racist arguments rested on what purported to be scientific foundations. The religious opposition to immigrants, on the other hand, resulted in part from the cluster of romantic and sentimental ideas that made up the faith of the Middle Border.[27] The differences between urban and rural progressive leaders who did not succumb to nativism are even more important as well as more suggestive of the same dichotomy. Seeking rational solutions to immigration problems, urban reformers stressed the duties of citizenship, demanded that newcomers meet their responsibilities, engaged in slum clearance, and provided settlement houses for the underprivileged. The rural progressives who followed Bryan would use even nativists in the war against sin; they fought conspiracy, not environment.

T.R. and the Commoner

Much of Bryan's opposition to Theodore Roosevelt can be traced to the contrast between rural and urban attitudes toward reform. Although a member of that class threatened by status revolution, Roosevelt was, to be sure, an imperfect symbol of the urban progressive impulse. He was certainly not one to view public issues with calm, scientific detachment. Muckrakers such as Ray Stannard Baker, John S. Phillips, and Charles Edward Russell, who prided themselves on their objectivity, thought him too partisan and ambitious to further significantly the cause of reform.[28] To many reformers he seemed no less equivocal than most politicians. "Mr. Roosevelt's reconstructive policy does not go very far in purpose or achievement," admitted Herbert Croly in 1909. But at the same time he added that "limited as it is, it does tend to give the agitation for reform the benefit of a much more positive significance and a much more dignified task." [29]

In this strange combination of positive force with moderation and dignity Roosevelt typified an important segment of progressive thought. His violence was usually expressed in words, not deeds, but it was not without influence. It served to provide Americans with a kind of moral purgative. To the urban progressive mind the psychic function of reform became increasingly important as the movement gained momentum. William Allen White thought that Roosevelt was "a force for righteousness" because his power was a spiritual one.[30] While they did not think in terms of conversion, progressives of metropolitan mentality, like agrarian reformers, sought an awakened conscience for America.

Legislative or material results, desirable though they always seemed, were not the sole object of urban progressive endeavor. In 1900 *The Public* printed a fable:

> Once upon a time some Reformers, looking very ferocious, came upon some Ordinary Persons. All this in a certain large and populous town.
>
> "Can you show us any tiger's tracks?" asked the Reformers.
> "We can show you a tiger," replied the Ordinary Persons.
> "All we want is tracks!" protested the Reformers, and went their way with much noise and were presently elected to fat offices, it being possible to fool enough of the people enough of the time.[31]

Urban progressives sought tracks and they found them; yet they often did not take the lead in suggesting means of preventing tigers from running about. Their programs were moderate, for they trusted tigers to behave once their tracks had been exposed to public scrutiny. Meanwhile, Bryan believed that he had treed a tiger. Having done so, he could not see much point in tracking its spoor; it should be killed or caged, he thought, and he called on "the people" to aid him in disposing of the beast. Roosevelt with his forceful language and moderate policies was a representative product of urban progressivism. Bryan, leading agrarian progressives, helped to bring about action by constantly demanding it.

T.R.'s debt to the Commoner has often been noted.[32] And the points at issue between the two were, in William Allen White's view, "so entirely technical, so nice in their adjustment, that it will strain democracy to its utmost to furnish public wisdom to see the truth and keep the demagogue's foot off the scales."[33] Yet while differences between the programs advocated by Bryan and Roosevelt may have been subtle, they should not be obscured by similarities. Apart from the obvious fact that the support which each man received came from different sources, there was sufficient conflict on public questions to encourage debate and criticism.

The most fundamental disagreement concerned foreign policy, where Bryan's desire for world peace ran counter to the bellicose imperialism of the Rough Rider. Perhaps Henry Blake Fuller was unfair when he suggested that T.R. delighted in "the spatter of brains upon the plains—and the gore that is mushy and thick."[34] Nevertheless, it was the combative side of Roosevelt's character that drew some of Bryan's sharpest criticism. The Commoner thought the strenuous life, as defined by T.R., was a reversion to a barbaric conception of virtue, for it placed "physical courage above mental greatness and moral worth." He was scandalized when Roosevelt told the cadets at West Point, "A good soldier must not only be willing to fight; he must be anxious to fight." This "fit of animal enthusiasm," thought Bryan, "revealed a moral deformity which must shock such of his friends as are not wholly carried away with the bloody and brutal gospel of imperialism."[35]

The evidences of brutality in Roosevelt's character are less significant than the relationship between imperialism and the progressive movement. Many of the progressives were, in fact, carried away by the "bloody and brutal gospel."[36] Herbert Croly, who was highly influential in shaping urban progressive opinion, believed that "the irresponsible attitude of Americans in respect to their national domestic problems may in part be traced to freedom from equally grave international responsibilities." The United States was manifestly justified in assuming responsibilities in Cuba and Puerto Rico. The Philippines constituted a more expensive obligation and their possession seemed to result in no obvious benefits to the United States. But Croly argued that they did have a peculiar value: they helped "American public opinion to realize more quickly than it otherwise would the complications and responsibilities created by Chinese political development and by Japanese ambition." Croly did not urge war for its own sake, nor did he plead for American intervention where the interests of the United States were not involved. He did contend that if the nation wanted peace, "it must be spiritually and physically prepared to fight for it." His argument—one that many progressives found attractive—was that "peace will prevail in international relations, just as order prevails within a nation, because of the righteous use of superior force." [37]

In the first decade of the twentieth century not many reformers associated, as did Bryan, the fight against imperialism abroad with the fight for progressivism at home. On the contrary, most of them found a certain harmony between the ideological content of imperialism and that of progressivism. Roosevelt refused to consider American withdrawal from the Philippines because the Filipino would "wallow back into savagery." He believed that in working for the Panama Canal despite objections from Colombia he was "certainly justified in morals, and therefore justified in law." In his famous "Corollary" to the Monroe Doctrine, he said that the American desire "to see all neighboring countries stable, orderly, and prosperous" might require intervention in their affairs.[38] Brandishing his "Big Stick," the President leaped onto the horns of a dilemma: it was sometimes impossible to combine humanitarian ideals with imperialistic or nationalistic aspirations. And when urban progressives were faced with a choice between the two, they usually chose imperialism or nationalism. Herbert Croly, for example, was highly critical of Tolstoy. The saintly Russian had "merely given a fresh and exalted version of the old doctrine of non-resistance, which, as it was proclaimed by Jesus, referred in the most literal way to another world. In this world faith cannot dispense with power and organization." [39]

On the home front the struggle between Bryan and the urban progressives centered around the problem of organization. This conflict demanded consideration of two basic questions: how far big business should be permitted to expand, and how far the national government should be permitted to go in controlling the activities of business. Both Bryan and the urban progressives condemned the abuses of big business. The Commoner was never more critical of captains of industry than Roosevelt was during the anthracite strike of 1902. While negotiations were taking place, T.R. commented upon the "gross blindness" of the mine operators. He thought they had failed "absolutely" to recognize that they had duties with respect to the public.[40] When they said that they would die of cold before yielding to arbitration, Roosevelt pointed out that *"they* were not in danger of dying of cold," for they would pay higher prices and suffer no discomfort. What they were really saying was "that they would rather somebody else should die of cold than that they should yield." This, thought the President, was an impossible position. "May heaven preserve me," he wrote, "from ever again dealing with so wooden headed a set, when I wish to preserve their interests." [41]

In spite of his invective Roosevelt was ambivalent toward big business. He did, after all, wish to protect business from socialism and "anarchic disorder." William Howard Taft, writing to the President from Manila during the furor of 1902, gave clear expression to the Rooseveltian and urban progressive point of view. "The blindness and greed of the so-called captains of industry would pass my comprehension," he confessed, "if I had not been made acquainted with the unconscious arrogance of conscious wealth and financial success. By your course you are saving these gentlemen from a cataclysm that they do not seem to understand the danger of." Taft thought that as a result of the anthracite settlement Roosevelt was in a position "to guide the feeling against trusts and the abuses of accumulated capital, in such a way as to remedy its evils without a destruction of those principles of private property and freedom of contract that are at the base of all material and therefore of spiritual and intellectual progress." [42] Unlike Bryan, Roosevelt and Taft did not fear bigness in business; their concern, and the concern of most urban progressives, was that trusts be controlled to prevent abuses. "What we believe in, if I understand it," wrote Taft somewhat uncertainly during the campaign of 1908, "is the regulation of the business of the trusts as distinguished from its destruction." [43]

The urban progressive was willing to concede that the formation of trusts was not only inevitable, but in many respects beneficial. Herbert Croly believed that huge corporations, even though sometimes guilty of abuses, had contributed to American "economic efficiency." They had brought order out of industrial and commercial chaos by substituting cooperative for competitive methods. And where the small businessman was not able to hold his own, Croly saw "no public interest promoted by any expensive attempt to save his life." Legislation designed to maintain competition was not only expensive; it was discriminatory. The Sherman Antitrust Act, for example, encouraged small business at the expense of big business, and it therefore discriminated for small business against the general good. Corporations should not be hampered in their natural growth, Croly thought, for this growth resulted in efficiency. On the other hand, in order to prevent abuses, large business organizations should be limited by broad powers exercised in the national interest.[44] Because powers so extensive could only be lodged in the national government, Croly and the urban progressives demanded centralization.

Bryan and the rural progressives did not accept either the logic or the conclusion of this argument, and the struggle over organization thus developed into a conflict involving principles of federalism. In 1907 Bryan observed that there were two forces at work within the nation, "one force tending to bring the government nearer to the people and the other tending to carry the government away from the people." He thought that "opposition to the rule of the people usually takes the form of the advocacy of legislation which removes authority from a point near to the people to some point more remote from them." [45] Senator Beveridge suggested that Bryan need have no fear of centralization of power in the national government, for the national government was nothing more than the people of the forty-six states acting in the mass. Bryan replied that "when the people of a state act together on a local matter they are nearer to the subject under discussion, and, therefore, can act more intelligently." [46]

The Commoner remained firm in the belief that "every attempt to take authority away from the community and vest it in some power outside of the community contains a certain amount of infidelity to the democratic theory of government." The true Jeffersonian democrat would not take from the national government any power necessary to the performance of its responsibilities, Bryan admitted, but he would regard the consolidation of all political power in Washington as "a menace to the safety of the nation." [47] National legislation dealing with the trusts should be supplemental to statutes already in existence in the states.

In 1910 when Roosevelt enunciated his New Nationalism—the very phrase suggests his debt to Herbert Croly—at Osawatomie, Kansas, Bryan was highly critical. T.R. was travelling a perilous road at breakneck speed. Indeed Bryan thought the Rough Rider had already galloped past a number of milestones: he had wished to put "the national need before sectional or personal advantage"; he had insisted that "every man holds his property subject to the general right of the community to regulate its use to whatever degree the public welfare may require it"; he had declared that "combinations in industry are the result of an imperative economic law which cannot be repealed by political legislation" and that the only solution to problems resulting from such combinations was to control them completely "in the interest of the public welfare"; he had confessed his impatience with "the impotence which springs from overdivision of governmental powers" and he had hailed the executive as "the steward of the public welfare." [48] Although this might have been acceptable urban progressive dogma, Bryan thought that Roosevelt had here raised issues which must in time separate him from Republican insurgents and alienate those Democrats who had been in sympathy with policies T.R. had stolen from Democratic platforms.

The Commoner had no doubt that the Hamiltonian doctrines of the New Nationalism were dead, yet he felt compelled to whistle in the graveyard. Even the Rough Rider, Bryan assured himself, could not popularize such a program, for "the trend is toward democracy and away from the aristocratic ideas of Alexander Hamilton." The New Nationalism was not really new; it was merely the latest indication of that "restiveness" which Roosevelt had always displayed when confronted by constitutional limitations. And what of this doctrine of executive stewardship? Did Roosevelt mean that "the executive department is to exercise a fatherly interest and act independently of the wishes of the people?" If so, thought the Commoner, he was advancing a doctrine as dangerous as it was strange to Americans: "the doctrine of monarchies, not the doctrine of republics." [49] Two years later, during the campaign of 1912, Democrats insisted that the New Nationalism demanded a new version of "America" for T.R.'s exclusive use:

> My country, 'tis of thee,
> Sweet land of mostly—Me,
> > Of Me I yell.
> All rule belongs to Me,
> Perkins, Bill Flinn and Me,
> For President, take Me,
> > Or, go to ――
>
> I am the Chief Bull Moose
> Bulwark of liberty
> > Of Me I sing,
> Land where my fathers died,
> I am thy joy and pride,
> From every mountain side,
> > Let my name ring.[50]

Bryan and the Muckrakers

Few periods in American history have been characterized by a livelier popular interest in issues than the progressive era. In a period before radio and television the media through which these issues could be discussed were limited. The speaker's rostrum was widely used, but its limitations were many. Chautauqua companies marshalled speakers and did much to eliminate difficulties in getting those speakers before audiences. Even so, only a small percentage of the American people was reached, and much time was consumed in reaching those few. The written word, therefore, proved a more effective medium for the discussion of issues, and the journalistic outpourings of the progressive period constitute one of its salient features. Although Bryan's fame rested in large part upon his oratory, his weekly newspaper

The Commoner was as important an organ as his matchless voice in the expression of his views. And newspapers and magazines—particularly the latter—were even more vital for the urban wing of the progressive movement. The literature of exposure, which is as old as the bawdy planet, took on a new intensity when packaged in magazines of national circulation. The titans of progressive journalism were the muckrakers, and a more zealous body of fact-finders would be difficult to imagine. They were not purveyors of a romantic sensationalism; their readers were sophisticated and respectable. The muckrakers were, in other words, representative of the urban progressive impulse. Examination of the relationship between editor Bryan and the muckrakers is therefore essential to an understanding of the relationship between the urban and rural progressives.

Paradoxically, it was Theodore Roosevelt who in 1906 first employed the figure which popularized the term "muckraker." Some of his contemporaries, he said, were like the Man with the Muckrake in Bunyan's *Pilgrim's Progress,* the man who would not look up even to receive a celestial crown and "continued to rake to himself the filth of the floor." T.R. conceded that filth needed raking, but he felt that those who did nothing else were dangerous. Although the President's charges caused a flurry of excitement in the press, they were so ambiguous that the object of his attack was uncertain. And Roosevelt did little to clear up the point. It was not Lincoln Steffens, he assured that writer, nor was it any of several others who had been associated with reform journalism. In any case, the term came to be used indiscriminately to describe all those engaged in the exposure of evil and corruption.[51]

The mass-circulation magazines found a ready market for such exposures. *Collier's, Munsey's, Hampton's, Everybody's,* the *Independent, Cosmopolitan,* the *American Magazine, McClure's*—all these served up dishes that were not so dainty to set before fact-hungry reformers. The virile articles in which Thomas Lawson analyzed stock-market practices and Charles Edward Russell's damning exposure of the beef trust appeared in *Everybody's.* Readers of *Collier's* were shocked by Samuel Hopkins Adams' treatment of patent-medicine frauds. *Cosmopolitan* published the famous series of David Graham Phillips, "The Treason of the Senate." Nothing escaped the teeth of the rake; even women's clubs and churches were not immune. The day had passed, thought Mr. Dooley, when magazines "was very ca'ming to the mind" and he could enjoy them as he did "a bottle iv white pop now an' thin." Even poetry had been influenced: "All th' pomes be th' lady authoresses that used to begin: 'Oh moon, how fair!' now begin: 'Oh, Ogden Armour, how awful!' " [52]

Although muckraking became a widespread journalistic activity, the most influential pioneer of the movement was the irascible S. S. McClure, founder of *McClure's Magazine*. Flitting hither and yon in his search for new authors and new subjects of potential interest to readers, he had, before the day of the muckraker dawned, already secured a large circulation through the imaginative use of popular fiction and biography.[53] Ida M. Tarbell's account of her first interview with McClure in Paris is a vivid portrayal of the man's character. He ran up four flights of stairs to her apartment, breathlessly informed her that he could stay only ten minutes, remained two hours chatting enthusiastically about his life and work, commissioned her to write a series of articles, borrowed her last forty dollars, and was off like a will-o'-the-wisp.[54] Yet McClure seems to have had no clear idea of where this furious activity was leading him or his magazine. Ray Stannard Baker thought him "one of the most unorganizable, impatient, and disorderly men I ever knew." [55]

In 1901 McClure hired Lincoln Steffens as an editor; characteristically, it was the unpremeditated consequences of this action that were the most far reaching. Although Steffens enjoyed the confidence of his chief, he was hardly a sparkling success during his first months with the magazine. And no one saw this more clearly than McClure himself. "Get out of here, travel, go—somewhere," he told his editor. "Go out in the advertising department. Ask them where they have transportation credit. Buy a railroad ticket, get on a train, and there, where it lands you, there you will learn to edit a magazine." Steffens landed in Chicago and there, he recalled later, "sure enough, I learned—not exactly how to edit a magazine, but I started our political muckraking." [56]

Perhaps Steffens was presumptuous, but it is clear that in its origins muckraking was unplanned and accidental. It was not until January 1903, when the Big Three of his staff—Tarbell, Baker, and Steffens—were hard at work digging up facts and writing exposures, that S. S. McClure paused to take a long, hard look around him and write a famous editorial. "How many of those who have read through this number of the magazine noticed that it contains three articles on one subject?" he asked. Confessing that it had not been so planned, he suggested that Miss Tarbell's current chapter on the history of Standard Oil, Baker's exposure of law-breaking during the anthracite strike, and Steffens' article on "The Shame of Minneapolis" constituted an arraignment of American character which should give the nation pause:

> Capitalists, workingmen, politicians, citizens—all breaking the law, or letting it be broken. Who is left to uphold it? The lawyers? Some of the best lawyers in this country are hired, not to go into court to defend cases, but to advise corporations and business firms how they can get around the law without too great a risk of punishment. The judges? Too many of them so respect the laws that for some "error" or quibble they restore to office and liberty men convicted on evidence overwhelmingly convincing to common sense. The churches? We know of one, an ancient and wealthy establishment, which had to be compelled by a Tammany hold-over health officer to put its tenements in sanitary condition. The colleges? They do not understand.
>
> There is no one left; none but all of us. . . . We all are doing our worst and making the public pay. The public is the people. We forget that we all are the people; that while each of us in his group can shove off on the rest the bill of to-day, the debt is only postponed; the rest are passing it on back to us. We have to pay in the end, every one of us. And in the end the sum total of our debt will be our liberty.[57]

Thus was muckraking born. The next three years were militant ones, and in 1906 the rake uncovered filth in virtually every nook and cranny of the United States. By 1908 muckrakers appeared to have exhausted themselves, but dissatisfaction with the Taft administration breathed new life into the movement, and 1911 was replete with exposures. The end was nevertheless in sight. Although many of the muckrakers were active during the campaign of 1912, the final decline had begun.[58] This span of years, as well as the urban-rural dichotomy in progressivism, demands a comparison of muckraking journals and *The Commoner,* and for these purposes *McClure's* may be considered representative of the former.

In appearance the two publications were quite different. *McClure's* was not an expensive magazine, but new processes had made possible an attractive, low-priced format. The glazed paper on which it was printed was made from wood pulp and was therefore much cheaper than rag paper, but it had many of the characteristics of high-quality paper. Improvements in photography and in the printing of photographs and paintings were a boon to the muckraking journals; each issue of *McClure's* was agreeably flavored with pictorial reproductions.[59] *The Commoner,* for many reasons, embodied few of these refinements so characteristic of the muckraking periodicals. It was a weekly newspaper, not a magazine, and it was made up like a newspaper. Photographs appeared rarely, although cartoons were a regular feature for several years. Advertising provided some relief from eyestrain, but it was distinguished chiefly for its gaucherie.[60]

Differences in appearance between *McClure's* and *The Commoner* were matched by differences in content. *McClure's* never concentrated its efforts wholly on muckraking. Even the famous issue of January 1903, which launched the movement, contained four fictional pieces, an installment on the autobiography of actress Clara Morris, an article on "English Men of Letters," and a scientific report on "Dr. Lorenz, Straightener of Children." While *McClure's* was a magazine with wide appeal, Bryan's only concession to broad reader interest in *The Commoner* was a "family page" devoted to anecdotes and recipes. Other content differences were perhaps more significant, however, for they reveal that the primary concern of *McClure's* was in accurate and objective description, while emphasis in *The Commoner* was upon remedies for abuses.

Few would deny that the muckrakers became interested in securing reforms. They nevertheless believed that exposure of evil was a necessary prelude to reform. In his introduction to Ray Stannard Baker's article, "The Right to Work," which concerned problems faced by nonstriking workers, McClure wrote, "We believe that the presentation of the facts . . . will be helpful to the public, which is the final arbiter, and beneficial to those also who have in charge the administration of labor unions." [61] And again, in an introduction to a study of child labor in the coal mines by Francis H. Nichols, he asserted, "The editors of McClure's know that, in this great controversy, what their readers want first of all is simply the facts." [62]

McClure was willing to pay for facts, and members of his staff were subsidized for doing research as well as for writing. Circulation figures justified his policy, but it produced other results too. The typical muckraker's devotion to accuracy has never been surpassed in American journalism. Steffens went out to find facts, not because they built circulation, but because he wanted to study cities scientifically and discover through inductive methods the causes of their shame.[63] No one more clearly stated the muckraker's point of view than did Ray Stannard Baker during a conversation with Jack London. When London asked him why he was not a socialist, Baker replied:

> You see, I'm not a reformer. I'm a reporter. I have only begun to look at the world. I want to see it all more clearly and understand it better, before I pledge myself to any final solution for the evils we both see. I'm not sure yet that if either you or I made over the world, it would be any better than the one we now have. We don't know enough.[64]

Muckraking, as it appeared in McClure's, was an expression of the urban progressive impulse: scientific, objective, unbiased, suggesting few specific solutions or answers and no sweeping alterations in the American social and economic system. "Th' noise ye hear is not th' first gun iv a rivolution," Mr. Dooley informed his friend, Mr. Hennessy, "It's on'y th' people iv th' United States batin' a carpet." [65]

The contents of The Commoner, aside from the family page, were almost exclusively editorial, for Bryan thought it his principal duty to present his point of view on every issue and event. He perhaps could not have adopted McClure's approach even had he so desired; his resources were too limited. He did not, however, feel any need to engage in muckraking. While *Mc-Clure's* was devoted to facts, *The Commoner* was devoted to arguments. The people, thought Bryan, were like jurors. "The most upright judge cannot decide fairly until both sides have been presented," he wrote, "and so a citizen, however well-meaning, must have a chance to read the arguments presented by those opposed to his views as well as the arguments advanced by those of his own party, if he would be sure of his ground." He therefore concluded that "there should be papers representing different schools of thought and different views on public questions for truth is born of conflict." [66] His function as editor, as he conceived it, coincided with his function as leader of a political opposition, and *The Commoner* provides a running commentary on current affairs from the rural progressive point of view.

Although Bryan himself did not engage in muckraking, he was in some measure both responsible for it and dependent upon it. Ray Stannard Baker thought the writing of the muckrakers captured American readers because the country had for years been berated by agitators with their charges of corruption and privilege "which everyone believed or suspected had some basis of truth, but which were largely unsubstantiated." This agitation was the result of a deep-seated unrest, and Bryan's campaigns seemed to Baker "vigorous, if blind, expressions of the same unrest." [67] After years of dissatisfaction, then, during which the search for a bête noire led to confusion through the multiplication of unproved assertions, the muckrakers arrived with their accurate and objective articles of exposure. Perhaps they would have appeared had there been no unrest, no Populist party, no silver crusade, and no reform pressure, but this seems doubtful. Certainly Baker's thesis that readers were more receptive to the muckrakers for having experienced late nineteenth-century agitation has much to recommend it. Insofar as Bryan had some share in this agitation, he helped to make muckraking possible.

The Commoner's association with the muckrakers goes further, however, for he used their findings to support his arguments. Again and again he was able to point to their articles as proof of what he had been saying since his entry into public life. In 1905 after citing a series of investigations before the courts, together with the work of Thomas Lawson, Ida M. Tarbell, and Charles

Edward Russell, Bryan made an observation similar to the one S. S. McClure had made two years before: "Here we have bankers, railroad magnates, promoters, manufacturers and speculators all vieing with each other in the use of methods which offend against both statute and moral law." But McClure had suggested that existing evils were attributable to society as a whole and that reform must come from "all of us." Bryan, uncompromising, never gave up the idea that the "money trust" was responsible for the sins of society. "The thimbleriggers at a street fair," he wrote, "are engaged in more honorable business for they cheat those who are foolish enough to risk their money on a game known to be dishonest, but these thimbleriggers of high finance rob the helpless and the dependents under the guise of doing an honest business." [68] Working from this assumption, it was easy for Bryan to suggest a program for the reform of abuses; it is always easier to pass laws preventing the misdeeds of a few than to legislate for a whole people.

Failure in Success

The interaction between Bryan and the muckrakers in the journalistic sphere parallels the interaction between the rural and urban wings of the progressive movement in the realm of political action. The urban progressives, feeling the pressures of a status revolution, demanded reform and through the muckrakers provided concrete evidence of evils in American society. Yet the urban progressives were reluctant to suggest specific policies for making reform effective. The rural progressives started with a program they had inherited from the Populists, and this program, modified, seemed to meet the problems which troubled the urban wing of the movement. Thus it would not be too much to say that the two wings of progressivism were complementary; the urban group demonstrated the need for a change, while the rural group led by Bryan produced a program which became the basis for change.

Roosevelt's adoption of plank after plank from the Bryan platform becomes intelligible when it is seen as the result of this dialectic at work within the progressive movement. T.R.'s support of rural planks of course drew considerable comment from political observers and indeed from Bryan himself. Such comment began to appear in quantity shortly after the election of 1904. Bryan then took occasion to point out that in the advocacy of freight regulation for railroads, Roosevelt was on Democratic territory. The President was receiving support from Democrats everywhere, he said, "not because he has discovered a new reform, not because democrats have abandoned their principles or that republican doctrines have become acceptable to them, but rather because Mr. Roosevelt has taken up a reform which was long ago and repeatedly suggested by the democratic party." [69]

T.R., however, appropriated more than rate regulation. In 1906 the New York *World* printed a remarkable editorial entitled "The Roosevelt-Bryan Merger." Using Bryan's recent Madison Square Garden speech and the President's annual message as a basis for comparison, the editorial discussed the basic agreement between the two men on the income tax, publicity for campaign contributions, enforcement of the Sherman Act, licensing corporations, government by injunction, the eight-hour day, arbitration of labor disputes, free trade for the Philippines, and the inspection of meat. After examining the points on which there was a difference of opinion, the editorial concluded that

if Mr. Roosevelt would advocate tariff revision and Mr. Bryan would stop advocating government ownership of railroads they would be substantially in accord. . . . Accepting Mr. Roosevelt and Mr. Bryan as the leaders of their respective parties we defy anybody to say where the dividing line is beyond which a voter has ceased to be a Roosevelt republican and becomes a Bryan democrat. There has been no such obliteration of party lines in American politics for three-quarters of a century. The Roosevelt-Bryan merger is one of the most extraordinary events in American history, especially in view of the fact that Mr. Bryan claims to be "more radical than ever," while Mr. Roosevelt persists in regarding himself as a rational conservative battling manfully "against the demagogue and the agitator." [70]

Bryan was soon speaking to this point with increasing frequency, for both parties were preparing for the presidential campaign ahead. In May 1907 at Newark, New Jersey, he addressed the People's Lobby, a nonpartisan organization. "I have so many opportunities to be partisan that I welcome an opportunity to be non-partisan," he began. Then with tongue in cheek he confessed that "I find it very difficult to be partisan now even when I want to be, for if I make a straight-out democratic speech, the first thing I know the president makes one of the same kind and then the subject immediately becomes non-partisan." [71] During the campaign of 1908, after the nominations were made, the Nebraskan frequently asserted that he, and not Taft, was Roosevelt's legitimate political heir. In a typical utterance, Bryan said:

> There are certain things that come naturally by descent, and reforms come by descent. You can not convey a reform by will. The President has tried to bequeath certain reforms to the Republican candidate, but I am the next of blood in the reform business, and they come to me. In fact, I think I could make it stronger than that. If a man dies and leaves no children the property goes back to his parents, and so far as reforms are concerned the Republican party has died without heirs, and the reforms go back to the one from whom the Republican party got the reforms. So I think I have a right to expect a good many Republican votes this year.[72]

The victory of Taft in November did not ring down the curtain on this line of argument. When T.R. began to expound his New Nationalism, Bryan repeated many of his old allegations. In 1911 he encouraged his followers to rejoice that Roosevelt had "AT LAST thrown his influence on the side of the popular election of senators and the initiative and referendum." The former President had become a convert on several propositions, however, and so far as he had supplemented his original commentary on the New Nationalism, "it is simply democracy under another name, and the new name does not fit it as well as the old name." [73]

While Bryan's influence on the urban progressives has received much emphasis, little attention has been paid the urban progressive influence on Bryan. To say with Vachel Lindsay that T.R. aped Bryan is to voice a partial truth; equally accurate would be the observation that Bryan aped T.R. Roosevelt at heart was conservative, and were it not for his desire to thwart radicalism by correcting some of the evils of the status quo, he might never have become a progressive at all. Even as a progressive he made a habit of balancing good and evil: the good trust as opposed to the bad trust, for example. In politics he dealt with machines, but he did so to buy votes for good legislation. "T.R. saw the machine; he did not see the system," thought Lincoln Steffens. "He saw the party organizations of the politicians; he saw some 'bad' trusts back of the bad politics, but he did not see the good trusts back of the bad trusts that were back of the bad machines." [74] Roosevelt represented the powerful but neutral state, or thought he did. And in the eyes of his followers he doubtless appeared to be standing righteously above partisan strife and acting in the interests of the public welfare. His position as a neutral resulted in equivocation—bristling equivocation, for Roosevelt was by nature a violent man and his nervous energy required an outlet. It resulted also in a modification of what had originally seemed a radical platform; in his hands the Bryan planks were cut and planed and used to construct a moderate program.[75]

It took no keen perception to see that Roosevelt was immensely popular with voters, and before long Bryan was taking pains to point out that he too was fundamentally conservative. "Not only is the reformer the real defender of property rights, but he is the best friend of the very persons who abuse him," he wrote in 1905. "Just as that physician is the best one who points out to his patient the dangers of the disease from which he suffers and proposes the best remedy, no matter how severe, so those are the best friends of the rich who attempt to restrain excesses and to correct abuses." [76]

The new moderation of the Commoner created a stir in the press during the campaign of 1908. The New York *Evening Post* observed that twelve years earlier Bryan had been regarded as a kind of "bogey man," an agitator and innovator, a "stirrer-up" of class hatred. "But today," commented the editorial writer, "Bryan has changed all that." Eastern newspapers which had been overwhelmingly opposed to the Nebraskan in his earlier campaigns were impressed with the Democratic platform of 1908. The New York *Times, Press,* and *Herald* all agreed that it was a platform on which Roosevelt could stand as comfortably as Bryan, and the *World* was pleased that it avoided the disastrous blunders of the past.[77] The *World* also thought that Bryan was an entirely new personality: "The old-time impulsiveness has utterly vanished and exaggerated caution has taken its place." [78] In his speeches the Commoner substantiated this impression. "The Democratic party seeks not revolution, but reformation," he said in accepting his nomination. "I have such confidence in the intelligence as well as the patriotism of the people, that I cannot doubt their readiness to accept the reasonable reforms which our party proposes, rather than permit the continued growth of existing abuses to hurry the country on to remedies more radical and more drastic." [79]

Just before the election one of the few prominent Bryan Democrats in New York, William J. Gaynor, sent a message of good will to the Commoner. "You will *probably* bring your party into power now; certainly four years hence," he wrote. "The day of raillery and tirade against you is gone by even in New York newspapers. I suppose you are aware of their changed tone of respect and good will toward you. Those of us who were with you from the first are now respectable citizens again." After Taft's election Gaynor wrote again, this time in the spirit of *ave atque vale:* "You will have a larger place in the history of the country than most of our Presidents. . . . The opposition in a constitutional government often does more good and achieves a greater reputation than those in actual control of the government." [80]

These two letters are suggestive of the paradoxical relationship between Bryan and the urban progressives. After his defeat, Bryan continued to urge the efficacy of a two-party system, a system which had, for all its shortcomings, led to progress. And he continued to argue against the formation of a third party by Republican and Democratic reformers because he thought the two historic parties provided the best means for securing reform legislation:

Let the democratic reformers fight for the control of their party, and let the republican reformers fight for the control of the republican party. If the democratic reformers control the democratic party, and the republican reformers fail to control the republican party, then let democrats appeal to republican reformers to cross the party line and put reforms above party. The appeal will be heeded by a multitude of republicans. If, on the contrary, the republican reformers secure control of their party and the democratic reformers lose control of theirs, there is no doubt that the republicans could count on the support of many democrats.[81]

The one possibility that Bryan omitted here—that both parties should become parties of reform—was the one that did, in fact, occur when T.R. occupied the White House.

As a critic Bryan found much to discuss during these years; although he failed to win election to the presidency, he did see the enactment and adoption of many reforms he had proposed. Gaynor was certainly justified in crediting Bryan's opposition with some share in bringing about the positive results of the progressive era. At the same time the very success of a modified Bryan program tended to make the Commoner himself more moderate and respectable, and, toward the end of Roosevelt's administration, less effective as a leader of political opposition. The conservatism of Taft soon aroused Bryan's antipathy, and once again the issues which separated the Nebraskan from the party in power seemed more clearly defined. But temporarily at least, success in failure had been accompanied by failure in success.

VII

*

* * *

*

BRYAN AND HIS PARTY

WRITING ON AMERICAN POLITICS in the late nineteenth century, Lord Bryce was unable to discover in either of the two major parties any distinctive principles which might have served to unite its adherents and give cohesion to its program. Both Republicans and Democrats had traditions, war cries, and organizations. But their interest in securing the patronage of the government was so overwhelming that the differences between parties on tenets and policies, points of political doctrine and political practice, had all but disappeared. "All has been lost," concluded the observant Englishman, "except office or the hope of it." [1] Half a century later Henry Steele Commager echoed these sentiments when he wrote, "This period, so barren of political thought, was likewise the ebb tide of statesmanship." [2] The seas fall only to rise again, however, and the emergence of William Jennings Bryan coincided with the flow of the tide. The metaphor is not to be pressed too far; the forces of nature often follow predictable patterns, while the actions of men confound determinists. Nevertheless, during the years of Bryan's ascendancy, the Democracy broke with part of its past and began to move in a new direction. His efforts to mold his party into one committed to principles consistent with the moralistic heritage of the Middle Border, his unremitting discussion of issues, and his ability to elicit a significant response from his countrymen helped to raise the level of political debate in the United States. Beyond this, his leadership of the Democratic party helped to force enactment of legislation the previous generation had felt no need even to consider.

Yet American political parties in the period from 1896 to 1912 did not become principled parties; they did not divide on fundamental tenets or principles. The Democratic party under Bryan became the party of reform, but much the same thing could be said of the Republican party of Theodore Roosevelt. Although the reform movement of the progressive period was strong enough to capture the leadership of both parties, there were many who preferred the old nineteenth-century system and techniques. In spite of progressive victories such individuals were never without influence in both parties. Thus the Commoner fought his battles on two fronts. As spokesman for the agrarian wing of the progressive movement, he tilted against the urban wing led by T.R. And within his own party he fought for the same causes in opposition to a conservatism that obstinately held to late nineteenth-century ideas and practices. The story of the struggle inside the Democracy from 1896 to 1912 is one of initial victory, temporary defeat, and ultimate triumph.

The Boy Orator and Gold Democrats

Bryan's differences with the conservatives of the Democratic party went back to 1892, when he was re-elected to the House of Representatives on a platform that included a silver plank. On August 16, 1893, during the debate on repeal of the Sherman Silver Purchase Act, he treated his colleagues and packed galleries to an eloquent three-hour plea for bimetalism. That speech cost the young Nebraskan his seat in the House. President Cleveland, who held the Sherman Act responsible for the depression he was struggling to overcome, had had enough. After consulting with Secretary of Agriculture J. Sterling Morton, he sent his orders out to Nebraska; Bryan was to be prevented from returning to Washington. But the upstart silverite let fly a few more shafts before leaving Capitol Hill. One of these was his speech in favor of an income tax, an issue that filled Cleveland and his friends in financial circles with apprehension. It was evident that the President had acted wisely in calling a halt to the political career of the young Nebraskan.[3] While Bryan might be shipped back to the plains, however, he could not be muzzled. Nor could the protests of prairie farmers be silenced by the pressure of patronage. By the summer of 1896 the silver movement had become rampant, and the Old Guard was overwhelmed in the Democratic national convention.

This changing of the guard was not an orderly process. With 16-to-1 Democrats, Silver Republicans, Populists, and what the Chicago *Tribune* called "riotous Debsites" all converging on Chicago along with followers of Cleveland and professional politicians, confusion was inevitable. One thing only was clear, and that was the death of the old sound-money party.[4] "Did Tammany Hall and New York machine delegates ever start for a convention before without knowing whom they were going to vote for?" asked a reporter of a New York delegate. "They never went to a hayseed silver convention until now," was the reply.[5] In the end, after the smoke of five hot, brawling days had cleared and the echoes of the "Cross of Gold" speech had died, administration men counted the cost. The hayseeds had not only adopted a silver platform and repudiated the only Democrat to occupy the White House since the Civil War, but they had nominated the Nebraskan who dared to risk Presidential wrath for silver's sake. The stone that Cleveland rejected had become the head of the corner.

After Chicago the aggrieved supporters of the President withdrew to Indianapolis to organize the Gold Democrats. They listened to Colonel W. C. P. Breckinridge of Kentucky denounce Bryan as a preacher of "dissatisfaction, dissension and discord," and then they proceeded to nominate Senator John M. Palmer and a former Confederate general, Simon Bolivar Buckner, on a gold platform.[6] Cleveland supported the move, and others who had long been high in the councils of the Democracy joined in the bolt. When Bryan campaigned in Kentucky, Henry Watterson branded him editorially: "He is a boy orator. He is a dishonest dodger. He is a daring adventurer. He is a political faker."

David B. Hill of New York told Charles S. Hamlin confidentially that he would not "come out for Bryan" and that he was "working hard for sound money." Publicly he would only say, "I was a Democrat before the Chicago convention, and I am a Democrat still—very still." [7]

The antagonism of conservative Democrats helped to bring about Bryan's defeat in 1896; yet within four years all but the most irreconcilable were back in the party fold. Doubtless the return of the bolters can be explained in terms of expediency. Bryan came so close to being elected in 1896 that he could not be denied a second nomination; and because success at the polls, or the possibility of success, was the chief evocator of political fealty, many of those who disagreed with Bryan on principle flocked to his banner in 1900. Pragmatic in their political relationships, they did not wish to forfeit patronage opportunities in order to maintain a proud independence of the dominant faction in the party. Two developments of the years between 1896 and 1900, however, suggest another explanation for the awakening of Democratic loyalties among disaffected elements. One was the return of prosperity, and the other was the movement of the United States toward a policy of imperialism. In the atmosphere of peace and self-satisfaction resulting from the former, some members of the business community—and opposition to Bryan was centered here—had serious doubts about the wisdom of the latter. Ironically, it was what John P. Mallan has called "materialist complacency" that provided the conditions for a face-saving compromise between the Commoner and the conservatives of his party.[8]

The terms of that compromise required little of Bryan. He was not asked to repudiate his stand on the silver question, but he was asked to shift from the advocacy of silver to the condemnation of imperialism. In 1899 Rollo Ogden of the New York *Evening Post* admitted to Bryan that "the silver question should have a place in your programme; but, if you are to win, it must be a subordinate place." [9] Before the campaign began in 1900, Bryan received a communication from Senator Francis G. Newlands forwarding suggestions from J. F. Merriam of the distinguished family of publishers. Merriam, Newlands informed Bryan, had indicated "Democratic tendencies" even though his family had had strong Republican connections since the heyday of the abolitionists. "Don't let Altgeld's name figure too conspicuously as a Bryan supporter," warned Merriam. "Let the matter of the *ratio* be left out of the Kansas City platform." [10] And in May, D. L. Baumgarten, who was to become a delegate to the Kansas City convention from Ohio, was authorized to convey to the Nebraskan the sentiments of Joseph Pulitzer. Pulitzer did not think it "wise, politic or to his interest" for Bryan to press the silver issue in eastern states. "Let him simply pledge himself to keep silent on *Silver* east of the Blue Ridge Mountains and leave us in the east to fight the battle on the balance of the platform, and as we may deem expedient," said the publisher of the *World*. "Tell him that if he must take up and talk Silver, I do not care how much he discusses it in the West, but most certainly it cannot and should not be discussed in the Eastern and Middle States. Under these conditions we can meet upon common ground." [11]

So great was the desire of many gold Democrats to work out a *modus vivendi* with Bryan that even his insistence upon a silver plank did not quell their ardor. W. Bourke Cockran, an influential figure in New York Democratic politics, rendered yeoman service to this cause by producing a rationale for returning bolters.[12] He began by facing the fact that while many easterners approved of Bryan's position on imperialism, they regarded his views on other questions with "distrust and apprehension." Yet he argued that the inclusion of the silver plank in the Kansas City platform was not sufficient cause for voting against the Commoner. "The Democratic platform declares that Imperialism is the paramount issue of the campaign," he wrote, "and Mr. Bryan's speech at Indianapolis accepts this conception of the issue, emphasizes it and vindicates it. But a declaration that Imperialism is the paramount issue is equivalent to a declaration that it is the sole issue, for no Presidential election ever decided more than one question." The platform, then, rather than arousing hostility toward Bryan's candidacy, should be regarded as "highly creditable to his honesty"; inasmuch as his views on the silver question had not changed, it was his duty to say so.[13] This honesty and integrity was actually a guarantee that the gold standard would remain intact. Even though Bryan was pledged to recommend revision of the coinage laws if elected, Cockran was certain that at least one house of Congress would oppose the recommendation and that Bryan's sincerity "makes it absolutely certain that he would enforce every existing law with unflinching loyalty." [14]

With men like Cockran working so effectively, the hopes of Bryan supporters ran high. The key state in the East was New York, and reports from there were most encouraging. In April Congressman William Sulzer wrote the Nebraskan that he did not think there would be any "serious opposition" to renomination. By convention time he was more confidant. "I believe matters in the State are in better shape than any of us had any reason to expect a few months ago," he exulted. "The delegates to the National Convention will be instructed for you. This was the object most desired and it has been brought about without causing friction or bad feeling." [15] Dr. John H. Girdner, whose devotion to the Commoner helped to compensate for his political inexperience, served as a medium for the exchange of views and information between Bryan and the returning Gold Democrats. The dominant note in Girdner's correspondence during the spring and summer of 1900 was one of optimism. He was pleased to inform Bryan long before the convention met that "all effective opposition is at last broken down." David B. Hill, New York party wheelhorse, had asked him to say that he wanted as conservative a platform as possible, and that he would "make a sham fight" against it, contending that it was not conservative enough. But after his prearranged defeat, he would make a speech saying "he and those who left the party in '96 must return now and all must sink every difference of every kind and save the country from destruction, etc., etc." Happily, Tammany Hall had also decided to go with Bryan. "I know for a fact that Croker will gladly do anything you wish," wrote Girdner. "The Tammany Tiger will come to K. C. tamed and chained and ready to do your bidding both before and after the convention." [16]

Apparently these reports were accurate. The convention came and went. "Four years ago," wrote Norman E. Mack, national committeeman and publisher of the Buffalo *Times*, "it took two columns a day for several days to print the names of the bolters in this country, but so far this year, they have not been able to print half a column." [17] And James K. McGuire, chairman of the Democratic State Committee in New York, reported that "from more than fifty counties in the State, we learn that the Gold Democrats are back into the Party." [18]

Yet all was not well within the Democracy, for the Cleveland faction remained aloof if not hostile. In the preconvention scrambling Cleveland openly opposed Bryan's nomination, but he recognized the strength of the Commoner's support. "Hundreds of thousands of our prominent Democrats are convinced that Bryan's nomination means defeat," he asserted, "and yet they are silent. Our press (if we have a democratic press) is see-sawing about afraid to take any position until it can find out to its satisfaction which side has the butter on. What a sad condition!" [19] The former President confessed to Richard Olney that "the political situation is too much for me." He referred scornfully to the activities of Henry Cabot Lodge ("Massachusetts' sweet-scented 'scholar in politics' "), and as for his own party, he wrote, "the old Adam occasionally dominates me." [20]

With the nomination of Bryan, Cleveland and his intimates were faced with what were for them the disagreeable alternatives of returning to the party and supporting the Nebraskan, or maintaining their independence and voting for either McKinley or a third candidate. In view of the action taken in 1896, talk of a third party was inevitable. The New York *Sun,* however, argued convincingly against putting up another slate: "For those who want to protect the honor of the nation against the Bryanite program of repudiation, renunciation and revolution, it is folly to think of wasting one-half of the defensive efficiency of their ballots by giving them to a third ticket." [21] Evidently Cleveland, along with others in his faction, accepted this reasoning, yet he was "very far from wishing to affirmatarily [sic] aid McKinleyism." If, therefore, he would satisfy his own conscience and avoid as much criticism as possible, his only escape was to keep silent. "This is a thing very hard for me to do at a time when I am so clear in my convictions," he confessed.[22] But keep silent he did. Although permitting himself an occasional outburst of a confidential nature, he said nothing in public. When the national committee made overtures, he wired a reply to Democratic headquarters: "My silence is the best certification I can make and I beg you to forego an interview as it would be unsatisfactory to you and vexatious to me." [23]

In spite of his notorious obstinacy, and perhaps because of it, appeals continued to pour in. Again and again he commented on the volume of his correspondence, and he felt himself "pestered to death nearly" by importunities.[24] Not all of these requests came from those who wanted advice on how to vote, or from those who wanted Cleveland to lend his support to Bryan's cause. James H. Eckels, who had served in the Treasury Department under Cleveland, was among a small but influential minority who thought that "it would be a good thing for the country and a more excellent thing for Democracy" if the former President made a public declaration demanding Bryan's overwhelming defeat. "My view," wrote Eckels, "is that it is not enough to barely defeat him. The real good to the party must come through discrediting him with the organization by showing in the largest way possible how unalterably opposed the business and other interests of this country are to the things for which he stands." [25] But no arguments, however plausible, could force Cleveland to take the stump, and in the final analysis it was J. Sterling Morton who gave expression to the true feelings of the Cleveland faction: "It is a choice between evils, and I am going to shut my eyes, hold my nose, vote, go home and disinfect myself." [26]

Unresponsive though he was to the call of his party, Grover Cleveland could not be made to bear the responsibility for Bryan's defeat in 1900; the faction he led was too small to have great influence. Other Gold Democrats also escaped blame, for they had re-enlisted under the party banner. Paradoxically, the return of prosperity during McKinley's first term, which had helped make reunification of the Democracy possible, was probably the chief cause of the Commoner's defeat. As early as May, before the campaign began in earnest, the Philadelphia *Press* had printed an incisive commentary on the chances of the Populists, who in its view had provided the driving power of the Democratic effort of 1896:

But the edge is off this kind of thing this year. Populism has small chance in a year of full work and fair wages. When the masses are busy, Populist meetings are empty. The specious socialism of the Populist platforms, its paper money, direct vote, initiative and referendum are but a mark for the unrest and agitation which rises to a flood in bad years and sinks to an ebb in seasons of prosperity. When the world goes well, Populism goes ill. It only carries states where men are losing money.[27]

When the returns were in, Bryan and his supporters were able to see clearly what they had been unable or unwilling to see earlier: that the full dinner pail had irresistible appeal for voters.[28] Democratic Campaign Manager James K. Jones marveled that in his own county "men who have voted the Democratic ticket all their lives, voted the Republican this time, openly boasted of it, and gave as the reason, that they did not want any more '5 cent cotton.'" William Sulzer could come to only one conclusion: "The power of money is stronger than the power of logic; plutocracy has won; the people are beaten." And another follower of Bryan lamented, "The porcine ego is a great factor in life—greater often than humanity, justice or even liberty." William H. Rogers of Wisconsin was "convinced that the wrecking record of Grover Cleveland's last term was the most potent factor in securing the re-election of Mr. McKinley; it was the prosperity argument, while the voters failed to appreciate the importance of the 'paramount issue.'" Nevertheless Rogers was not despondent. "Your last campaign has brought you added strength," he wrote Bryan. "Today you are the only hope of the liberty loving sons and daughters of America."[29]

The Harmony Movement

The comforting words had a hollow sound. Bryan's defeat did not bring him added strength; on the contrary, it gave the conservatives within the Democracy an opportunity they had long awaited. For some time there had been talk of reorganizing the party under the old leadership. In 1899 John Peter Altgeld had warned Bryan that "the gold standard people of the East have been actively, systematically and persistently at work, in a quiet way, all over the land," but he hoped that a death blow might be delivered "to all the intrigues and schemes of the gold standard corruptionists." [30] Early the next year Bryan received a communication from John S. Seymour, a conservative member of the Cleveland faction. Seymour thought those occupying positions of responsibility in the party were "in the main zealous but puny men, who, while having some vogue with the people, do not enjoy the confidence of the thoughtful and judicious, and with whom, as with the Orleanists, a kind of intriguing cleverness supplies the place of real political wisdom." After commenting favorably on Bryan's "purity of character" and "absolute fidelity," he suggested that the Commoner was so identified with the silver issue that he could never be elected. He therefore urged that Bryan "withdraw voluntarily and irrevocably from the candidacy for the Presidency in 1900." If such action were not taken, he thought that the Democrats would be defeated and that this defeat would force a reorganization of the party in 1904.[31]

Although Bryan was not convinced of the merits of this suggestion, Seymour was accurate as a political seer. And there is evidence that the groundwork for reorganization was laid even while Bryan was still campaigning. "When the Democratic party is rid of the populism and socialism of Bryan those who stand out against him now will be welcomed back without conditions," wrote James H. Eckels.[32] Grover Cleveland found satisfaction in only two developments during the Commoner's second campaign: "the hopping and jumping in certain cages of Democratic zoological specimens," and growing indications that party workers were beginning to learn that "no Bryanism or Bryan conciliation will gather enough votes to do the business." [33] He had "some idea that the party may before long be purged of Bryanism, and that the rank and file, surprised at their wanderings, and enraged at their false leaders, will be anxious to return to the old faith; and in their desire to reorganize under the old banners will welcome the counsel of those who have never yielded to disastrous heresy." These hopes were echoed by most of the eastern conservatives. There were, to be sure, differences of opinion on the best means for achieving the goal. Richard Olney, for example, was sympathetic to the views of his old chieftain, but like most of the Gold Democrats he voted for Bryan in 1900. He reasoned that those who did so would be in a better position to command the confidence of the party in the future.[34]

Timing was important. With four years ahead of them the reorganizers moved slowly at first; to have brought the movement along too rapidly would have been a fatal blunder. Yet their determination did not languish, and no one was more determined than Grover Cleveland. "I am so attached to the old Democratic faith," he wrote, "that no political activity but an attempt to bring the party back to its old way, has any present allurement for me." [35] At times he grew impatient; he was in his sixties, his health was uncertain, and he did not want to be deprived of the opportunity to render one last service to his party. "Isn't it a shame that the old Democratic party is in such a wretched condition to retake its abandoned vantage ground?" he queried Don Dickinson in 1902. "No punishment or humiliation would be too great for those who have betrayed the best cause, and the best fighters that ever met an enemy or won a battle. What an inspiration it would be to hear Democratic leadership proclaim 'Bryanism is not Democracy.' " [36]

The former President did not have long to wait, for the year 1902 saw increased activity among the reorganizers. They went out under the banner of "Democratic Harmony," pleading that there were "more ways than one of killing a rabbit" and that someone other than Bryan should be allowed to try his way. It was Henry Watterson who asked the question uppermost in their minds: "Why should Mr. Bryan insist upon the repetition of a series of abstractions upon which the party, encountering a dwindling, not an increasing vote, has lost in succession two presidential elections, well nigh effacing itself in all the determinate states?" [37]

One thing was necessary for the reorganizers. If Bryan was to be ousted as party leader, they had to find someone to take his place. Yet there were few Gold Democrats who were available, and hence it was not surprising that Grover Cleveland's name should be mentioned as a possible candidate in spite of his age, his health, and the traditional opposition to a third term. Frank Campbell, chairman of the New York State Committee, wrote Cleveland in 1903, "I hear expressions day after day wishing for your nomination." Another admirer expostulated, "God knows it is time our party gave us a chance to vote for a Democrat instead of a man imbued with 'isms.' " Thoroughly convinced that

Cleveland was the "man of the hour," Senator John Lowndes McLaurin of South Carolina offered his services.[38]

Nevertheless, Cleveland's candidacy could not be taken seriously. "You have well earned, and surely paid, for everything that is pleasant in your retirement," wrote Don Dickinson. "After what you have gone through, even the American people have no *right* to ask you to give that up, and take up a life, risking all that you have gained, and to have again to undergo the evils, the anguish and suffering, the misunderstandings, betrayals and abuse, which you have suffered." [39] Henry Watterson was more vitriolic than usual in his opposition to Cleveland's re-entry into public life:

In his recent manifestations of political activity Mr. Cleveland may have been a disinterested man. If he was he made a serious mistake in supposing that he could contribute to Democratic harmony. But we do not think he was a disinterested man. On the contrary, it is our opinion that he never drew an unselfish breath in all his life; that he goes out after all there is in sight, or he does not go out at all; . . . and that all his PRETEN-TIOUS POSING as a retired sage and patriot is but the crafty and spectacular performance of a man who had been—like his younger prototype, Theodore Roosevelt—a candidate for office ever since he became of age. . . . He is an artful, selfish, ignorant, and vulgar professional politician, having had amazing good fortune and being possessed of rare skill in the pursuit of his own ambition and desires. . . . No real Democrat can regard Mr. Cleveland other than as a marplot and wrecker. Between him and Bryan we would support Bryan ten times over; between him and Roosevelt we would support Roosevelt. Of course the suggestion of his candidacy is A KIND OF AB-SURDITY. But not in his opinion, nor in the opinion of the wealthy nincompoops behind him.[40]

Even Theodore Roosevelt, who was usually inclined to overestimate the strength of his political opponents, thought that Cleveland would be a weak candidate. The former President had never had any direct contact with wageworkers or with the poor; he knew nothing of sweatshops or slums. He was surrounded by men "incapable of taking anything but the corporation attitude," and although T.R. respected him, he did not doubt that he would become the "unconscious ally" of big business. And only business interests would be entirely satisfied with him.[41]

Facing squarely Cleveland's limitations as a candidate, conservatives of the Democracy were forced to look elsewhere. But the search was not fruitful. The most likely possibility was Alton B. Parker, a New Yorker and chief justice of the court of appeals, who had avoided factional struggles within the party and whose campaign was being managed by David B. Hill. Early in 1904 former Secretary of War Daniel Lamont and Charles F. Murphy of Tammany Hall had a long talk about party prospects. Dutifully Lamont reported to Cleveland. Murphy, he said, was opposed to Parker because there was "nothing in Parker to campaign on." The Tammany boss would not hear of Gorman, and he thought that Bryan "should be absolutely turned down and ignored." As for Hearst, Murphy said, "He cuts no figure whatever."[42] Cleveland, who had never wanted to be considered as a candidate for a third term, was inclined to favor either Richard Olney or Senator Gray of Delaware. The elder statesman finally decided to support Parker, however, because of "a large concentration of sentiment and preference in his favor." He thought there would be "elements of so malign a character" in the convention that "the Parker solid front could not be broken without danger." It was comforting to know that Parker was at least "a clean decent man."[43]

Clean and decent, yes, thought many a good party worker, but distinguished chiefly for his lack of color and political appeal. "Bryan, Hearst, Tom Johnson—these are your Democrats—your genuine article," commented the New Orleans *Harlequin*. "Grover isn't a Democrat. He is a stomach. Parker isn't a Democrat. He is a ladada."[44] Fearful that such attacks would eliminate their candidate, supporters of Parker apparently chose to use Cleveland as a stalking horse. The former President would draw the fire of those opposed to reorganization, and Parker could then be presented to the convention as satisfactory to all factions. The plan worked well despite the fact that Bryan and others were suspicious of the Cleveland boom.[45] Yet conservatives themselves had limited confidence in Parker. "I still think he will be nominated," Cleveland wrote Daniel S. Lamont in June, "but I cannot feel sure of his election."[46] Already it was becoming evident that although they might dominate the convention and agree on a candidate, the Old Guard would be unable to effect the one thing that mattered most: victory over the Republicans in November.

While the hopes of conservative Democrats rose and fell, Bryan never wavered in his opposition to the reorganization of his party; steadfastly he resisted appeals to Democratic harmony under conservative leadership. This could easily have been predicted. And the form his opposition took was equally characteristic. So far as he could discern, the harmony advocates and the reorganizers were nothing more than "unrepentant bolters." They were backed by the "money power" and they dwelt in the tents of wickedness: the metropolitan centers of the East. They were "false prophets" of politics, for their design was to deceive and mislead. "They stand in the market places and talk about harmony—the very thing that they themselves destroyed," said Bryan in a speech at Columbus, Ohio, in 1903. "They demand the leadership and say to the party: 'Did we not hold office in thy name, and in thy name draw large salaries?'" The Commoner thought that if the party had gained wisdom from experience, it would say, "Depart, I never knew you, ye that work iniquity." [47]

His deep-seated suspicion was not the only reason for Bryan's opposition to the reorganization movement. He believed the real basis for harmony resulted from certain fixed rules, and in his view reorganizers had ignored all basic principles of democratic government. He reviewed the ideas of Thomas Jefferson and found that the Sage of Monticello had expounded two of those rules: acquiescence in the will of the majority and frequent elections. If Jefferson were still alive, he would certainly suggest a third, "the ascertainment of the will of the majority by methods so direct, so fair and so honest that the minority cannot doubt that that will has been actually expressed." Harmony could always exist, Bryan argued, among those who accepted such principles—among those who believed in government by the people. But while differences of the mind might be compromised, differences of purpose were irreconcilable. "Between one who is at heart an aristocrat and one who is in reality a democrat," he wrote, "there is a great gulf fixed." He thought any attempt to patch up an "apparent harmony" with those not in sympathy with democratic purposes would be disastrous.[48] The reorganizers, said Bryan, had been "conspicuous for their treachery" in the past. What alarmed him, however, was "their treachery not so much to the ticket as to the principles of the democratic party." [49]

Bryan was quite certain that the reorganization movement was an aristocratic maneuver; yet he found no lucid statement of its basic objectives. Leaders of the Old Guard were "indefinite in their language." They talked only of "getting together," and Bryan wished to know what they were getting together for, "whether to defend rights or to enter upon a course of pillage." The condition of the Democracy reminded him of a story:

> A visitor to an old graveyard once ran across an epitaph on a neglected tombstone which concluded with the lines: "As I am now so you shall be, Prepare, my friend, to follow me." Being a cautious man and not willing to share the company of the deceased without first investigating his surroundings, he penciled the following postscript: "To follow you, I am not content, Until I know which way you went." [50]

Thus the most grievous fault of the reorganizers was not their preference for aristocratic government, bad as that was. Their worst sin was their failure to state clearly what ideas they represented. "With them success is the only thing to be considered," Bryan noted. "Instead of regarding politics as the science of government they look upon it as a game in which offices are awarded as prizes to the most skillful players. Instead of discussing as leaders those who study public questions and seek to discover the best solution of each new problem, they measure men by their shrewdness in political management." [51] If such men were successful in gaining control of the Democracy, Bryan believed his party would differ from the Republican in name only.[52]

The Commoner's opposition to the reorganization and harmony movement does not mean that he was uncharitable toward those who had opposed his candidacy. In 1900 he accepted support from the bolters of 1896. He believed in welcoming the prodigal son. While he confessed to "some little sympathy" for the son who did not go astray, he appreciated the forgiveness of which the heart was capable. Had he been convinced that the prodigal sons who were now attempting to reorganize the party were truly repentant, he would doubtless have worked with them. But he was not convinced, and his course was dictated in part by their attitudes. Again he dipped into his fund of anecdotes and drew out one of the dialect stories for which he was notorious:

> I think the old colored minister described this forgiving spirit very accurately. He said that the father saw the son coming back, that he could see as the son came that he was sorry. The son had his head down, and he walked hesitatingly, almost ashamed to look his father in the face, and the father's heart went out to him, and the father hastened forth to meet him, and the son was glad and the father was glad. But, said the colored preacher, if the son had come back swaggering as if he owned the place, and said to his father, "Wha's dat caff?" do you suppose the father would have killed the fatted calf for him? [53]

Withdrawal from Bryanism

No one hastened forth to meet Bryan when he arrived in St. Louis for the Democratic National Convention of 1904. He was not a candidate himself, and in any case the Old Guard apparently had been successful in one respect: it had destroyed the possibility that a Bryan man would receive the nomination. Nevertheless the Commoner had long ago made up his mind that the conservatives should not dominate the convention. During the summer of 1902, Bryan, in company with others of his party, had addressed a rally at Bangor, Maine. The day had been hot, and he had no fresh underwear with him. As was his habit in such emergencies, he retired to his room, hung up his perspiration-soaked underclothing to dry, and went to bed. While thus enthroned as befitting a commoner, he held court for party workers. With Charles S. Hamlin, who was then bending every effort to secure the nomination of Olney, he discussed the future of the party. "He talked to me for over an hour—" Hamlin recorded in his diary. "He sd. he did not expect nor did he want the nomination in 1904 but that he was determined that no one shld have it who did not support the ticket in 1896—He seemed to ignore 1900 but made 1896 the test."[54] Such a test was, from Bryan's point of view, justifiable. He was conscious of the fact that many of the Old Guard had supported him in 1900 out of expediency, not principle.

The battle lines were therefore drawn, but the outcome of the struggle was never in doubt. Conservative sappers had seen to that; in the last three years they had undermined every key position held by Bryan in 1900. The professional soldiers of the Democracy, who had experienced years of defeat in fighting under the banner of the Commoner, recognized those positions as untenable and went over to the enemy. And with the professionals encamped on the convention floor, Bryan and his ragged regiment in the galleries were doomed. The Peerless Leader, clad as always in the armor of a righteous cause, nevertheless refused to accept unconditional surrender.

Not all of Bryan's followers understood or approved of his tactics, however. There were those who felt that he might have thwarted the nomination of Parker had he so desired. These were the men who were pledged to William Randolph Hearst. Hearst did, indeed, show amazing strength, and he and his supporters believed that if Bryan could be persuaded to use his influence in behalf of the eccentric publisher, the nomination would be his. The Commoner, while he had earlier regarded Hearst as "one of the men who are to be considered," decided finally to support Senator Cockrell of Missouri. It was a decision to fight on other grounds, for Cockrell obviously had no chance. Hearst was, of course, sorely disappointed. He had supported Bryan faithfully during the campaigns of 1896 and 1900, but he now came to the conclusion that the Commoner was an ingrate of insatiable ambition. Never again was Bryan to receive the endorsement of Hearst newspapers.[55]

The ground on which the Peerless Leader had chosen to make his stand was a room where the committee on resolutions met to work out a platform, and it became the "bloody angle" of the convention. It was entirely in keeping with the Commoner's principles to expend his mightiest efforts in securing a platform that would reaffirm the position his party had taken during the two previous campaigns. A candidate, he believed, was morally bound to adhere to his platform if elected. And if the platform adopted were a progressive one, the retreat from "Bryanism" could be prevented from becoming a rout. So Bryan fought to defend his ideas and his program. In the final session of the committee he fought, thought Charles S. Hamlin, like one gone mad.[56] For sixteen hours he crossed swords with the champions of the Old Guard—and held them off. When the committee finally emerged, it was with a platform which the Commoner could accept. "You may dispute whether I have fought a good fight," he told the delegates, "you may dispute whether I have finished my course, but you cannot deny that I have kept the faith."[57] Then fatigued almost to the point of collapse, he finally went to his hotel room with a cold so severe his physician feared pneumonia.[58]

The platform produced by the resolutions committee became controversial not so much for what it contained as for what it left out. The most conspicuous of the omissions was a gold plank which the conservatives had hoped to include. The vote in committee was thirty-five to fifteen against any mention of the money question, but the opposition of the Commoner was not the only reason for its defeat. Hamlin, who was a member of the committee, thought "leaders like Williams, Tillman, Bayley, Carmack and others were against us *in spite of Bryan* also opposing. They recognized that silver was dead & had no desire to revive it, but they said they wld never consent to putting gold plank in the platform, thus discrediting them w. their constituents at home." There was some talk of presenting a minority report on the gold question, but the Old Guard decided against doing so. Such action would, they reasoned, give Bryan an opportunity to raise a host of other questions before the convention. It seemed more prudent to secure his support of the platform and let the candidate "in his letter of acceptance fully attone [*sic*] for any silence in the platform."[59]

Judge Parker did not wait until time for his letter of acceptance to clarify his position. He sent a telegram to the convention saying, "I regard the gold standard as firmly and irrevocably established, and shall act accordingly." He urged the delegates to select another nominee if his views on the money question were repugnant to them. Bryan left his sickbed to make a speech denouncing Parker, but his efforts were to no avail. The convention sent the Judge a conciliatory answer which was widely regarded as the death knell, not only for silver, but for Bryan's political career.[60]

With mingled feelings toward the Commoner, William Allen White wrote his political obituary for *Collier's:*

He stood there surrendering his power, that had come to him in his youth so suddenly. He had carried the banner of social democracy in America further than any other man had carried it. It is not free silver that Bryan stands for, and he knew it, in the breaking day, when his party told him to stand aside.

Bryan has stood for as much of the idea of socialism as the American mind will confess to. He believes that his idea (whether he defines it clearly or not is immaterial) is important to the welfare of his country. Probably he is wrong; but as he stood there sadly appealing to his party for his old cause, which he knew was a lost cause, he seemed bidding farewell—a long farewell—to all the power and glory that has been the breath of his nostrils. He has lived cleanly, and has acted fairly and squarely according to his lights. He is the idol of that party, of his branch of his party, which stood for his ideas. These men live in the Middle West. Thousands of them came hundreds of miles to see his surrender. He quit like a gentleman, with his colors flying. Whatever his enemies may say of him, they must admire the pluck which he showed at the last.[61]

Others were not so sympathetic. "Just as his power over his party was testimony to American admiration for honesty," commented the Philadelphia *North American,* "so his downfall is testimony to American common sense." The New York *World* could not rejoice over Bryan's "political suicide" even though it thought he had attempted to establish a dictatorship over the party. It could only regret that "brilliant talents have been thrown away, a mighty prestige ruined, and an influence dissipated that might have accomplished great things for the national welfare had it been exercised intelligently." Unfortunately, however, "Mr. Bryan has shown no talent for building up. He could only destroy, and in the end he has succeeded in destroying himself." [62]

Two men whose familiarity with the presidency had been gained by firsthand experience differed in their attitudes toward

Parker but agreed that his chances in November were good. Grover Cleveland, feeling more optimistic now that the convention was over, was gratified with the results "as brought about by Providence and a gentleman living in Esopus." He wrote Richard Olney that "such Democrats as you and I ought to be pretty well satisfied. Bryan and Bryanism are eliminated as influential factors in Democratic councils, true Democracy has a leader, and its time honored and time approved principles again are set before the people of the land without apology or shamefacedness." [63] Theodore Roosevelt thought Parker's telegram to the convention had been a "bold and skillful move." He did not believe his Democratic opponent had any strong "sound money" principles, for when the New York platform had been drafted Parker had not objected to the omission of a gold plank. But after his nomination by the Democracy, when the possibility of offending delegates was slight, he had played a "perfectly safe but spectacular game." He had, thought Roosevelt, "become a very formidable candidate and opponent; for instead of being a colorless man of no convictions he now stands forth to the average man—and this at astonishingly small cost—as one having convictions compared to which he treats self-interest as of no account." [64]

As the campaign got under way, Judge Parker proved far less formidable than T.R. had thought he would be. Roosevelt's electioneering activities were limited by responsibilities of his office, and Parker was presented with a perfect opportunity for a vigorous campaign. Yet for various reasons he was unable to make the most of it. It was difficult for a man of his juristic temperament to project himself as a forceful and dynamic personality. As Richard Olney pointed out, Roosevelt was a young man who appealed strongly to the young men of the country and "to their admiration of success and their love of adventure." Parker had none of this magnetism. While T.R.'s idiosyncrasies were legion, the gentleman from Esopus had only one: he went swimming every morning at dawn. After all, conservatives did not expect him to live strenuously; he had been nominated because he was "safe and sane." And Democratic conservatives based their campaign on the assumption that financiers and men of property would prefer him to the potentially dangerous Rough

Rider. It was a false assumption, and it took the sting from what attacks Parker did launch.[65] "If we can only keep peanut methods out of our campaign management, I believe there is a good chance to rid the country of Rooseveltism and its entire brood of dangers and humiliations," Grover Cleveland wrote Olney. Yet it was soon evident that the peanut methods Bryan had employed in 1896 and 1900 were worth almost 1,500,000 more votes than the "safe and sane" appeal.[66]

Resurgence of Bryan Democracy

"When you preach the funeral of the democratic donkey be sure to stand at the head," quipped party workers; "otherwise you might get hurt." To men like Josephus Daniels, Bryan was the donkey personified, for the defeat of Parker breathed new life into the Commoner's political career.[67] While the candidate of the Old Guard was yet on the stump, Bryan announced in *The Commoner* that "Democracy must move forward." He pointed out that in 1896 and 1900 he had felt bound by the doctrines of the party platform. But now that leadership had devolved upon another, his was a responsibility borne by every private citizen— responsibility for his opinions, utterances, and conduct. "I am free to undertake a work which until now I have avoided," he announced, "namely, the work of organizing the radical and progressive element in the Democratic party." [68]

Bryan nevertheless supported Parker's candidacy.[69] He resisted appeals to form a third party, and before long the wisdom of his course began to manifest itself. He gained a new respect among conservatives who could not understand or appreciate his ideas, but appreciated his fidelity to the Democracy. Alfred B. Williams, editor of the Richmond, Virginia, *News Leader,* was such a conservative. In a letter to Grover Cleveland he confessed that Bryan's efforts in behalf of Parker had seemed impressive, so impressive that he had been led to criticize Cleveland adversely for the first time in twenty years. "In the present political campaign," commented a *News Leader* editorial, "Mr. Bryan figures very much more handsomely than Mr. Cleveland." While the Commoner defied "threats of throat and lung trouble" in lending his oratory and influence to the party cause, Cleveland refused to exert himself for a candidate nominated by conservatives.

> If Judge Parker should be disastrously defeated or should fail to make a better showing in the returns than Mr. Bryan did [concluded the editorial], a revival of Bryanism will be inevitable. The Bryan element of the Democrats magnanimously and sensibly surrendered after two defeats and handed the party over to the conservatives to demonstrate their strength and show what they could do. If this conservative element does not prove its strength the radical, or Bryan element will promptly resume control, and with very good reason. There is no sense in surrendering party control and machinery to a faction which can not win nor offer a hope of victory.[70]

The editor was too critical of Cleveland; the former President had done all he could. Parker's failure and Bryan's loyalty did, however, have the results predicted. The Commoner was never more influential within his party than he was after the fiasco of 1904. Circumstances gave him an opportunity to fight again for his lost leadership; when he spoke on questions of political policy and strategy, Democrats listened to what he had to say. And speak he did. "The Democratic party has nothing to gain by catering to organized and predatory wealth," he said. "It must not only do without such support, but it can strengthen itself by inviting the open and emphatic opposition of these elements." It was not enough that the party maintain its stand on old issues; it was essential that it advance to meet new issues as they might arise. Bryan urged the party faithful to take courage, for he was confident that the Democracy had "passed through the Valley of the Shadow of Death." [71]

For a time the Peerless Leader worked at fever pitch as though the campaign of 1908 were already under way. Because the national Democratic committee was still controlled by conservatives, a Washington bureau was established to provide a rallying point for Bryan's friends.[72] In *The Commoner* he announced a plan by which the rank and file could cooperate to secure victory in the next campaign. Each was to sign a card pledging himself to attend all primaries and "use his influence to secure a clear, honest, and straightforward declaration of the party's position on every question upon which the voters of the party desire to speak." [73] The citizen could not perform his duty by merely voting for the ticket of his party. It was his responsibility to assist in choosing the ticket, and as never before the times called for each man to do his part. "It must be plain to everyone that the greatest political contest in history will be waged in 1908," warned the Peerless Leader, "if the special interests that now thrive at the expense of the general public are to be brought into obedience to law and justice." [74]

After striking swiftly and effectively to establish his primacy among Democratic leaders, Bryan left party councils, Chautauqua tents, and the offices of *The Commoner* to make a whirlwind trip around the world. It was a shrewd maneuver. From Honolulu to London, Bombay to Oslo, he chatted with princes and statesmen and graciously received their compliments. The Nebraskan was no bumpkin politician; he was a world figure. And when he returned to New York, Democrats of all varieties gathered to claim him as their own. *Harper's Weekly* printed a greeting saturated with the honeyed sarcasm in which its editor, George Harvey, was adept:

As we pen these words you are dancing over the billowy waves under the protection of the German flag, on your way to home sweet home. Presently you will be borne majestically into the most impressive of harbors, and remain at anchor long enough to explain to the customs officer why you found it necessary to purchase a suit of clothes manufactured by the pauper labor of Europe. Then you will go on deck, and the brass will crash and the trumpets bray along with a varied collection of statesmen eager to be kodaked while grasping your large, glad hand. It will be a grand reception. Even now the clans are gathered from Nebraska to Maine. A pity it is that bickerings and jealousies are but too apparent in many councils, but all are pardonable as springing from a laudable purpose. It is the highest ambition of each and every member of the multitude . . . to let you know how fully he appreciates your greatness, and to let the public know how graciously and fraternally you recognize his appreciation. When some years ago ULYSSES S. GRANT landed in San Francisco after passing around the world, he was It; you are They. You are not only the original, undiluted, and uncompromising radical of old . . . but, by the grace of THEODORE ROOSEVELT, you are by contrast the personification of conservatism. For the first time shivering plutocracy joins with rag-tag and bob-tail in doing reverence to one who was described not long ago as a statesman who never made a statute, a lawyer who never tried a case, a soldier who never fought a battle, and a farmer who never turned a furrow. Wide and deep, however, is the belief now in the hearts of your countrymen that all you lacked was the opportunity, and that the time of realization of glorious possibilities is rapidly approaching.[75]

Such causticity could not stop the Bryan boom, but the Old Guard continued to hack away ineffectually at the Commoner's prestige. Gradually it became clear that the Nebraskan's power was greater than it had been at any time since 1896. His views were solicited on many questions, but nothing better illustrates the scope of his influence than his relationship to the people of Oklahoma. At the time of Bryan's return, that territory was about to enter the sisterhood of states, and he was asked to address the constitutional convention meeting at Guthrie. Because of previous commitments, he was unable to do so. He did, however, send a letter with several suggestions, and virtually every one was incorporated into the constitution. "It is not necessary to say that the result in Oklahoma is a great victory for democrats," commented *The Commoner.* "The victory speaks for itself." [76]

To conservatives Bryan actually seemed to flaunt his power. When he was in England preparing for the last lap of his journey, he was approached by George Harvey acting in the interest of Thomas F. Ryan, captain of industry. Was there a ground for cooperation between the two men? "Tell Mr. Ryan," said the Peerless Leader, "that he is in a position to do one of the greatest services to his country that any man has ever rendered. He should rid himself of all personal pecuniary interest in, at least, all corporations having to do with public utilities, railroad stocks and bonds, traction stocks and bonds, and all such properties, and invest his money in Government bonds." Bryan's position must have shocked Harvey, for Bryan reminded him that "the young man who went to the Saviour and asked what he should do is said to have gone away sorrowing when told that he must divest himself of his property because he had great possessions; but that was the only way, although he did not follow it." [77]

Many of the Old Guard branded Bryan a "dictator," a name that in itself described his power if not the manner in which it was exercised. Others gave up the fight and closed ranks with the rural progressives whose devotion to the Commoner remained unquestioned. Yet despondency was almost universal among conservatives, whether they supported Bryan or not. Solicitous indeed were the letters Henry Watterson received when the *Courier-Journal* came out for the Nebraskan and when old "Marse Henry" began to take an active part in his campaign: "I do not see what else you could do"; "I see that you have fallen in with the Bryan crowd, and I well understand why it was necessary if you meant to save your journal as a valuable property," etc.[78] The Brooklyn *Eagle* gloomily reported that in the South newspapers were generally in favor of Bryan: "Many of them regard him as preferable. Others deem him to be inevitable. A few outrightly object to him, but will accept him if they can not overthrow him." [79]

While the press of other sections, particularly the Northeast, was not so friendly, Democrats from all over the country placed their names in the Bryan column at the Denver convention of 1908. The Commoner was in complete control. The platform reflected his views, and he was nominated on the first ballot. "He has built up a personal following unparalleled for one with a record of nothing but defeat, and with no patronage to strengthen his control," remarked the *Wall Street Journal*.[80] It was a remarkable performance, certainly, for this twentieth-century Lazarus to return to the leadership of his party after his political death had been so widely celebrated four years earlier. But it was a performance that occasioned no surprise, so thoroughly had the Old Guard been discredited.[81] A malevolent few among the conservatives took what comfort they could from the excellent chance that Bryan would be defeated again. "The Democrats will now resume their accustomed occupation of electing a Republican President," observed George Harvey.[82]

The Campaign of 1912

Colonel Harvey was right; Taft won a sweeping victory over the Commoner.[83] But what did the election of 1908 portend? Would another swing of the political pendulum carry the Democracy back to Old Guard conservatism? The Colonel thought so, and he set about grooming his candidate, the politically inexperienced president of Princeton, Woodrow Wilson. Tenable though it may have appeared, the pendulum theory did not fit the facts; conditions within the party were not the same as they had been after Parker's defeat. "The smoke of battle . . . is clearing away, and we are just beginning to understand the tremendous advance made by the Democratic party in the last four years," wrote Congressman Henry T. Rainey of Illinois. The Peerless Leader had received well over a million more votes than were cast for Parker. Democratic governors were elected in five states that had been Republican four years earlier. Victories had been registered in the House of Representatives and in every legislative body in the country. These gains, Rainey confided to Bryan, "indicate that the fight has been conducted along proper lines, and the warfare you have so relentlessly waged for Democratic ideals and against predatory wealth must continue." [84] The hopefulness of Democratic progressives after the election of 1908 contrasts sharply with the despondency of conservatives following Parker's annihilation in 1904.

Nevertheless Bryan virtually took himself out of contention for another nomination shortly after the results of the election were announced. He told his friends the parable of the inebriate who made three attempts to force his way into a club, and was thrice thrown out into the street. After his third encounter with the obstinate doorman, he got up, brushed off his clothes, and said, "I am on to those people. They don't want me in there." [85] But the Commoner was too canny a politician ever to state in unequivocal terms that he would not be a candidate in 1912, and this course gave him far greater influence than he otherwise might have expected.

There were, then, two factors which had a profound influence on intraparty battles between conservatives and Bryan progressives during the four years from 1908 to 1912. One of these was the prevalence of reform sentiment throughout the country, which gave rise to the optimism of Democrats favoring the progressive cause, and the other was the possibility that Bryan would again become the Democratic candidate. Although he had little desire for a fourth nomination, the threat of his own candidacy was a lever which might be used to force recalcitrant conservatives into line behind another progressive; further, his support was essential for any candidate with progressive inclinations. Bryan applied all the strength resulting from these factors to the achievement of two objectives: victory over the conservatives within his party, and nomination of the most progressive of Democratic candidates.

It is in this context that Bryan's criticism of President Taft must be viewed. Little would be gained if he fought for a progressive candidate but neglected to point out Taft's failure to live up to progressive ideals. For the first time since McKinley's death Bryan could combine his opposition to the Old Guard with his opposition to the Republican party. And he made the most of his opportunity. Shortly after Taft had taken the oath of office, the Peerless Leader detected a "community of interests between the president and the Aldrich-Cannon element of his party." Taft had not been in office a year before Bryan observed that "there seems to be no limit to the reactionary policies of the present administration." In 1910 the Commoner became even more critical, and he adopted a line of argument well suited to emphasizing Taft's conservatism. Republican insurgents, he noted, were proclaiming their loyalty to the administration but opposing its agents, Aldrich and Cannon, in Congress. If insurgents were to "serve their country effectually" and be consistent in their actions, "they must make war against Aldrichism and Cannonism in the White House, even as they make war against Aldrichism and Cannonism in the capitol building." [86] By campaign time Bryan was striking mighty sledge-hammer blows:

President Taft claims to be a progressive—it is a confession that progressivism is popular—and launches this paraphrase: "Progressive is as progressive does." Is he willing to be measured by that standard? Does he doubt that the people of the United States demand the election of senators by direct vote? Why has he been so late in recognizing the demand? In 1908 he said that PERSONALLY he was INCLINED to favor it—that was after Congress had declared for it five times, after nearly two-thirds of the states had indorsed it and after it had been included in three national platforms of the democratic party. What has he done since to help the people secure this great reform? Nothing. If "progressive does" how old will Ann be before Mr. Taft progresses as far on this question as the democratic party was nineteen years ago? We have a law compelling the publication, before the election, of the names of contributors to the national campaign fund. The principle had no opposition in the senate or house. This is a progressive measure. What was the president's part? He never said a word in behalf of the measure and when he signed the bill he was aware that if he did not sign the bill it would be passed over his veto. . . . Where does he stand on the income tax? He urged the submission of the amendment in order to defeat a statutory tax—he did it at the solicitation of Senator Aldrich and he has not in his travels urged ratification but has, on the contrary, elevated to the supreme bench Governor Hughes who asked the New York legislature to refuse to ratify. What progressiveness did he show here? . . . What a record! It is without a parallel. He spends so much time qualifying, explaining and hair splitting on the capacity of the people for self government that he has no time left—nor disposition—to assist the people to secure a larger and more effective control over the instrumentalities of government.[87]

Thus did Bryan seek to drive deeper the wedge that had already begun to split the Republican party, making a Democratic victory possible in 1912.

In the meantime, the critical eye of the Commoner scanned a host of presidential aspirants until two men stood out. One, Champ Clark of Pike County, Missouri, had been his friend and supporter for twenty years; the other, Woodrow Wilson, had been until recently one of his severest critics. Clark was of a type dear to the hearts of agrarian radicals whose speech and mannerisms he emulated. He even dressed the part; his long coat and broad-brimmed black slouch hat appealed to folk who expected eccentricities in their politicians. He had joined Bryan in the House of Representatives in 1892, but unlike the Commoner he was to serve in that body until his death in 1921. Loyal though he had been to Bryan, he bore the stigma of the party hack.[88]

Wilson was, of course, Clark's opposite in almost every respect. The scholarly academician had long preached against the "errors and heresies" of Bryan. From 1896, when he voted the Gold Democratic ticket, until 1908, when he refused to appear on the same platform with Bryan, Wilson regarded the Nebraskan as "foolish and dangerous in his theoretical beliefs." It was only after he entered politics in 1910 under the tutelage of George Harvey that the scholar began to retreat from his conservative position.[89] Before he entered the Governor's mansion, he denounced the New Jersey bosses who, through Harvey's machinations, had helped to elect him. It was then that Bryan first noticed with interest the star in the eastern sky.

Wilson's attack on the bosses was only a beginning. Repudiating the conservative Harvey and mounting a successful reform program, the Governor went through what seemed a miraculous metamorphosis. As a result relations between Bryan and Wilson became more intimate. They agreed that the need for tariff reform and regulation of trusts was urgent, that results of the alliance between big business and politics were iniquitous, that the primary concern of the state ought to be protection of individual rather than corporate rights. But Bryan still had some questions on his mind. What, he asked, did Wilson think of the various planks in the platform of 1908? When the Governor unequivocally endorsed them, Bryan was "greatly gratified." And the income tax? "There are few questions," thought the Commoner, "which furnish a better test of a man's sympathies." Wilson immediately dispatched a strong letter to the legislature recommending ratification of the amendment.[90] Early in 1912, when the final break between Harvey and Wilson came, Bryan issued a statement in support of the Governor. There was, he said, "an irrepressible conflict between aristocracy and democracy." Consciously or unconsciously, Wilson had been on the aristocratic side when Colonel Harvey launched his presidential boom. Then came the Wilson shift. "As soon as it became apparent that he was a progressive democrat, the predatory interests were shocked, and this anger has grown hotter and hotter every day." The violence of their attacks only proved Wilson's sincerity; the Governor was, thought Bryan, the modern Saul of Tarsus.[91]

But what of the old disciple, Champ Clark? By virtue of his seniority, the pride of Pike County had become Speaker of the House after the Democratic victories of 1910, and Bryan had hoped that he would assume leadership of the progressive forces. The Commoner's hopes were dashed. Apparently Clark had misconceptions about what was expected of him. In November 1911 Bryan noted that the Speaker's usefulness was limited, "partly by fear that he will be accused of imitating Cannon, and partly by the mistaken idea that it is his special mission to preserve harmony among the democrats in the house." Although Bryan still considered Clark the "best bet" for the Democratic nomination, he insisted that the Missourian could not remain a formidable candidate until he recognized that "progress is more important than harmony." [92] Shortly before the convention met in 1912, when congressmen were debating the tariff on wool, Bryan warned Clark that the debate might well be the crisis of his life:

A leader must *lead;* it is not always pleasant to oppose friends and one who leads takes the chances of defeat, but these are the necessary attendants upon leadership. Wilson is making friends because he *fights.* His fight against Smith was heroic. He fought for the income tax & for a primary law. The people like a fighter. You won your position by fighting and you must continue to fight to hold it. Enter into the wool fight. Don't be content to take polls and sit in the background. Take one side or the other and take it *strong.* If a tax on wool is right lead the protectionists to victory. If free wool is right, as I believe it is, lead the fight for it and get the credit for the victory, if victory comes. Don't inquire about how the fight is going to go—make it go the right way, if you can. If you fail you lay the foundation for a future victory. The right wins in the end—don't be afraid to wait. My opinion is that you will not have to wait long, but whether long or not one can better afford to be defeated fighting for the right than to win on the wrong side.[93]

Clearly, as the Commoner looked upon Wilson's candidacy

with increasing favor, he began to lose confidence in Clark. Yet Bryan maintained a neutral position between the two men, defending both against what he regarded as unwarranted attacks. Until the convention at Baltimore was well under way, Bryan continued to insist that both Wilson and Clark were progressives who could be trusted.[94] To contend, then, that Bryan labored to overthrow Clark and project Wilson into the White House, or to assume that he hoped for a stalemate that would result in his own nomination is to misinterpret his position. The Commoner was not interested in personalities: he was interested in a cause. His fight at Baltimore was against those elements of his party that had consistently worked to prevent it from being progressive.[95] In making this fight he helped to create a condition which worked in Wilson's favor, but Willis Abbot was probably right when he wrote that Bryan "would have been quite as ready to nominate Clark if that would have contributed to the success of what he thought the greater issue." [96]

Professor Arthur Link has shown that in the long climactic struggle, as balloting dragged on hour after tensive hour, Bryan played a role more spectacular than decisive. The Commoner's dramatic shift from Clark (for whom all Nebraska delegates had been instructed) to Wilson stirred the convention. Clark men booed and hissed while Wilson forces cheered, but there was no stampede. Bryan made his move on the fourteenth ballot, and Wilson was not nominated until the forty-sixth. Obviously the Peerless Leader could not be given credit—or blame—for the final outcome. Wilson's victory was more directly the result of other causes: the obstinacy of that bloc of delegates pledged to Oscar Underwood, who refused to give up the fight when Clark seemed to emerge as favorite of the convention; the success of Wilson's managers in making agreements with machine-controlled delegations; and the capitulation of Underwood to Wilson.[97]

The Commoner did play a decisive role, however, during the first hectic days of the Democratic conclave. It was then that he fought the selection of Alton B. Parker as temporary chairman on grounds that it would be "suicidal to have a reactionary for chairman when four-fifths of the country is radically progressive." [98] It was then that he introduced his famous Morgan-Ryan-Belmont resolution, which placed the convention on record as "opposed to the nomination of any candidate for president who is the representative of or under obligation to J. Pierpont Morgan, Thomas F. Ryan, August Belmont, or any other member of the privilege-hunting and favor-seeking class." [99]

In his account of the Baltimore struggle Ray Stannard Baker remarked, "Great Leadership consists in making issues so clear, so simple that common men who do not think may vote as they feel." [100] If this can be accepted, then Bryan demonstrated great leadership before balloting began by forcing a clear-cut alignment between conservatives and progressives. "This one thing I know," said Cone Johnson of Texas after Bryan had objected to Parker, "the fight is on and Bryan is on one side and Wall Street is on the other." [101] The Commoner had made his point, and with his strange resolution against the "money power" he drove it home. Charles S. Moore, the son-in-law of Senator Benjamin F. Tillman, wrote Wilson after the convention describing Bryan's action:

I shall never foreget [sic] as long as I live the impressive, the eloquent, and the courageous manner in which he attacked the special privilege class on that memorable Thursday night when he presented his resolution against Morgan, Ryan and Belmont naming the candidate. When he pronounced the words "You shall not deliver the Democratic party in bondage to the interests of this country" it seemed to me I could hear the voiceless millions lending applause to the cries and cheers of those within the walls of the armory. When he spoke that word "bondage" in the sentence above quoted you could all most [sic] see the great money power of this country reaching out its tentacles around the throats of the people.[102]

A final word on Bryan's part in nominating Wilson must be added. Victory did not come until after Roger Sullivan, the Chicago boss, swung his delegation into line behind the Governor. Why did Sullivan so act at the eleventh hour? He had previously promised William McCombs, commander of Wilson's forces, that should the Governor's men muster enough strength to make Wilson's nomination probable, Illinois would lend its support. Furthermore, Sullivan's archrivals in state politics, the William Randolph Hearst–Carter Harrison faction, had been active advocates of Clark. And finally, Sullivan apparently believed that Bryan, whom he despised, was manipulating the delegates to secure his own nomination.[103] He acted then, not so much out of love for Wilson as out of hatred for Bryan, and the political shrewdness of the Peerless Leader in refusing clearly to disavow his own candidacy bore fruit that was sweet to the taste of Wilson's followers.

VIII

*

* * *

*

THE TRUMPET SOUNDETH

WHEN BRYAN RELINQUISHED LEADERSHIP of the Democratic party to Woodrow Wilson, he might have looked back over the past twenty years with justifiable satisfaction. His political and economic views had been shaped by the moralism of the Middle Border, and he had displayed remarkable consistency in adhering to those views. He had labored—for the most part successfully—to have his ideals, his analysis of shortcomings in American life, and his remedies adopted by the Democracy. He had seen many of his proposals enacted into law. Even though he had spent but four years in public office, he was widely respected at home and abroad. Few statesmen have been so honored—or so influential. Yet when Bryan delivered his valedictory in an emotion-charged atmosphere at Baltimore in 1912, the structure of American politics had not been changed drastically from what it had been when he electrified the Chicago convention with his "Cross of Gold" speech in 1896.

The Commoner had always maintained that political parties should be distinguished by their principles; on that he and the advocates of responsible party government were agreed. Yet the period from 1896 to 1912 did not produce a system in which the two major national parties differed on fundamentals. Although Bryan's "first battle" seemed to presage political realignment, conservative Democrats gained strength after his second defeat. With Parker's nomination in 1904 they attempted a reorganization that would rid the party of "Bryanism." During those years of internal discord, the Commoner's hopes of placing the Democracy under commitment to his principles remained unfulfilled.

When he was successful in once more persuading a majority of his party to accept his views, a development in another quarter worked against the emergence of two parties differing on fundamentals. The development was, of course, Theodore Roosevelt's appropriation of large portions of Bryan's platform. The Commoner could not and did not abandon his program to the care of the Rough Rider in order to create differences between Republicans and Democrats; on the other hand, as he discovered when he proposed government ownership of railroads, to take further steps down the lonely pathway of radicalism would mean a loss of influence. What he did, therefore, was to modify the presentation of his ideas, making them more acceptable to moderates. And in so doing he softened party differences.

After 1908 the apparent conservatism of President Taft seemed to provide Bryan with an opportunity once more to oppose the party in power on a fundamental level. But following his third defeat the chances of another Bryan candidacy were slight, and his opposition to Taft (whether the Commoner was aware of it or not) served a somewhat different purpose from his earlier opposition to Roosevelt. Prior to 1908 he had been instrumental in securing the adoption of many of his reforms by Republicans; in part to prevent Bryan's election, the G.O.P. had solicited reform votes. After Taft took office, Bryan's interest in the future of his party became perhaps his primary concern, and his opposition to the new Republican administration served to keep the Democracy committed to progressivism. But again a system of principled parties failed to develop, for with the Roosevelt-Taft split Republicans entered into a period of internal conflict similar to that experienced by Democrats after 1900.

That the heterogeneous composition of American parties remained unchanged did not, however, force a return to nine-teenth-century political techniques and practices. Although Bryan could claim a personal following of more than six million voters, he never created a political machine on the pattern set by the Old Guard. He almost invariably supported Democrats in national, state, and local elections, but he always tried to secure the nomination of progressives. In his personal relation-ships he was careful not to alienate machine politicians, yet he did not use them in the traditional way. The Commoner and the bosses could work together if they accepted his terms; he could compromise on men, not on principles.

Bryan cooperated with bosses when he thought their help freely given would aid his cause; at the same time he joined other reformers in urging the adoption of measures calculated to change the mechanics of American politics. Direct democracy (estab-lished through direct primaries, popular election of senators, initiative, referendum, recall, and similar changes) would, it was hoped, break up the machines and return control of the govern-ment to "the People." Bryan's support of these measures was a natural extension of the practices he himself followed. He often appealed directly to the people over the heads of machine leaders and party organizations. Of course he shared progressive opti-mism about political prospects under direct democracy. At last the people would rule.

Direct democracy had not been established when Bryan stepped down as the leader of his party, and the structure of American politics had not been significantly modified. But the tone of American political life had changed immeasurably, and Bryan was to an extent responsible for that change. No longer were candidates able to win elections without discussing live issues, and it may even be that victory itself seemed less important to some party workers than the position the party took on ques-tions of the day. The fight Bryan waged within his party and against the Republicans was more than a mere struggle for power, although any political struggle is certainly that; it was a fight for the sake of certain ideas and convictions. And it was, in a very real sense, a victorious fight. Under his aegis Bryan's Democracy did not follow the reorganizers back to the nineteenth century. It came to stand for progressivism, and partly through Bryan's efforts it nominated a progressive candidate in 1912.

What was the nature of the progressive program which Bryan persuaded his party to accept? It has been said that his reforms were superficial. Herbert Agar, for example, remarked, "It is something of an anticlimax to cry out against the degradation of democracy and the exploitation of the poor, and then suggest the direct election of senators." [1] With equal justification it might be shown that the whole progressive movement was in large part superficial and anticlimactic. The disparity between its enthusiastic discussion of issues and its meager concrete results stands out as one of the striking features of the period. Roosevelt was not alone when he stood at Armageddon; Bryan, La Follette, and even Wilson were capable of equally extravagant rhetoric. Nevertheless, in the legislative and administrative process the flood was dammed, and the grand torrent of reform oratory trickled out in a stream of measures later considered ineffectual by disappointed reformers.[2] For all the fury of the debate over trusts, big business continued to exist. For all the passion in the plea to let the people rule, bosses managed to survive until complex social changes deprived them of their old functions.[3]

Was it all futile then? Bryan never thought so, although his prestige declined during his last years, and at the end he was perhaps more despised than hated by some, more pitied than loved by others. In his opposition years he had, after all, raised and argued some questions that were vital to American democracy—some questions that urgently needed raising. If free silver was a delusion, it was the symbol for a movement of protest that called attention to far-reaching economic developments. If imperialism was not a good campaign issue in 1900, a half century later Americans might have wished that it had been considered more seriously. If reforms relating to the tariff, trusts, and the regulation of business did not land the Commoner in the White House, they did suggest that adjustments to profound social and economic change could be made without sacrificing values of the past.

It was those values that Bryan most wanted to preserve, and through his incessant preaching of middle western moralism he helped to keep them meaningful to his contemporaries. Ray Stannard Baker might treat with scorn "Bryan's comment that the financial problems of the country could be easily solved if 'our hearts were in the right place.' " [4] But to treat Bryan with scorn is to overlook the reasons for his influence. Perhaps only a devoted follower of the Peerless Leader—and he had many in the opposition years—could explain that influence. Louis F. Post did so by implication in 1909 when he defended Bryan against charges of inconsistency in dealing with the kaleidoscopic issues of the times:

> The test of [a public man's] consistency is that with all issues that take shape in the popular mind, he shall be found upon the same side of the principle they involve. For specific controversies are but outward forms or expressions, more or less perfect, of one general controversy over a principle. All of the many political issues in this country have in one way and another given expression to the essential controversy of equal rights against special privileges, of democracy against aristocracy or plutocracy; and to that controversy, whatever the special issue and whether he has been mistaken or not in his particular apprehensions, William J. Bryan has been consistent throughout. . . . To say of him that he veers like a weather-cock with every turn of the wind, is to confess to an utter lack of apprehension of the difference between constant political principle and the ephemeral policies through which political principle, from time to time and in changing form according to varying circumstances, finds concrete expression.[5]

The Commoner's progressivism was founded not on political contrivances or on economic panaceas; it was founded on the faith that was his heritage as a son of the Middle Border. His appeal to the hearts of his countrymen, his doctrine of love, his emphasis on sacrifice as the measure of greatness, his belief in majority rule, his devotion to the common man, his conception of good and evil, his revivalistic approach to social and economic problems, his confidence in God's purpose as he understood it— all these are traceable to a mentality that found the values of an agrarian environment completely satisfying. In a special sense Bryan was more conservative than Cleveland, Parker, and most of the Old Guard—far more conservative than Ryan, Belmont, or any of the captains of industry and finance. Yet the missionary movement of the nineteenth century which had helped to shape the midwestern faith also infused it with a sense of mission. To Bryan, American progress seemed part of a mighty movement, and the destiny of America seemed attainable because the nation was a divine instrument for improving the world.

In a Jackson Day address delivered in 1912 Bryan told of visiting Peru and finding innumerable sand dunes on the western slope of the Andes. The dunes were uniform in size and they "marched with the precision of an army" two hundred feet a year toward the mountain. The cause of this phenomenon was the wind blowing inshore from the ocean and carrying with it particles of sand as it swept across the terrain. As the wind moved Peruvian dunes, so back of every progressive reform was "the same irresistible force constantly at work that gives triumph to every righteous cause." Bryan confessed that he could not worship God as he did were it not for his belief that the reform movement in which he had played such a significant part would triumph in the end. Now after a long career as the leader of his party he was preparing to turn that responsibility over to another. In a characteristic peroration he quoted Lord Byron in what was both a confession of faith and a call to action based upon its premises:

> The dead have been awakened—shall I sleep?
> The World's at war with tyrants—shall I crouch?
> The harvest's ripe—and shall I pause to reap?
> I slumber not; the thorn is in my Couch.
> Each day a trumpet soundeth in mine ear,
>   Its echo in my heart—[6]

*

*   *   *

*

NOTES

CHAPTER I

Patterns of Culture on the Middle Border

1. Walter P. Webb, *The Great Frontier* (Cambridge, Mass., 1952), p. 34.
2. Peter Mode, *The Frontier Spirit in American Christianity* (New York, 1923), pp. 106-107; Robert Hastings Nichols, "The Influence of the American Environment on the Conception of the Church in American Protestantism," *Church History*, XI (June, 1942), pp. 185-186; William Warren Sweet, *American Culture and Religion, Six Essays* (Dallas, Texas, 1951), pp. 37-38.
3. Winthrop S. Hudson, *The Great Tradition of the American Churches* (New York, 1953), pp. 28-32; Sidney Mead, "In Search of God," *The Heritage of the Middle West,* ed. John J. Murray (Norman, Okla., 1958), pp. 152-155; Sidney Mead, "Denominationalism: The Shape of Protestantism in America," *Church History*, XXIII (December, 1954), p. 299; Sidney Mead, "The Rise of the Evangelical Conception of the Ministry in America (1607-1850)," *The Ministry in Historical Perspectives,* ed. H. Richard Niebuhr and Daniel D. Williams (New York, 1956), pp. 207-208.
4. Excellent brief discussions of sectarian rivalry may be found in Timothy L. Smith, *Revivalism and Social Reform* (New York, 1957), pp. 15-33, and in R. Carlyle Buley, *The Old Northwest, Pioneer Period, 1815-1840* (Indianapolis, 1950), II, 417-488.

5. Peter Cartwright, *Autobiography,* ed. Charles L. Wallis (New York, 1956), p. 35.

6. Quoted in Buley, *The Old Northwest,* II, 488.

7. David M. Potter, *People of Plenty* (Chicago, 1954), pp. 92-97; William G. McLoughlin, Jr., *Modern Revivalism* (New York, 1959), pp. 21-22.

8. Bernard A. Weisberger, *They Gathered at the River* (Boston, 1958), pp. 82-84; Smith, *Revivalism and Social Reform,* pp. 32-33.

9. William B. Sprague, *Lectures on Revivals of Religion* (Albany, 1832), appendix, pp. 17-18, as quoted in McLoughlin, *Modern Revivalism,* p. 22 n.

10. Tocqueville, *Democracy in America,* trans. Henry Reeve (New York, 1958), II, 24-28.

11. Weisberger, *They Gathered at the River,* p. 228; McLoughlin, *Modern Revivalism,* pp. 25-26.

12. H. Richard Niebuhr, *The Social Sources of Denominationalism* (New York, 1957), pp. 149-151; Bernard A. Weisberger, "Pentecost in the Backwoods," *American Heritage,* X (June, 1959), pp. 79-80; Charles A. Johnson, *The Frontier Camp Meeting* (Dallas, Texas, 1955), pp. 69-80.

13. Mead, "Denominationalism: The Shape of Protestantism in America," pp. 307-310; Mode, *The Frontier Spirit in American Christianity,* pp. 107-108; William Warren Sweet, *Revivalism in America* (New York, 1944), p. 139. H. Richard Niebuhr suggests that "the camp meeting was an early form of denominational co-operation in which Presbyterian, Methodist and Baptist preachers united." *The Social Sources of Denominationalism,* p. 179.

14. Colin Goodykoontz, *Home Missions on the American Frontier* (Caldwell, Idaho, 1939), pp. 25-27; F. A. Michaux, "Travels to the West of the Allegheny Mountains," *Early Western Travels,* ed. Reuben Gold Thwaites (Cleveland, 1904), III, 144. Peter Cartwright thought the reports of "these newly-fledged missionaries" highly exaggerated, as indeed they were. Yet throughout his *Autobiography* he gives many examples of frontier crudity. What he really resented in eastern missionary reports was the implied criticism of workers already in the field, especially itinerant Methodist preachers like himself.

15. Lyman Beecher, *Autobiography* (New York, 1864), I, 241. See also Goodykoontz, *Home Missions on the American Frontier,* pp. 130-139.

16. Mode, *The Frontier Spirit in American Christianity,* pp. 112-113; Goodykoontz, *Home Missions on the American Frontier,* pp. 172-188.

17. Lyman Beecher, *Plea for the West* (3d ed., Cincinnati, 1836), p. 10.

18. Quoted in Goodykoontz, *Home Missions on the American Frontier,* p. 236. The American Home Missionary Society, founded in 1826, always viewed its efforts as related to American destiny. The

Missionary Herald, giving editorial assistance to the new society, printed a number of reports on the need for missionaries in the West. It prefaced those reports with the following comment: "Every one who believes, that in order to [insure] the permanent prosperity of our country, our religious institutions should be co-extensive with our population, should stop on reading such statements as the following and reflect on what will be the consequence to our nation of not making an increased effort to supply every part of it with the preaching of the Gospel." *The Missionary Herald,* XXIII (May, 1827), p. 161.

19. Quoted in Goodykoontz, *Home Missions on the American Frontier,* p. 238.
20. Quoted in Mode, *The Frontier Spirit in American Christianity,* pp. 38-39.
21. Richard D. Mosier, *Making the American Mind: Social and Moral Ideas in the McGuffey Readers* (New York, 1947), pp. 168-169.
22. Lewis Atherton, *Main Street on the Middle Border* (Bloomington, Ind., 1954), pp. 65-66.
23. Harvey Minnich (ed.), *Old Favorites from the McGuffey Readers* (New York, 1936), p. viii.
24. *Ibid.,* pp. 11-12.
25. In this study, citations are to the "Eclectic Educational Series" (Cincinnati, 1879). Full titles of the textbooks in this series are as follows: *McGuffey's First Eclectic Reader, McGuffey's Second Eclectic Reader, McGuffey's Third Eclectic Reader,* etc. *Fourth Reader,* pp. 64-67.
26. *Third Reader,* pp. 151-155.
27. *Fifth Reader,* p. 231.
28. *Fourth Reader,* p. 28.
29. *Second Reader,* pp. 44-46.
30. *Fourth Reader,* pp. 38-39.
31. *Third Reader,* pp. 123-126.
32. *Ibid.,* pp. 67-69.
33. Minnich (ed.), *Old Favorites from the McGuffey Readers,* pp. 188-189.
34. *Fifth Reader,* p. 351; Atherton, *Main Street on the Middle Border,* p. 68.
35. *Fourth Reader,* pp. 152-153.
36. *Third Reader,* pp. 115-117.
37. Minnich (ed.), *Old Favorites from the McGuffey Readers,* p. 113.
38. Commager, *The American Mind* (New Haven, 1950), p. 38.
39. Atherton, *Main Street on the Middle Border,* p. 107.
40. *Sixth Reader,* pp. 120-121.
41. Harry P. Harrison and Karl Detzer, *Culture Under Canvas* (New York, 1958), pp. 39-49; Gay MacLaren, *Morally We Roll Along* (Boston, 1938), p. 75.
42. Atherton, *Main Street on the Middle Border,* pp. 324-325; Mac-

Laren, *Morally We Roll Along,* p. 79; Harrison and Detzer, *Culture Under Canvas,* pp. 51-55.

43. Donald L. Graham, "Circuit Chautauqua, A Middle Western Institution" (unpublished Ph.D. dissertation, State University of Iowa, 1953), p. 25. Senator Jonathan P. Dolliver of Iowa was a popular speaker at independent Chautauquas and he had earlier noted the receptivity of midwestern audiences to the type of program the circuit Chautauqua brought to the plains. "These little Kansas cities are wonders of the intellectual world—places of 3000 people turning out their whole adult population to the entertainments of their lecture course." Dolliver to Mrs. Dolliver, November 13, 1899, *Jonathan P. Dolliver Papers,* Iowa Historical Society Library, Iowa City.

44. Graham, "Circuit Chautauqua," pp. 2-3; R. B. Tozier, "The American Chautauqua" (unpublished Ph.D. dissertation, State University of Iowa, 1932), p. 54.

45. MacLaren, *Morally We Roll Along,* pp. 147-148.

46. Gregory Mason, "Chautauqua, Its Technics," *American Mercury,* I (March, 1924), p. 275.

47. MacLaren, *Morally We Roll Along,* pp. 146-148; Harrison and Detzer, *Culture Under Canvas,* p. 182.

48. MacLaren, *Morally We Roll Along,* p. 97.

49. Quoted in Graham, "Circuit Chautauqua," p. 134.

50. Victoria and Robert Ormond Case, *We Called It Culture* (Garden City, New York, 1948), pp. 74-75; MacLaren, *Morally We Roll Along,* pp. 178-179; Harrison and Detzer, *Culture Under Canvas,* pp. 138-144. Even informative speeches carried titles with moralistic or religious overtones. Senator Dolliver's lecture on labor, for example, was entitled "The Working Man of Nazareth." Dolliver to A. E. Palmer, November 25, 1899, *Dolliver Papers.*

51. Typewritten MS, William Rainey Bennett file, *Chautauqua Collection,* State University of Iowa Library. This vast collection contains a wealth of Chautauqua materials, but they have not been catalogued or arranged. The only work which fully exploits these holdings is Donald Graham's excellent Ph.D. dissertation, "Circuit Chautauqua, A Middle Western Institution."

52. Quoted in Tozier, "The American Chautauqua," pp. 57-58.

53. Harrison and Detzer, *Culture Under Canvas,* p. 138.

54. MacLaren, *Morally We Roll Along,* pp. 163-164.

55. *Ibid.,* pp. 176-177; Atherton, *Main Street on the Middle Border,* p. 270; Harrison and Detzer, *Culture Under Canvas,* pp. 183-184.

CHAPTER II

A Son of the Middle Border

1. Charles F. Horner, *Strike the Tents* (Philadelphia, 1954), pp. 126-127.
2. Paxton Hibben, *The Peerless Leader, William Jennings Bryan* (New York, 1929), p. 27.
3. E. G. Dewey to Mary Baird Bryan, June 17, 1912, *William Jennings Bryan Papers*, Division of Manuscripts, Library of Congress. Dewey was principal of the Salem school in 1874-1875.
4. Hibben, *Peerless Leader*, p. 49.
5. J. C. Long, *Bryan, The Great Commoner* (New York, 1928), p. 26. Whether or not Bryan actually studied the lessons in the McGuffey Readers is an open question. Bryan himself said that he did. See William Jennings Bryan and Mary Baird Bryan, *Memoirs* (Philadelphia, 1925), p. 40. Yet Bryan's sister, Mrs. T. S. Allen, has written that she does not remember the Readers being used in the Bryan home. Mrs. T. S. Allen to the author, April 9, 1956. The point is minor, however, for Bryan unquestionably used either McGuffey's textbooks or others very similar in content.
6. William Allen White, *Masks in a Pageant* (New York, 1928), p. 252.
7. Richard Hofstadter, *The American Political Tradition* (New York, 1949), pp. 191-192.
8. Paolo E. Coletta, "The Youth of William Jennings Bryan—Beginnings of a Christian Statesman," *Nebraska History*, XXXI (1950), p. 17.
9. Paul R. Anderson, "Hiram K. Jones and Philosophy at Jacksonville," *Journal of the Illinois State Historical Society*, XXXIII (1940), p. 518.
10. William Jennings Bryan, *The First Battle* (Chicago, 1896), p. 38.
11. See, for example, Hibben, *Peerless Leader*, pp. 55-56, 65-88.
12. Charles Henry Rammelkamp, *Illinois College, A Centennial History, 1829-1929* (New Haven, 1928), p. 24; Albert Schmidt, "Blazing a Trail to Higher Education," *The Heritage of the Middle West*, ed. John J. Murray, pp. 236-239.
13. Rammelkamp, *Illinois College*, p. 39.
14. *Ibid.*, pp. 262-265, 297-299, 324; Coletta, "The Youth of William Jennings Bryan," pp. 12-13; George R. Poage, "The College Career of William Jennings Bryan," *Mississippi Valley Historical Review*, XV (1928), pp. 166-167.
15. Poage, "The College Career of William Jennings Bryan," pp. 168-169.
16. Donald E. Polzin, "Curricular and Extra-Curricular Speech Train-

ing at Illinois College: 1829-1900" (unpublished M.A. thesis, University of Illinois, 1952), pp. 21-25.

17. The Illinois College newspaper, the *College Rambler*, contains many references to Bryan's oratorical activities. See especially the issues for April, May, and November, 1880; April 2, May 21, and June 4, 1881.

18. Bogus commencement programs attacking graduating seniors were sometimes surreptitiously printed and circulated during this period. One which commented on Bryan was particularly vicious: "It sounds well to hear him say: 'Cromwell, I charge thee fling away ambition,' in view of the fact that his college life has been one continuous endeavor to secure place and power." Quoted in Poage, "The College Career of William Jennings Bryan," p. 181. A copy of this program is now in the archives of Illinois College.

19. The societies purchased books with funds secured from dues and lectures which they sponsored. By the end of the century each society had a library of some 2,000 books. Polzin, "Curricular and Extra-Curricular Speech Training at Illinois College," p. 65.

20. Benjamin P. Thomas, *Abraham Lincoln* (New York, 1952), p. 15.

21. *The College Rambler*, March 5, 1881; Coletta, "The Youth of William Jennings Bryan," p. 13.

22. Quoted in Poage, "The College Career of William Jennings Bryan," pp. 171-172. Bryan's Jacksonville acquaintances had occasion to recall his academic record when he became a candidate in 1896. Commented one: "All through his college life he bore a good character and was faithful in his attendance at church and Sunday school and acted as a gentleman. He was a hard student, and while he could hardly be called brilliant, he studied hard and what he did learn he remembered, as he excelled in that respect." Jacksonville *Daily Journal*, July 11, 1896.

23. Bryan, *Memoirs*, pp. 48-50; Hibben, *Peerless Leader*, pp. 48-49; Long, *The Great Commoner*, p. 27.

24. Nichols, "The Influence of the American Environment on the Conception of the Church in American Protestantism," p. 190.

25. *The Commoner*, February 17, 1905.

26. William Jennings Bryan, "The Next Awakening," *Public Opinion*, XXXVIII (May 27, 1905), p. 805.

27. Paul Carter, *The Decline and Revival of the Social Gospel* (Ithaca, N.Y., 1954), p. 47. Carter here points out that logically fundamentalism could be combined with political radicalism, and that "Bryan himself sometimes saw the controversy over evolution in Social Gospel terms." To this I would add that Bryan's attitude toward theology enabled him to combine the moralistic faith of the Middle West with fundamentalism. He saw no reason to question the Bible, which he took as the given Word of God to be applied by men. He sought not to analyze its content but to define its ethical implications for American society. One reason

for his poor showing at the Scopes trial, it may be observed here, is that he had never studied Scripture from a theological or scholarly point of view.

28. Bryan, "The Next Awakening," p. 805.

29. William Jennings Bryan, *The Making of a Man* (New York, 1914), pp. 25-27.

30. William Jennings Bryan, "The Prince of Peace," printed in *The Commoner*, February 1, 1907.

31. Helen Edith Marshall, "The Social Philosophy of William Jennings Bryan" (unpublished M.A. thesis, University of Chicago, 1929), p. 47.

32. William Jennings Bryan, *The First Commandment* (New York, 1917), p. 23.

33. William Jennings Bryan, "Faith," printed in *The Commoner*, July 19, 1907.

34. William Jennings Bryan, "Tolstoy, The Apostle of Love," printed in *The Commoner*, February 19, 1904; William Jennings Bryan, *The Old World and Its Ways* (St. Louis, 1907), p. 561.

35. William Jennings Bryan, *The Forces that Make for Peace* (Boston, 1912), p. 11.

36. Bryan, "Tolstoy, The Apostle of Love."

37. Bryan, "The Prince of Peace."

38. *The Commoner*, April 4, 1902.

39. William Jennings Bryan, "Democracy's Appeal to Culture," printed in *The Commoner*, February 17, 1905.

40. *The Commoner*, April 4, 1902.

41. *Ibid.*

42. William Jennings Bryan, *The Value of an Ideal* (New York, 1914), pp. 27-39.

43. Bryan, *The First Battle*, p. 205.

44. White, *Masks in a Pageant*, p. 260.

45. Mrs. T. S. Allen to the author, April 9, 1956.

46. Horner, *Strike the Tents*, pp. 107, 112-113. Bryan's enemies accused him of making speeches only to obtain his fees, which they intimated were exorbitant. It is true that Bryan did do well financially, but Chautauqua managers thought him fair and reasonable. Unlike other speakers, Bryan did not share in season ticket income, but drew his fee at the gate. He took the first $250, and his sponsor the second $250. All that came from single admissions in excess of $500 was equally divided. Very few other speakers could have made money under such a contract. Clipping in *Chautauqua Collection*, State University of Iowa Library, from *Lyceum Magazine*, July 16, 1916.

47. Booker T. Washington to Mary Bryan, January 2, 1899, Booker T. Washington to William Jennings Bryan, November 14, 1901, *Bryan Papers*.

48. The story of the Bennett will, which was contested by Bennett's

widow, is told in Bryan's *Memoirs,* pp. 129-144. Although Bryan's opponents attempted to discredit him as the recipient of a bribe in this matter, they were unsuccessful in doing so.

49. *The Commoner,* July 24, 1903.
50. William Jennings Bryan, *Man* (New York, 1914), p. 15; *The Commoner,* May 30, 1902.
51. *The Commoner,* May 30, 1902.
52. Bryan, *Man,* p. 18.
53. Bryan, *The Making of a Man,* p. 20. Bryan recalled that his own father did much to encourage education: "My father was wont to say that if a man had the big head, you could whittle it down, but that if he had the little head there was no hope for him." Bryan, "Faith."
54. *The Commoner,* August 9, 1901.
55. *The Commoner,* March 8, 1901.
56. Bryan, *Man,* p. 19. Cf. McGuffey's view of education, p. 12.
57. Bryan, "Democracy's Appeal to Culture."
58. Bryan, "The Prince of Peace."
59. William Jennings Bryan, "Commerce," *Speeches of William Jennings Bryan* (New York, 1913), II, 413. Hereafter cited as *Speeches.*
60. William Jennings Bryan, *Heart to Heart Appeals* (New York, 1917), p. 7.
61. *Ibid.,* p. 8; Bryan to Henry Watterson, August 4, 1908, *Henry Watterson Papers,* Division of Manuscripts, Library of Congress.
62. *The Campaign Textbook of the Democratic Party of the United States, 1908* (n.p., 1908), p. 220.
63. *The Commoner,* February 24, 1905, and June 28, 1907. See also Bryan to Dr. R. H. Reemelin, July 17, 1901, *Bryan Papers.*
64. Bryan to C. M. Hubener, June 6, 1892, *William Jennings Bryan Papers,* Nebraska State Historical Society, Lincoln, Nebraska.
65. Bryan, *The Value of an Ideal,* p. 42; *The Commoner,* September 20, 1907.
66. Bryan, "Radical and Conservative," *Speeches,* II, 207-208.
67. Bryan, "Patriotism," *Speeches,* II, 193.
68. Bryan, "Radical and Conservative," pp. 208-209.
69. Bryan, *The Value of an Ideal,* p. 47.
70. *The Commoner,* October 25, 1901.
71. *The Commoner,* March 1, 1907.
72. *Ibid.;* Bryan, *Heart to Heart Appeals,* pp. 11-12. Bryan was, of course, shifting the ground of the argument here, a technique he often employed in debate.
73. *The Commoner,* February 6, 1901, and January 20, 1911.
74. Bryan, "The Next Awakening," p. 806.
75. Clipping in the *Bryan Papers* from the Helena *Daily Independent,* October 27, 1908.
76. Transcript of a speech delivered at the Jefferson Day Banquet,

New York, April 13, 1912, *Maurice F. Lyons Papers,* Division of Manuscripts, Library of Congress.

77. Bryan, "Thanksgiving Day," *Speeches,* II, 203.
78. Bryan, "Missions," *Speeches,* II, 316.
79. Bryan, "America's Mission," *Speeches,* II, 15.

CHAPTER III

The Cross of Gold

1. Ralph Gabriel, *The Course of American Democratic Thought* (New York, 1956), p. 54.
2. For an excellent review of recent works on the economic history of this period, see Thomas LeDuc, "Recent Contributions to Economic History: The United States, 1861-1900," *Journal of Economic History,* XIX (March, 1959), pp. 44-63.
3. Richard Hofstadter, *The Age of Reform, From Bryan to F. D. R.* (New York, 1955), pp. 24-25. For the Jeffersonian background of these beliefs, see A. Whitney Griswold, *Farming and Democracy* (New York, 1943), pp. 18-46.
4. John D. Hicks, *The Populist Revolt* (Minneapolis, 1931), p. 6. In accounting for the movement of settlers into Kansas in the seventies, one observer credited the "flaming handbills" posted in railroad stations and post offices with great influence. Headed "Ho! for Kansas," they pictured in glowing colors the "wonderful fertility of its plains," and the "cheapness of its lands." Paul W. Gates, *Fifty Million Acres: Conflicts over Kansas Land Policy, 1854-1890* (Ithaca, N.Y., 1954), pp. 246-247.
5. Raymond C. Miller, "The Economic Background of Populism in Kansas," *Mississippi Valley Historical Review,* XI (1925), pp. 277, 486; John D. Barnhart, "Rainfall and the Populist Party in Nebraska," *American Political Science Review,* XIX (1925), p. 532.
6. William Allen White, *Autobiography* (New York, 1946), pp. 280-282.
7. Fred A. Shannon, *The Farmer's Last Frontier* (New York, 1945), p. 143. Tables demonstrating the relationship of farm machinery to hours of labor required for the putting in and securing of one acre of wheat may be found in Leo Rogin, *The Introduction of Farm Machinery in Its Relation to the Productivity of Labor in the Agriculture of the United States during the Nineteenth Century,* "University of California Publications in Economics," IX (Berkeley, 1931), pp. 216-220, 234-235. See also Fred A. Shannon, *America's Economic Growth* (New York, 1940), pp. 376-378, 705-708.
8. John D. Hicks, "The Third Party Tradition in American Politics," *Mississippi Valley Historical Review,* XX (1933), p. 15. See also

Harold U. Faulkner, *Politics, Reform and Expansion* (New York, 1959), pp. 48-49.

9. Hofstadter, *The Age of Reform*, pp. 40-46. James C. Malin has commented upon the speculative tendencies of American farmers: "When mortgage financing practices were introduced, speculation in land took on a character not too dissimilar to futures trading on margins, except that it was not done on an organized market such as a stock exchange or a board of trade. For the most part each farmer was a speculator who made a living from the farm until he could sell it at an advance in price. Often he miscalculated and lost his land by foreclosure of mortgage; that is, he was sold out on a falling market when his margin was too small. Technical owner- ship was of little more permanence than the possessory rights of the miner, or the ownership of stocks, wheat or cotton in margin trading." "Mobility and History; Reflections on the Agricultural Policies of the United States in Relation to a Mechanized World," *Agricultural History*, XVII (1943), pp. 181-182. See also Allan Bogue, *Money at Interest, The Farm Mortgage on the Middle Border* (Ithaca, N.Y., 1955), pp. 143-144, 274-275. For a detailed study on the instability of farm population see James C. Malin, "The Turnover of Farm Population in Kansas," *Kansas Historical Quarterly*, IV (1935), pp. 339-372.

10. Among the most active of speculative groups were the railroads. Perhaps the best discussion of railroad land policies during the period of agrarian unrest may be found in Gates, *Fifty Million Acres*, pp. 249-294. The relationship between mechanization and expansion is suggested by James C. Malin, *Winter Wheat in the Golden Belt of Kansas* (Lawrence, Kans., 1944), pp. 104-106. Malin argues that large horse-drawn machines were necessary in the sub- humid climate of the trans-Missouri plains. Soil there had to be worked when moisture content was adequate, and the speed which such machines could provide was essential to survival. Furthermore, yield per acre was lower than in other areas, and the possibility of crop failure greater. It seemed advisable, there- fore, to farm more acres of land less intensively. And this could be done only through mechanization.

11. Benton H. Wilcox, "An Historical Definition of Northwestern Radicalism," *Mississippi Valley Historical Review*, XXVI (1939), pp. 383-384.

12. *Yearbook of the United States Department of Agriculture, 1901* (Washington, 1902), pp. 699, 709, 718, 727, 754. These pages con- tain tables showing prices for major crops during the years from the close of the Civil War to 1901. The figures are those of Decem- ber 1, however, and because of lack of storage facilities most farmers were forced to sell earlier at lower prices. Furthermore, these statistics make no allowances for commissions to dealers, warehouse charges, variations among different grades of produce,

and distance to market. The only conclusion these statistics justify is that there was a general downward trend in prices. This conclusion is supported by James C. Malin, *Winter Wheat*, pp. 43, 197-199, 143, 148. See also Solon J. Buck, *The Granger Movement* (Cambridge, Mass., 1913), pp. 28-34, and Shannon, *The Farmer's Last Frontier*, pp. 292-295. The summary of the figures issued by the Department of Agriculture here reproduced may be found in Hicks, *The Populist Revolt*, p. 56.

Average Market Price of Three Crops, 1870-1897

Years	Wheat (per bushel)	Corn (per bushel)	Cotton (per pound)
1870-1873	106.7	43.1	15.1
1874-1877	94.4	40.9	11.1
1878-1881	100.6	43.1	9.5
1882-1885	80.2	39.8	9.1
1886-1889	74.8	35.9	8.3
1890-1893	70.9	41.7	7.8
1894-1897	63.3	29.7	5.8

13. Shannon, *America's Economic Growth*, pp. 389-390.
14. Quoted in Eric Goldman, *Rendezvous with Destiny* (New York, 1953), pp. 37-38.
15. Shannon, *The Farmer's Last Frontier*, pp. 298-301; Faulkner, *Politics, Reform and Expansion*, pp. 56-57.
16. Hallie Farmer, "The Economic Background of Frontier Populism," *Mississippi Valley Historical Review*, X (1924), p. 424.
17. Quoted in Hicks, *The Populist Revolt*, p. 66.
18. Shannon, *The Farmer's Last Frontier*, p. 306; Hicks, *The Populist Revolt*, p. 23. According to the Census Bureau, in the United States as a whole there were thirteen persons for every mortgage in force on January 1, 1890. Abstract of the Eleventh Census, 1890 (Washington, 1896), p. 217.
19. Wilcox, "An Historical Definition of Northwestern Radicalism," p. 385. Allan Bogue has shown that abundant loan capital tended to drive interest rates down, while the maximum hovered at 10 or 12 per cent in the plains areas. In addition to interest, there were also commission and service charges which greatly increased the cost of the loan. Nevertheless, the assertions of agrarian writers that rates of interest ran as high as 35 or even 50 per cent were not well grounded. Bogue, *Money at Interest*, pp. 114-121, 142-143, 263.
20. Shannon, *The Farmer's Last Frontier*, p. 313. The foreclosure of mortgages was as disastrous to the loan agencies as it was to the farmer. A source of revenue in good times, the real estate holdings of mortgage companies were costly in bad times because they froze

the working capital which was the life blood of such organizations. Bogue, *Money at Interest,* pp. 146-147, 193-194.

21. Hofstadter, *The American Political Tradition,* p. 184.

22. Hicks, *The Populist Revolt,* p. 88.

23. Farmer, "The Economic Background of Frontier Populism," p. 314.

24. Hofstadter, *The Age of Reform,* p. 35; Henry Nash Smith, *Virgin Land* (Cambridge, Mass., 1950), pp. 192-193.

25. Hofstadter, *The Age of Reform,* p. 72. Faulkner suggests that Hofstadter has overstated his case. The farmer, he feels, did pay higher prices than were warranted for transportation services and commodities he received. Farmers were mistaken, however, in thinking that their difficulties were the result of a conspiracy. Faulkner, *Politics, Reform and Expansion,* pp. 55-56.

26. Leon W. Fuller, "Colorado's Revolt Against Capitalism," *Mississippi Valley Historical Review,* XXI (1934), pp. 351, 353.

27. Quoted in Farmer, "The Economic Background of Frontier Populism," p. 424; Roger V. Clements, "The Farmers' Attitude Toward British Investment in American Industry," *The Journal of Economic History,* XV (1955), pp. 151-159. The speeches and writings of Populist leaders are shot through with references to the iniquity of the British. See the *Ignatius Donnelly Papers* and the *James Manahan Papers,* Minneosta Historical Society, St. Paul; the *John P. Altgeld Papers* and the *George A. Schilling Papers,* Illinois State Historical Library, Springfield; the *James B. Weaver Papers,* Iowa Historical, Memorial and Art Department, Des Moines. The Jews, too, were frequently charged with complicity in an international conspiracy against the farmer. As John Higham has suggested, however, the Populists were ambivalent in their attitude toward Jews. John Higham, "Anti-Semitism in the Gilded Age," *Mississippi Valley Historical Review,* XLIII (1957), pp. 562-565. In a speech given in Chicago during the campaign of 1896, Bryan said: "Our opponents have sometimes tried to make it appear that we were attacking a race when we denounced the financial policy advocated by the Rothchilds. But we are not; we are as much opposed to the financial policy of J. Pierpont Morgan as we are to the financial policy of the Rothchilds. We are not attacking a race; we are attacking greed and avarice, which know neither race nor religion." Printed in Bryan, *The First Battle,* p. 581.

28. Campaign speeches made at Springfield, Ohio, and Washington, D.C., printed in Bryan, *The First Battle,* pp. 361-362, 461.

29. Flavius VanVorhis to Bryan, November 19, 1900, *Bryan Papers.*

30. Quoted in Hicks, *The Populist Revolt,* p. 160.

31. Chicago *Tribune,* September 19, 1895. See also Harvey Wish, "John Peter Altgeld and the Background of the Campaign of 1896," *Mississippi Valley Historical Review,* XXIV (1938), p. 504.

32. Hicks, *The Populist Revolt,* pp. 210, 439-444; Shannon, *The Farmer's Last Frontier,* pp. 320-321; Carl C. Taylor, *The Farmers'*

Movement, 1620-1920 (New York, 1953), pp. 297-300; Kirk H. Porter, *National Party Platforms* (New York, 1924), pp. 166-169.

33. Topeka *Mail*, July 3, 1901, quoted in Farmer, "The Economic Background of Frontier Populism," p. 426.

34. Quoted in Faulkner, *Politics, Reform and Expansion*, p. 58.

35. Quoted in Hicks, *The Populist Revolt*, p. 151. This is to say of the farmer's attempt to make his influence felt what H. L. Mencken said later of the gentleman reformer's entry into politics: Those who argue for it simply argue "that the remedy for prostitution is to fill the bawdy houses with virgins," a reform that would accomplish little since "either the virgins would leap out of the windows, or they would cease to be virgins." H. L. Mencken, *Notes on Democracy* (New York, 1926), p. 107.

36. Hofstadter, *The Age of Reform*, pp. 101-102.

37. Faulkner, *Politics, Reform and Expansion*, pp. 141-157; Charles Hoffman, "The Depression of the Nineties," *Journal of Economic History*, XVI (1956), pp. 137-164.

38. Barnes, "Myths of the Bryan Campaign," *Mississippi Valley Historical Review*, XXXIV (1947), p. 369.

39. Quoted in Hicks, *The Populist Revolt*, p. 317. See also Barnes, "Myths of the Bryan Campaign," p. 383.

40. H. E. Taubeneck to Ignatius Donnelly, May 15, 1896, *Donnelly Papers*.

41. A case in point is Arthur Sewall, shipbuilder, railroad executive, bank president, and vice-presidential nominee of the Democratic party in 1896. Sewall was an ardent devotee of free silver and was regarded as something of a political renegade in Republican Maine where he made his home. While his advocacy of silver placed him on common ground with Populists, his background was so completely different from that of western farmers that their support of him was made to appear ludicrous. Hicks, *The Populist Revolt*, pp. 362-365; Bryan, *The First Battle*, pp. 229-232.

42. Elmer Ellis, "Silver Republicans in 1896," *Mississippi Valley Historical Review*, XVIII (1932), p. 524. See also Elmer Ellis, *Henry Moore Teller, Defender of the West* (Caldwell, Idaho, 1941), pp. 265-280.

43. H. E. Taubeneck to Ignatius Donnelly, May 15, 1896, *Donnelly Papers*. Other Populists were not so sanguine. "The only fear I now have," wrote one, "is that both the old parties are going to stampede, frightened by the red flag of the free silverites, and land their putrescent old carcasses in the 'middle of the road' where we have traveled since 1892." Frank Ives to Ignatius Donnelly, June 7, 1896, *Donnelly Papers*.

44. William Jennings Bryan to Ignatius Donnelly, January 1, 1896, *Donnelly Papers*. For views on Populist prospects see also H. H. Fuller to Donnelly, February 6, 1896, and H. E. Taubeneck to Donnelly, June 10, 22, and 29, 1896, *Donnelly Papers;* J. B. Ro-

mans to Jonathan P. Dolliver, January 11, 1896, *Dolliver Papers;* J. J. McInerney to William R. Morrison, May 16, 1896, *William R. Morrison Papers,* Illinois State Historical Library, Springfield.

45. Ignatius Donnelly, Diary, July 18, 1896, *Donnelly Papers.*

46. W. E. Stacy to Ignatius Donnelly, July 21, 1896, *Donnelly Papers.*

47. Most of the arguments for endorsement of Bryan may be found in the following correspondence in the *Donnelly Papers:* William Welch to Donnelly, July 11, 1896; Davis H. Waite to Donnelly, July 12, 1896; H. L. Bassett to Donnelly, July 28, 1896; Thomas D. O'Brien to Donnelly, July 18 and August 20, 1896; Marion Butler to Donnelly, September 18, 1896. See also S. P. Van Patten to George Schilling, October 27, 1896, *Schilling Papers.*

48. Quoted in Hicks, *The Populist Revolt,* p. 369.

49. Ignatius Donnelly, Diary, September 1, 7-9, and October 10, 1896, *Donnelly Papers;* James Manahan to Mrs. Manahan, September 5, 9, 1896, *Manahan Papers.*

50. James Manahan to Mrs. Manahan, September 12, 1896, *Manahan Papers.*

51. Thomas Beer, *Hanna* (New York, 1929), p. 153.

52. Bryan, *The First Battle,* p. 397; *Republican Campaign Text Book* (Washington, 1896), pp. 202-206. The techniques employed by Republican campaign strategists are well described in Herbert Croly, *Marcus Alonzo Hanna* (New York, 1923), pp. 209-227.

53. Faulkner, *Politics, Reform and Expansion,* pp. 203-211; Barnes, "Myths of the Bryan Campaign," pp. 399-400; Wayne C. Williams, *William Jennings Bryan* (New York, 1936), p. 195.

54. William Diamond, "Urban and Rural Voting in 1896," *American Historical Review,* XLVI (October, 1940), p. 285. West of the Mississippi, McKinley won Minnesota, Iowa, North Dakota, and Oregon. He also received the electoral votes of Maryland and West Virginia. Kentucky and California were divided.

55. Ignatius Donnelly, Diary, November 6, 1896, *Donnelly Papers.*

56. Quoted in Caro Lloyd, *Henry Demarest Lloyd* (New York, 1912), I, 264.

57. Professor John D. Hicks, while cautioning against *post hoc* argument, saw a close correlation between Populist demands and progressive reform. Hicks, *The Populist Revolt,* pp. 407-416. Another point of view is presented in George E. Mowry, *The Era of Theodore Roosevelt, 1900-1912* (New York, 1958), pp. 87-88. A third alternative, one that concedes Bryan's influence, may be found in Hofstadter, *The Age of Reform,* pp. 131-134.

58. *The Commoner,* September 13, 1901. In his "Cross of Gold" speech, Bryan said, "They tell us that this platform was made to catch votes. We reply to them that changing conditions make new issues; that the principles upon which Democracy rests are as everlasting as the hills, but that they must be applied to new conditions as they arise." Bryan, *The First Battle,* p. 203.

59. Porter, *National Party Platforms*, pp. 181-187; Bryan, *The First Battle*, pp. 406-409.

60. *The American Mercury*, VI (October, 1925), p. 159.

61. Harold Faulkner, *The Decline of Laissez-Faire, 1897-1917* (New York, 1951), pp. 22-27; Shannon, *The Farmer's Last Frontier*, pp. 326-327. For an interesting study of the census of 1900, see Fred Shannon, "The Status of the Midwestern Farmer in 1900," *Mississippi Valley Historical Review*, XXXVII (December, 1950), pp. 491-510.

62. Bryan to Altgeld, September 29, 1897, *Altgeld Papers*. See also A. N. J. Crook to William M. Springer, December 5, 1897, *William M. Springer Papers*, Chicago Historical Society.

63. James Creelman to Bryan, June 2, 1900, *Bryan Papers*.

64. William Randolph Hearst to Bryan, May 20, 1900, *Bryan Papers*.

65. William J. Stone to Bryan, June 25, 1900, *Bryan Papers*. Other letters in the *Bryan Papers* play upon the same theme, especially Andrew Carnegie to Bryan, December 18, 27, 1898; Rollo Ogden to Bryan, September 23, 1899; S. E. Morse to Bryan, February 17, 1900; D. L. Baumgarten to Bryan, May 3, 1900; T. T. Hudson to Bryan, May 16, 1900; Norman E. Mack to Bryan, July 19, 1900. See also *Public Opinion*, XXVIII (February 1, 1900), p. 133; New York *Tribune*, July 4, 1900; Willis J. Abbot, *Watching the World Go By* (Boston, 1933), p. 237.

66. Bryan to William J. Stone, June 30, 1900, *Bryan Papers*.

67. Bryan to James K. Jones, July 2, 1900, *Bryan Papers*. See also C. H. Jones to Bryan, June 26, 1900, *Bryan Papers;* John W. Springer to William M. Springer, January 21, 1899, *Springer Papers*.

68. Bryan to Carter Harrison, July 12, 1900, *Carter Harrison Papers*, Newberry Library, Chicago; Bryan, *Memoirs*, p. 125. See also Louis R. Ehrich to Bryan, December 5, 1900, John H. Girdner to Bryan, November 29, 1900, Flavius J. VanVorhis to Bryan, November 19, 1900, *Bryan Papers;* Bryan to Altgeld, July 11, 1900, Moreton Frewen to Altgeld, September 26, 1900, *Altgeld Papers;* Thomas A. Bailey, "Was the Presidential Election of 1900 a Mandate on Imperialism?," *Mississippi Valley Historical Review*, XXIV (June, 1937), pp. 43-44.

69. *The Commoner*, September 13, 1901.

70. *The Commoner*, November 1, 1907.

CHAPTER IV

Party Politics and Imperialism

1. Hofstadter, *The Age of Reform*, p. 60.

2. Austin Ranney, *The Doctrine of Responsible Party Government*,

"Illinois Studies in the Social Sciences," XXXIV (Urbana, 1954), p. 4.

3. Hicks, "The Third Party Tradition in American Politics," p. 3; E. E. Schattschneider, *Party Government* (New York, 1942), pp. 67-68.

4. Austin Ranney and Willmoore Kendall, *Democracy and the American Party System* (New York, 1956), pp. 151-152, 525-527.

5. Woodrow Wilson, *Congressional Government* (Boston, 1885), pp. 98-99. E. E. Schattschneider makes essentially the same point when he emphasizes the lack of party discipline in Congress and suggests that parties have both a private and a public personality. The unity that Wilson saw in the party outside the government is a reflection of what Schattschneider calls its public personality, while the decentralization of the parties in Congress (its private personality) is indicative of the local interests of party bosses. Schattschneider, *Party Government*, pp. 130-137.

6. This discussion relies heavily on the superb summary of Wilson's reasoning in Ranney, *The Doctrine of Responsible Party Government*, pp. 34-39.

7. Wilson, *Congressional Government*, pp. 91-92.

8. James Bryce, *The American Commonwealth* (New York, 1895), I, 78-85; Wilson, *Congressional Government*, pp. 42-43; Ranney, *The Doctrine of Responsible Party Government*, p. 35. Theodore Roosevelt held a similar view: "If a man has a very decided character, has a strongly accentuated career, it is normally the case of course that he makes ardent friends and bitter enemies; and unfortunately human nature is such that more enemies will leave their party because of enmity to its head than friends will come in from the opposite party because they think well of that same head. In consequence, the dark horse, the neutral-tinted individual, is very apt to win against the man of very pronounced views and active life. The electorate is very apt to vote with its back to the future!" Roosevelt to G. O. Trevelyan, May 28, 1900, *Theodore Roosevelt Papers*, Division of Manuscripts, Library of Congress.

9. Woodrow Wilson, *Constitutional Government in the United States* (New York, 1908), p. 60.

10. Wilson, *Constitutional Government*, pp. 210-211.

11. Woodrow Wilson, *The New Freedom* (Garden City, N.Y., 1913), pp. 225-226; Ranney, *The Doctrine of Responsible Party Government*, p. 37.

12. Wilson, *Constitutional Government*, pp. 213-217; Ranney, *Responsible Party Government*, pp. 37-38.

13. Bryce, *The American Commonwealth*, II, 59.

14. Hofstadter, *The American Political Tradition*, pp. 162-167.

15. Bryan, "Shall the People Rule?" *Speeches*, II, 100-101.

16. Bryan to R. H. Reemelin, July 17, 1901, *Bryan Papers*.

17. Bryan to Louis F. Post, October 8, 1910, *Louis F. Post Papers,* Division of Manuscripts, Library of Congress.

18. *The Commoner,* October 4, 1901. See also *The Commoner,* July 16, 1909, and *The Public,* X (November 23, 1907), p. 794.

19. George Norris, "Bryan as a Political Leader," *Current History,* XXII (September, 1925), p. 862.

20. Bryan, for example, supported Democratic nominee Alton B. Parker in 1904. *Public Opinion,* XXXVII (November 3, 1904), p. 549. In the *Bryan Papers* there is a form letter sent out to the Democratic leaders of Indiana which contains the following statement: "While I would have preferred candidates fully in sympathy with the platforms of 1896 and 1900, I feel that the election of the Democratic ticket will rid the country of imperialism and militarism, retire the race issue, and substitute a spirit of peace for the war-like spirit which pervades the White House. We shall be in a much better position to renew our fight for economic reforms when these issues are out of the way."

21. Abbot, *Watching the World Go By,* p. 204.

22. John Girdner to Bryan, August 18, 1899, *Bryan Papers; The Public,* II (August 19, 1899), p. 1. Bryan believed that Croker had been sincerely converted to free silver after reading *The First Battle.* Furthermore, he thought Croker's support was "entirely disinterested." Bryan, *Memoirs,* pp. 126-127.

23. Hay to Theodore Roosevelt, July 27, 1898, in William Roscoe Thayer, *The Life and Letters of John Hay* (New York, 1915), II, 337.

24. Margaret Leech, *In the Days of McKinley* (New York, 1959), pp. 326-327; Charles S. Olcott, *The Life of William McKinley* (Boston, 1917), II, 110-111.

25. Bryan to Mrs. Bryan, September 5, October 12, 26, 1898, Victor Vifquain to Charles H. Gere, September 23, 1899, *Bryan Papers.* For comments on Bryan's enlistment, see *The Public,* I (June 4, 1898), p. 2; *The New York Times,* May 17, 25, 29, June 1, 2, 1898; Bryan *Memoirs,* pp. 270-273.

26. Hibben, *The Peerless Leader,* p. 210.

27. Richard Hofstadter, "Manifest Destiny and the Philippines," *America in Crisis,* ed. Daniel Aaron (New York, 1952), pp. 180-181, 198; Leech, *In the Days of McKinley,* p. 184.

28. Quoted in Atherton, *Main Street on the Middle Border,* p. 106.

29. Hibben, *The Peerless Leader,* pp. 216-217; Merle Curti, *Bryan and World Peace,* "Smith College Studies in History," XVI (Northampton, Mass., 1931), pp. 118-119. Later, Bryan was astounded when Theodore Roosevelt told West Point cadets: "A good soldier must not only be willing to fight; he must be anxious to fight." Roosevelt, he said, "entirely overlooks the distinction between the exercise of force in defense of a right and the use of force for the

creation of a right." *The Commoner,* August 8, 1902. See also Bryan, *The First Battle,* pp. 64-65.

30. William Jennings Bryan, *British Rule in India* (Westminster, 1906), p. 5.

31. Bryan, "Imperialism," *Speeches,* II, 25-26. The manuscript from which Bryan read is in the *Bryan Papers.* The platform of 1900 viewed "with indignation the purpose of England to overwhelm with force the South African Republics." Porter, *National Party Platforms,* p. 216. See also Philip Wessels to Bryan, June 14, 1900, *Bryan Papers;* Leonard A. Rosing to John Lind, February 20, 1900, *John Lind Papers,* Minnesota Historical Society, St. Paul.

32. *The Commoner,* November 22, 1901.

33. *The New York Times,* June 15, 1898; William Jennings Bryan, *The Second Battle* (Chicago, 1900), p. 83.

34. Hofstadter, "Manifest Destiny and the Philippines," p. 190; Gabriel, *The Course of American Democratic Thought,* pp. 368-372.

35. Quoted in Claude Bowers, *Beveridge and the Progressive Era* (Cambridge, Mass., 1932), p. 69; Albert Weinberg, *Manifest Destiny* (Baltimore, 1935), p. 274.

36. *Webster County* (Nebraska) *Argus,* September 14, 1900. For the views of other clergymen see Julius W. Pratt, *Expansionists of 1898* (Baltimore, 1936), pp. 279-316.

37. Andrew Carnegie to Bryan, December 15, 18, 26, 1898, and January 10, 1899, *Bryan Papers.*

38. Bryan to Andrew Carnegie, January 13, 1899, *Andrew Carnegie Papers,* Division of Manuscripts, Library of Congress.

39. Bryan, "Imperialism," *Speeches,* II, 21; Bryan, *The Second Battle,* p. 105.

40. Bryan to Carnegie, January 13, 1899, *Carnegie Papers.*

41. Bryan to Carnegie, January 30, 1899, *Carnegie Papers;* Bryan to Wilkinson Call, January 12, 1899, *Bryan Papers.*

42. Bryan to Carnegie, January 30, 1899, *Carnegie Papers.*

43. Leech, *In the Days of McKinley,* pp. 353-358; Paolo Coletta, "Bryan, McKinley, and the Treaty of Paris," *Pacific Historical Review,* XXVI (May, 1957), pp. 133-138.

44. New York *Tribune,* December 26, 1898, and September 16, 1900; Springfield *Republican,* December 15, 1898; George F. Hoar, *Autobiography of Seventy Years* (New York, 1903), II, 322-323; R. F. Pettigrew, *Imperial Washington* (Chicago, 1922), pp. 269-271.

45. Coletta, "Bryan, McKinley, and the Treaty of Paris," pp. 139-143.

46. Bryan to Carnegie, December 30, 1898, *Carnegie Papers.*

47. Bryan to Carnegie, December 24, 1898, *Carnegie Papers.* To have accepted Carnegie's support on imperialism, it should be pointed out, would have meant losing the support of significant groups. This was the argument contained in a telegram from Arthur Brisbane: "Strongly advise against permitting public endorsement of

you by promoter of Homestead riots." Brisbane to Bryan, December 23, 1898, *Bryan Papers.*

48. Bryan to Carnegie, December 30, 1898, *Carnegie Papers.*

49. Josephus Daniels, "Behind the Scenes with William Jennings Bryan," *Josephus Daniels Papers,* Division of Manuscripts, Library of Congress.

50. *Republican Campaign Text-Book, 1900* (Philadelphia, 1900), p. 74. Moreton Frewen wrote Governor Altgeld: "Show the electors a good slice of the universe and they will scramble after it as children after a Christmas snapdragon!" Frewen to Altgeld, September 26, 1900, *Altgeld Papers.*

51. David Starr Jordan to Bryan, March 7, 1900, *Bryan Papers.*

52. Grover Cleveland to Judson Harmon, July 17, 1900, *Grover Cleveland Papers,* Division of Manuscripts, Library of Congress.

53. Bryan to Henry Watterson, June 7, 1900, *Watterson Papers;* Watterson to Bryan, June 14, 1900, *Bryan Papers;* Porter, *National Party Platforms,* p. 212. See also the speech made by John P. Altgeld to the Ohio Association of Democratic Clubs, Toledo, August 1, 1900, *Altgeld Papers; The Commoner,* May 15, 1903.

54. Bryan, "Imperialism," *Speeches,* II, 33. The summary of Bryan's arguments presented here is taken from this speech.

55. In the first issue of *The Commoner,* which Bryan began to publish after his defeat in 1900, he quoted Tolstoy: "You Americans are worse than the Mohammedans. They preach war and they fight; you preach liberty and peace and yet you go out to conquer through war." *The Commoner,* January 23, 1901.

56. Printed in *The Public,* III (November 3, 1900), p. 479.

57. Weinberg, *Manifest Destiny,* p. 254; Ray A. Billington, "The Origins of Middle Western Isolation," *Political Science Quarterly,* LX (1945), pp. 49-50.

58. Bryan, "America's Mission," *Speeches,* II, 11.

59. Bryan, "Imperialism," *Speeches,* II, 47.

60. Bailey, "Was the Presidential Election of 1900 a Mandate on Imperialism?," p. 49.

61. *The Commoner,* March 8, 1901.

62. *The Commoner,* June 14, 1901.

63. Mowry, *The Era of Theodore Roosevelt,* pp. 168-169.

64. *The Commoner,* February 10, 1905.

65. Theodore Roosevelt to William Howard Taft, August 21, 1907, *William Howard Taft Papers,* Division of Manuscripts, Library of Congress.

66. Mowry, *The Era of Theodore Roosevelt,* pp. 188-189.

67. *The Democratic Text-Book, 1912* (New York, 1912), pp. 351-352; *The National Democratic Campaign Book, Presidential Election, 1900* (Washington, 1900), p. 3; *The Campaign Text Book of the Democratic Party of the United States, 1904* (New York, 1904), pp.

17-18; *Campaign Textbook of the Democratic Party, 1908,* p. 224; Porter, *National Party Platforms,* pp. 211-213, 246-247, 284, 332.

CHAPTER V

Shall the People Rule?

1. Paolo Coletta, "The Morning Star of the Reformation: William Jennings Bryan's First Congressional Campaign," *Nebraska History,* XXXVII (1956), p. 110.

2. *Congressional Record,* 52 Cong., 1 sess., vol. 23, pt. 3, pp. 2124-2136. See also *The New York Times,* March 17, 1892; Myron G. Phillips, "William Jennings Bryan," *A History and Criticism of American Public Address,* ed. William Norwood Brigance (New York, 1943), II, 901.

3. Bryan, "The Tariff," *Speeches,* I, 7. Hereafter cited as "The Tariff" (1892); *Congressional Record,* 52 Cong., 1 sess., vol. 23, pt. 3, p. 2125.

4. Bryan, "The Tariff," *Speeches,* I, 307-312. Hereafter cited as "The Tariff" (1908). *The New York Times,* August 22, 1908; Des Moines *Register and Leader,* August 22, 1908; *Campaign Textbook of the Democratic Party, 1908,* pp. 251-254.

5. Bryan to Louis F. Post, June 2, 1909, *Post Papers.* Bryan's distinction between tariff reduction and free trade was probably disregarded by protectionists. Senator Joseph B. Foraker believed that to describe anyone as a "low tariff man" was to give him "only another name for a free trader." Foraker to J. G. Schurman, November, 1912, *Joseph Foraker Papers,* Division of Manuscripts, Library of Congress.

6. Bryan, "The Tariff" (1892), *Speeches,* I, 35; *Congressional Record,* 52 Cong., 1 sess., vol. 23, pt. 3, p. 2129.

7. *The Commoner,* March 11, 1904.

8. Bryan, "The Tariff" (1892), *Speeches,* I, 42-43; *Congressional Record,* 52 Cong., 1 sess., vol. 23, pt. 3, p. 2130.

9. Bryan, "The Tariff" (1892), *Speeches,* I, 18; *Congressional Record,* 52 Cong., 1 sess., vol. 23, pt. 3, p. 2126.

10. Bryan, "The Tariff" (1908), *Speeches,* I, 298, 318.

11. *The Commoner,* December 12, 1902.

12. Roosevelt to William Howard Taft, July 15, 1901, Roosevelt to John C. Rose, May 19, 1902, Roosevelt to Nicholas Murray Butler, August 12, 1902, *Roosevelt Papers.*

13. Taft to Mrs. Taft, July 30, 1909, Taft to Horace Taft, August 11, 1909, *Taft Papers.* Taft had reasons for thinking as he did. The act provided for a tariff commission and established a tax on corporations engaged in interstate commerce. The President himself had been responsible for reductions on several items. Taft to

Charles Taft, August 1, 1909, Taft to Roosevelt, May 26, 1910, *Taft Papers*.

14. *The Commoner,* August 13, October 22, 1909.

15. *The Commoner,* August 25, 1911.

16. Bryan, "The Tariff" (1892), *Speeches,* I, 34; *Congressional Record,* 52 Cong., 1 sess., vol. 23, pt. 3, p. 2129; Bryan, "The Tariff" (1908), *Speeches,* I, 311.

17. Bryan, *The Second Battle,* p. 213; Bryan, "The Tariff" (1908), *Speeches,* I, 308. See also Albert Cummins to James D. Hall, April 4, 1901, William Spencer to Cummins, July 3, 1908, Cummins to William Spencer, July 6, 1908, *Albert Baird Cummins Papers,* Iowa Historical, Memorial and Art Department, Des Moines.

18. Bryan, "An Income Tax," *Speeches,* I, 159-160; New York *World,* January 31, 1894; New York *Tribune,* January 30, 1894; *Congressional Record,* 53 Cong., 2 sess., vol. 26, pt. 2, pp. 1655-1658.

19. *Pollock v. Farmers' Loan and Trust Company,* 157 U.S. 429 and *Pollock v. Farmers' Loan and Trust Company,* 158 U.S. 601.

20. Bryan, "At the New York Reception," *Speeches,* II, 71; New York *World,* August 31, 1906; *The New York Times,* August 31, 1906.

21. Taft too should be given a large share of credit for the amendment. Accepting the Court's decision of 1895, he thought an amendment, not legislation alone, was the best means of securing an income tax. It was with Taft's support that the amendment was proposed, and he worked for its ratification. Taft to Horace White, March 28, 1909, Taft to Francis G. Newlands, May 14, 1909, Taft to Horace Taft, June 27, 1909, *Taft Papers*.

22. *The Commoner,* May 10, 1907; *Campaign Textbook of the Democratic Party, 1908,* p. 259.

23. Bryan, *The Second Battle,* pp. 210-214.

24. Bryan, "Conservation of Natural Resources," *Speeches,* II, 399. See also *The Literary Digest,* XXXVI (May 23, 1908), pp. 741-744.

25. H. J. W. Seamark, "Campaign Song of 1900," Nebraska State Historical Society, Lincoln.

26. Bryan, *The Second Battle,* p. 209.

27. Bryan, "Commerce," *Speeches,* II, 410. See also Bryan, *Heart to Heart Appeals,* p. 38.

28. Bryan, "A Remedy for the Trusts," *Public Opinion,* XXXVIII (April 25, 1905), p. 645.

29. *The Commoner,* December 13, 1901; James D. Richardson, *A Compilation of the Messages and Papers of the Presidents* (Washington, 1902), Supplement 1, pp. 313-354. Roosevelt made similar remarks on the trusts at Cincinnati in 1902. The Kansas City *World* thought them "as lucid as a puddle on a moonless night." Kansas City *World,* September 2, 1902. See also *The Commoner,* May 30, September 5, December 12, 1902, and April 17, 1903.

30. *The Commoner,* June 6, October 24, 1902.

31. *The Commoner,* August 8, 1902.

32. *Campaign Textbook of the Democratic Party, 1908,* pp. 222-223; Bryan, *The Second Battle,* pp. 215-216, 220-224; Porter, *National Party Platforms,* pp. 213-214, 276-277; Bryan, "A Remedy for the Trusts," p. 647.

33. W. J. Bryan to C. W. Bryan, n.d., *Bryan Papers.* This is one of several hundred telegrams passing between Bryan's home and Denver, where the Democratic convention was held in 1908.

34. Louis F. Post to Bryan, June 13, 1900, *Bryan Papers; The Public,* III (April 28, 1900), pp. 35, 130.

35. Roosevelt to William Dudley Foulke, November 16, 1907, *William Dudley Foulke Papers,* Indiana State Library, Indianapolis.

36. Bryan to F. D. Butler, June 5, 1900, *Bryan Papers.*

37. *The Commoner,* August 30, 1907.

38. *Senate Report* 848, 60 Cong., 2 sess., p. 9.

39. Taft to Seth Low, February 10, 1910, Taft to Frank B. Kellog, October 12, 1910, *Taft Papers; The Commoner,* December 3, 1909, June 2, 1911; Henry F. Pringle, *The Life and Times of William Howard Taft* (New York, 1939), II, 658-659; Mowry, *The Era of Theodore Roosevelt,* pp. 286-287.

40. Bryan, "The Trust Question," *Speeches,* II, 125; Wilson, *The New Freedom,* pp. 207, 212. Bryan held Taft responsible for the position of the Supreme Court in the Standard Oil and American Tobacco cases. The "rule of reason" therein enunciated involved judicial interpretation of what constituted "undue restraint" on the flow of commerce. Bryan agreed with Justice Harlan, who concurred in the illegality of Standard Oil's activities but disagreed with the reasoning of the majority, that the way had been opened to "judicial legislation." The decision, he thought, was little more than "a license to reorganize under a pledge of greater security." *The Commoner,* May 26, June 16, 23, October 27, 1911; *Standard Oil Company of New Jersey et al. v. United States,* 221 U.S. 60; William Howard Taft, *The Anti-Trust Act and the Supreme Court* (New York, 1914), pp. 85-95. See also Richard Olney to Lewis Cass Ledyard, May 17, 1911, *Richard Olney Papers,* Division of Manuscripts, Library of Congress.

41. Bryan, "The Trust Question," *Speeches,* II, 125.

42. *The Commoner,* August 25, 1905.

43. Bryan, "The Next Awakening," p. 806; *The Commoner,* December 6, 1901.

44. *The Commoner,* February 13, 1903.

45. *The Commoner,* February 8, November 8, 1907. Bryan opposed the Aldrich-Vreeland Act after the panic of 1907. Although the purpose of the act was to provide an emergency currency based upon government bonds or other qualified securities or commercial paper, Bryan thought it "would simply increase Wall Street's control over the nation's finances." *The Commoner,* February 21, June 5, June 12, 1908.

46. Bryan, "Guaranteed Deposits," *Speeches,* II, 147. See also *Congressional Record,* 53 Cong., 1 sess., vol. 25, pt. 2, p. 1700.

47. Norbert R. Mahnken, "William Jennings Bryan in Oklahoma," *Nebraska History,* XXI (1950), p. 271; Bryan, "Guaranteed Deposits," *Speeches,* II, 145-146.

48. Roosevelt to Taft, July 17, 1908, *Taft Papers.*

49. William B. Ridgely to Taft, October 14, 1908, George B. Cortelyou to Taft, August 25, September 2, 1908, J. L. Bristow to Taft, August 28, 1908, *Taft Papers;* Albert Cummins to W. M. Wright, October 26, 1908, *Cummins Papers;* J. H. Ingwersen to Jonathan Dolliver, January 20, 1908, S. J. Patterson to Jonathan Dolliver, January 18, 1909, *Dolliver Papers; Current Literature,* XLV (October, 1908), p. 365.

50. Bryan to Woodrow Wilson, March 1, 1911, *Woodrow Wilson Papers,* Division of Manuscripts, Library of Congress. See also Fritz Redlich, *The Molding of American Banking, Men and Ideas,* Part II, 1840-1910 (New York, 1951), pp. 215-217.

51. Bryan, *The First Battle,* pp. 379-380.

52. Bryan, "In Chicago on Labor Day," *Speeches,* II, 168-169.

53. Porter, *National Party Platforms,* pp. 185, 215, 248-249, 279-280, 328-329.

54. Bryan, "In Chicago on Labor Day," *Speeches,* II, 171-175.

55. *The Commoner,* October 10, November 28, December 12, 1902.

56. Taft to Roosevelt, July 10, 1908, *Taft Papers.* Bryan labeled Taft "the father of government by injunction." *The New York Times,* September 8, 1908. See also *The Commoner,* January 17, 1908; Taft's address at Lawrencebury, Kentucky, August 22, 1907, *Taft Papers;* Edgar A. Hornig, "Campaign Issues of the Presidential Election of 1908," *Indiana Magazine of History,* LIV (September, 1958), pp. 245-248; Mowry, *The Era of Theodore Roosevelt,* pp. 235-236.

57. Bryan, "In Chicago on Labor Day," *Speeches,* II, 171-179.

58. *Ibid.,* p. 178.

59. The concept to which Professor Daniel Boorstin has applied the term "givenness" was always apparent in Bryan's thinking on political questions. This concept is "the belief that values in America are in some way or other automatically defined: *given* by facts of geography or history peculiar to us." Daniel Boorstin, *The Genius of American Politics* (Chicago, 1953), pp. 8-10.

60. *The Commoner,* February 6, 1901.

61. Porter, *National Party Platforms,* p. 282; *Campaign Textbook of the Democratic Party, 1908,* pp. 11, 222.

62. A copy of Bryan's 1890 platform is in the *Bryan Papers.* See also Daniels, "Behind the Scenes with William Jennings Bryan," *Daniels Papers;* Bryan, *Memoirs,* p. 465; Bryan, *The First Battle,* p. 57; Coletta, "The Morning Star of the Reformation," p. 107.

63. Porter, *National Party Platforms,* pp. 215, 250, 282, 334.

64. *The Commoner,* February 6, 1901, February 21, 28, 1902.

65. Bryan, "At the New York Reception," *Speeches,* II, 69-70.

66. Daniels, "Behind the Scenes with William Jennings Bryan," *Daniels Papers.* In 1909 Bryan wrote President Taft urging him to support an amendment for popular election of senators. Taft, who was never a supporter of the proposal, replied: "I hardly deem this a party question, and a: there is a very wide difference of opinion in my own party in respect to it, I think it ought to be presented to Congress not as a party or as an administration question, but as a matter of individual opinion." Taft to Bryan, July 22, 1909, *Taft Papers; The Commoner,* July 23, 30, August 13, 1909.

67. Platform of 1890, *Bryan Papers;* Coletta, "Morning Star of the Reformation," p. 107. See also Bryan, *The First Battle,* pp. 57-58.

68. Bryan, "Shall the People Rule?," *Speeches,* II, 114-115.

69. *Ibid.,* pp. 102.

70. *The Commoner,* July 28, 1905.

71. Minutes of the Board of Trustees of Illinois College, January 5, 17, 31, May 9, June 7, November 6, 1905, February 12, 1906, Illinois College Archives, Jacksonville, Illinois; *The Public,* VIII (February 17, 1906), p. 759.

72. *The Commoner,* January 23, 1901.

73. *The Commoner,* January 30, 1901. Edward Alsworth Ross, who later taught at the University of Nebraska and the University of Wisconsin, was one of the six dismissed. At Nebraska Ross came to know Bryan personally, and at Wisconsin he served as an advisor to La Follette. For an account of the Stanford episode, see Ross, *Seventy Years of It* (New York, 1936), pp. 64-86.

74. *The Commoner,* June 28, December 20, 1907.

75. Bryan to Henry Watterson, May 26, 1908, *Watterson Papers;* Elbert F. Baldwin to Taft, July 16, 20, 22, 1908, *Taft Papers; The New York Times,* July 15, October 16, 1908; Pringle, *William Howard Taft,* I, 360-365.

76. Bryan to Harry Walker, January 20, 1915, *Bryan Papers; The Commoner,* February 17, 24, September 15, 1905; Bryan, "At the New York Reception," *Speeches,* II, 71.

77. Curti, *Bryan and World Peace,* pp. 145-148.

78. Bryan, "At the Peace Congress," *Speeches,* II, 228-229; London *Times,* July 25, 1906.

79. Bryan, "At the New York Reception," *Speeches,* II, 66; Bryan, *The Forces that Make for Peace,* pp. 12-13.

80. Bryan to Taft, June 29, 1910, *Bryan Papers;* Taft to Bryan, July 7, 1910, *Taft Papers;* Andrew Carnegie to Carter Harrison, November 25, 1911, *Harrison Papers.*

81. Bryan to Carnegie, April 13, 1911, *Carnegie Papers.*

82. Bryan to Taft, January 12, 1912, *Taft Papers.*

83. See Elting E. Morison and John M. Blum, eds., *The Letters of Theodore Roosevelt,* VII (Cambridge, Mass., 1954), especially the

following: Roosevelt to Lodge, June 19, August 14, September 12, 22, 1911, January 5, 1912; Roosevelt to Root, January 16, 1912. Cf. *The Outlook*, XCVIII (May 20, 1911), pp. 97-98; *ibid.*, XCIX (September 9, 1911), pp. 66-70; Richard Olney to Lodge, March 6, 1912, *Olney Papers*.

84. Pringle, *Taft*, II, 744-745; Mowry, *The Era of Theodore Roosevelt*, pp. 278-279; Taft to Bryan, January 16, March 29, 1912, *Taft Papers*.

85. Bryan, "At the Peace Congress," *Speeches*, II, 231.

86. Bryan to Post, November 12, 1904, *Post Papers*.

87. *The Commoner*, March 3, June 9, July 28, August 18, 1905.

88. Bryan, "At the New York Reception," *Speeches*, II, 84-85, *The Commoner*, September 6, 1906; *The Literary Digest*, XXXIII (September 8, 1906), pp. 300-301.

89. Bryan, "Government Ownership," *Speeches*, II, 95. Taft, in commenting on the question in 1905, had said: "Against this proposition, I feel confident the Republican party will always set its face like flint." Taft's address at Columbus, Ohio, May 24, 1905, *Taft Papers*.

90. *The Commoner*, July 26, 1907.

91. New York *World*, March 16, 1907.

92. *The Commoner*, March 22, 1907. See also *The Commoner*, March 15, April 5, 1907. Louis F. Post defended Bryan, pointing out that he had never said public ownership of railroads would be an issue in the election of 1908. *The Public*, X (July 27, 1907), p. 385.

93. W. J. Bryan to C. W. Bryan, n.d., *Bryan Papers*.

94. Coletta, "Morning Star of the Reformation," pp. 110-116.

95. *The Commoner*, August 12, 1910; James C. Olson, *History of Nebraska* (Lincoln, 1955), p. 254.

96. *The Commoner*, July 15, August 5, 12, 1910; Bryan to James B. Weaver, September 22, 1910, *Weaver Papers;* Daniels, "Behind the Scenes with William Jennings Bryan," *Daniels Papers*.

97. Watterson to Mack, May 28, 1910, *Watterson Papers*. For a critical discussion of Bryan's course during the prohibition fight, see Arthur F. Mullen, *Western Democrat* (New York, 1940), pp. 138-146.

98. *The Commoner*, December 6, 1901.

99. *The Commoner*, March 30, 1906.

100. *The Commoner*, March 1, 1901.

101. *The Commoner*, March 30, 1906.

102. Mowry, *The Era of Theodore Roosevelt*, pp. 186-189. See also Thomas A. Bailey, *Theodore Roosevelt and the Japanese American Crisis* (Palo Alto, 1934).

103. *The Commoner*, April 5, 1907.

104. New York *Tribune*, July 4, 1900.

CHAPTER VI

Bryan and the Progressive Movement

This chapter is an expanded and modified treatment of a paper read at the May, 1957 meeting of the Mississippi Valley Historical Association. The paper, "Bryan and the Urban Progressives," appeared in *Mid-America*, XXXIX (1957), pp. 169-179.

1. Hofstadter, *The Age of Reform*, p. 133.
2. Bryan, *The First Battle*, p. 300.
3. Ross, *Sin and Society* (New York, 1907), p. vii.
4. H. G. Day to Bryan, January 24, 1901, *Bryan Papers*.
5. *The Commoner*, January 20, 1905. Italics mine. See Thomas Lawson, "Frenzied Finance; The Story of Amalgamated," *Everybody's*, XII, XIII, XIV (January 1905–February 1906).
6. Hofstadter, *The Age of Reform*, pp. 135-138.
7. George Mowry, *The California Progressives* (Berkeley, 1951), pp. 87-88; Mowry, *The Era of Theodore Roosevelt*, pp. 86-87; Alfred D. Chandler, Jr., "The Origins of Progressive Leadership," *The Letters of Theodore Roosevelt*, ed. Elting Morison and John M. Blum, VIII, 1462-1465.
8. A penetrating contemporary comment on the middle-class protest of the early nineteenth century may be found in Walter Weyl, *The New Democracy* (New York, 1914), pp. 242-249. See also Hofstadter, *The Age of Reform*, pp. 146-148; Mowry, *The Era of Theodore Roosevelt*, pp. 95-96.
9. John Higham, *Strangers in the Land, Patterns of American Nativism, 1860-1925* (New Brunswick, N.J., 1955), pp. 4-11. Higham here defines nativism as "intense opposition to an internal minority on the ground of its foreign (i.e., 'un-American') conditions." This opposition, he points out, was directed against supposed revolutionaries, Catholics, and certain racial groups.
10. Roy L. Garis, *Immigration Restriction, A Study of the Opposition to and Regulation of Immigration into the United States* (New York, 1927), pp. 204-208; Carl Wittke, *We Who Built America* (New York, 1945), pp. 406-407.
11. Oscar Handlin, *The Uprooted* (Boston, 1952), pp. 124-129; Marcus Hansen, *The Immigrant in American History* (Cambridge, Mass., 1942), pp. 90-91.
12. Higham, *Strangers in the Land*, pp. 178-182.
13. Handlin, *The Uprooted*, pp. 218-221; Hofstadter, *The Age of Reform*, pp. 180-184; *The Public*, I (May 7, 1898), p. 3.
14. William L. Riordan, *Plunkitt of Tammany Hall*, ed. Roy V. Peel (New York, 1948), p. 63. See also Lincoln Steffens, *The Shame of the Cities* (New York, 1957), pp. 205-206.

15. E. A. Ross, who was closely associated with both urban and rural progressives, is perhaps the most conspicuous for his racist views. See Ross, "The Causes of Race Superiority," *Annals of the American Academy of Political and Social Science,* XVIII (1901), pp. 67-89; Ross, *Social Control* (New York, 1916), pp. 28-35; Ross, *The Old World in the New* (New York, 1914), *passim;* Ross, *Seventy Years of It,* pp. 223-229. For comments on the nativist elements in the progressive movement, see Mowry, *The Era of Theodore Roosevelt,* pp. 92-94; Goldman, *Rendezvous with Destiny,* pp. 77-79.

16. Roosevelt to St. Clair McKelway, April, 1902, *Roosevelt Papers.* The thinking of the Roosevelt administration on this matter can be traced through the President's correspondence. Letters in the *Roosevelt Papers* which reveal various ramifications of the difficulty are listed as follows: Roosevelt to Elihu Root, November 7, 1901; Roosevelt to Eugene A. Philbin, July 12, 1902; Roosevelt to Philbin, July 16, 1902; Roosevelt to James D. Fox, July 21, 1902; Roosevelt to Archbishop Ireland, July 23, 1902; Roosevelt to Taft, July 31, 1902; Roosevelt to Major John Crane, July 31, 1902; Roosevelt to the Reverend James A. McFaul, July 29, 1903; Roosevelt to Bellamy Storer, December 27, 1903; Roosevelt to Bishop F. Z. Rooker, July 22, 1904.

17. Pringle, *William Howard Taft,* I, 231.

18. *Pentecostal Herald,* July 15, 1908.

19. Roosevelt to Taft, October 12, 1908, *Taft Papers.*

20. Josephus Daniels to Mrs. Daniels, August 18, 1908, and a MS, "Will the Catholic Vote Be Delivered?" *Daniels Papers.* The *Taft Papers* contain letters indicating that some Catholics did, in fact, feel a certain obligation to Taft. See, for example, Michael Walsh to Taft, July 12, 1908, Judge John Gibbons to Taft, July 18, 1908, and Jerome Kuerty to Taft, August 22, 1908.

21. Charles Bryan thought that "this matter is changing more votes probably than any other single issue in the campaign." C. W. Bryan to Norman E. Mack, October 16, 1908, *Daniels Papers.*

22. Bryan to Watterson, August 17, 1908, *Watterson Papers.*

23. Taft to Roosevelt, November 17, 1908, *Taft Papers.*

24. C. S. Starr to Bryan, November 6, 1908, D. L. Savage to Bryan, November 9, 1908, G. L. Banks to Bryan, November 4, 1908, C. J. Lenmas to Bryan, November 6, 1908, Melvina Hildreth to Bryan, November 4, 1908, J. Clarke Dovell to Bryan, November 10, 1908, *Bryan Papers.* On the basis of 97 such letters in the *Bryan Papers,* nativism permeated all sections of the country. There were 39 sent from the Northeast, 11 from the South, 14 from the Middle West, and 33 from the trans-Mississippi West. New York accounted for 15 letters, more than any other state.

25. Father Nugent to Bryan, February 9, 1909, James K. McGuire to Bryan, January 23, 1909, *Bryan Papers.* See also Springfield, *Illinois*

State Register, November 1, 1908; James Manahan to T. T. Hudson, *Manahan Papers.*

26. Bryan to Wilson, n.d., stamped "Answered, July 31, 1912," *Wilson Papers.*

27. The best known racists such as Madison Grant and Henry Cabot Lodge were conservative. Further, racism was not as widespread in the urban East as it was in the South or on the Pacific Coast. Yet Theodore Roosevelt, E. A. Ross, and other progressives often pointed to Anglo-Saxon or Teutonic superiority over other races. Higham, *Strangers in the Land,* pp. 131 ff., 175-182; Oscar Handlin, *Race and Nationality in American Life* (New York, 1957), pp. 57 ff.

28. C. C. Regier, *The Era of the Muckrakers* (Chapel Hill, N.C., 1932), p. 198.

29. Croly, *The Promise of American Life* (New York, 1909), p. 167.

30. White, "Roosevelt: A Force for Righteousness," *McClure's Magazine,* XXVIII (January, 1907), p. 393; Hofstadter, *The Age of Reform,* pp. 210-212.

31. *The Public,* III (May 26, 1900), p. 107.

32. Hofstadter, *The Age of Reform,* pp. 132-133; Hibben, *The Peerless Leader,* p. 260; Henry F. Pringle, *Theodore Roosevelt* (New York, 1931), pp. 368-370; George E. Mowry, *Theodore Roosevelt and the Progressive Movement* (Madison, Wis., 1946), p. 33; Arthur W. Dunn, *Gridiron Nights* (New York, 1915), pp. 154-156. These are only a few of the many works that make this point.

33. White to Roosevelt, October 16, 1908, *William Allen White Papers,* Division of Manuscripts, Library of Congress.

34. Quoted in F. H. Harrington, "Literary Aspects of Anti-Imperialism," *New England Quarterly,* X (1937), p. 655.

35. *The Commoner,* August 8, 1902. See above p. 70.

36. Leuchtenberg, "Progressivism and Imperialism; The Progressive Movement and American Foreign Policy, 1898-1916," *Mississippi Valley Historical Review,* XXXIX (1952), p. 483. See also *Public Opinion,* XXXV (October 1, 1903), p. 421.

37. Croly, *The Promise of American Life,* pp. 308-312.

38. Roosevelt to E. E. Hale, December 17, 1901, Roosevelt to M. A. Hanna, October 5, 1903, Roosevelt to Elihu Root, May 20, 1904, *Roosevelt Papers; The New York Times,* May 21, 1904. See also Howard K. Beale, *Theodore Roosevelt and the Rise of America to World Power* (Baltimore, 1956), pp. 23 ff.

39. Croly, *The Promise of American Life,* p. 282; Leuchtenberg, "Progressivism and Imperialism," pp. 485, 503. There were, of course, progressives of considerable stature who did not agree with Croly's analysis, and who rejected its international implications as well as its Hamiltonian emphasis in domestic affairs. Robert La Follette was a prototype for such men, and in these matters he stood closer to Bryan than to Croly. For a commentary on the differences between Croly and progressives of the Middle West, see Russel B.

Nye, *Midwestern Progressive Politics* (East Lansing, Mich., 1951), pp. 274-278.

40. Roosevelt to J. B. Bishop, October 13, 1902, *Roosevelt Papers.*
41. Roosevelt to Mrs. W. S. Cowles, October 16, 1902, *Roosevelt Papers.*
42. Taft to Roosevelt, November 9, 1902, *Taft Papers.*
43. Taft to Roosevelt, July 12, 1908, *Taft Papers.* See also Hofstadter, *The Age of Reform,* pp. 213 ff.; Louis Filler, *Crusaders for American Liberalism* (New York, 1950), pp. 51-53; Walter Johnson, *William Allen White's America* (New York, 1947), pp. 145-146.
44. Croly, *The Promise of American Life,* pp. 358-362.
45. *The Commoner,* September 20, 1907.
46. *The Commoner,* April 19, 1907. Bryan at this time was conducting a debate with Senator Beveridge in the pages of the *Reader Magazine.* Much of the debate was reprinted in *The Commoner.* See also Claude Bowers, *Beveridge and the Progressive Era,* pp. 259-261.
47. *The Commoner,* September 20, 1907.
48. Hermann Hagedorn, ed., *Works of Theodore Roosevelt* (New York, 1923-1926), XIX, 16-27.
49. *The Commoner,* September 16, October 14, 1910. See also Fremont Older to Upton Sinclair, August 3, 1910, *Upton Sinclair Papers,* Special Collections, Indiana University Library, Bloomington.
50. Clipping from the Kootenai *Democrat,* August 13, 1912, *Daniels Papers.*
51. Regier, *The Era of the Muckrakers,* pp. 1-2; Lincoln Steffens, *Autobiography* (New York, 1931), p. 357, 581-582; Pringle, *Theodore Roosevelt,* pp. 427-428.
52. Lawson, "Frenzied Finance"; Charles E. Russell, "The Greatest Trust in the World," *Everybody's,* XII (February-September 1905); Samuel Hopkins Adams, "The Great American Fraud," *Collier's,* XXXVI, XXXVII (October 7, 28, November 18, December 2, 1905; January 15, February 17, April 28, July 14, 21, August 4, September 1, 22, 1906); Adams, "Fraud Above the Law," *Collier's,* XLIX (May 11, 1912), pp. 13-15; Adams, "Fraud Medicines Own Up," *Collier's,* XLVIII (January 20, 1912), pp. 11-12; Adams, "The Law, the Label, and the Liars," *Collier's,* XLIX (April 13, 1912), pp. 10-11; Adams, "Tricks of the Trade," *Collier's,* XLVII (February 17, 1912), pp. 17-18; David Graham Phillips, "The Treason of the Senate," *Cosmopolitan,* XL, XLI, XLII (1906); Goldman, *Rendezvous with Destiny,* pp. 174-175; Mark Sullivan, *Our Times* (New York, 1926-1935), III, 87.
53. Regier, *The Era of the Muckrakers,* pp. 55-56; Goldman, *Rendezvous with Destiny,* p. 172; Hofstadter, *The Age of Reform,* p. 191.
54. Tarbell, *All in the Day's Work* (New York, 1939), pp. 118-120.
55. Baker, *American Chronicle* (New York, 1945), p. 95.
56. Steffens, *Autobiography,* p. 364.
57. *McClure's Magazine,* XX (January, 1903), p. 336.
58. Regier, *The Era of the Muckrakers,* p. 194; Hofstadter, *The Age of*

Reform, pp. 194-195; Filler, *Crusaders for American Liberalism,* pp. 359 ff. The causes for the decline were many: the withdrawal of advertising, the adoption by bankers of discriminatory credit policies, even the use of espionage. Hofstadter suggests, too, that the "muckraking mood was tapering off."

59. Baker, *American Chronicle,* pp. 77, 97; Steffens, *Autobiography,* p. 358; Tarbell, *All in the Day's Work,* p. 121; Regier, *The Era of the Muckrakers,* p. 15; James P. Wood, *Magazines in the United States* (New York, 1949), p. 140.

60. Bryan refused to accept advertising for any product made or controlled by a trust, and this policy helps to account for the kind of advertising that appeared in *The Commoner.* Abbot, *Watching the World Go By,* p. 243. Particularly offensive were the patent medicine advertisements, but it should be noted that not all advertising in the muckraking periodicals was of a higher type.

61. *McClure's Magazine,* XX (January, 1903), p. 323.

62. *McClure's Magazine,* XX (February, 1903), p. 435.

63. S. S. McClure, *My Autobiography* (New York, 1914), p. 245; Steffens, *Autobiography,* pp. 375, 393-394, 398.

64. Baker, *American Chronicle,* p. 139.

65. Quoted in Sullivan, *Our Times,* III, 88.

66. *The Commoner,* November 28, 1902.

67. Baker, *American Chronicle,* pp. 183-184.

68. *The Commoner,* July 14, 1905.

69. *The Commoner,* February 17, 1905. Later in the year Bryan wrote: "President Roosevelt endorses the democratic doctrine of railroad rate legislation; Governor La Follette endorses rate legislation and also the democratic doctrine of primary elections; Governor Cummins endorses the democratic doctrine of tariff revision; editor [Victor] Rosewater endorses the democratic doctrine of election of senators by popular vote—next?" *The Commoner,* September 8, 1905.

70. New York *World,* December 5, 1905.

71. *The Commoner,* May 24, 1907.

72. *The Literary Digest,* XXXVIII (September 12, 1908), p. 335. Bryan also charged that Taft, as Roosevelt's nominee, had taken over many Democratic planks. "This does not injure me in the slightest, I think," wrote Taft to Roosevelt, "but indicates a testiness on his part, being deprived of some of the arguments which he might have made." Taft to Roosevelt, July 31, 1908, *Taft Papers: The New York Times* posed the question: "Will the American people have the Roosevelt policies continued and administered by Mr. Taft or by Mr. Bryan?" It then went on to compare the two, leaving no doubt that it considered Taft the better man. *The New York Times,* July 10, 1908.

73. *The Commoner,* March 3, 1911.

74. Steffens, *Autobiography,* p. 505. For an evaluation of Roosevelt as

a "broker of the possible," see Mowry, *The Era of Theodore Roosevelt*, pp. 110-115.

75. Hofstadter, *The Age of Reform*, pp. 232-234, 236-238. A typical example of Roosevelt's balancing of good and evil may be found in Baker, *American Chronicle*, p. 203.

76. *The Commoner*, July 7, 1905.

77. *Literary Digest*, XXXVI (May 30, 1908), p. 778; *ibid.*, XXXVII (July 18, 1908), p. 72.

78. New York *World*, July 5, 1908.

79. *Campaign Textbook of the Democratic Party, 1908*, p. 243; *The Commoner*, August 28, 1908; *Literary Digest*, XXXVII (August 22, 1908), pp. 233-235. For comments on Bryan's apparent conservatism see *The Public*, IX (April 7, 1906), p. 4; Chicago *Record Herald*, August 7, 24, 1908; Des Moines *Register and Leader*, August 22, 1908; Springfield *Illinois State Register*, November 3, 1908.

80. Gaynor to Bryan, October 19, November 13, 1908, *Bryan Papers*.

81. *The Commoner*, July 16, 1909.

CHAPTER VII

Bryan and His Party

1. James Bryce, *The American Commonwealth*, II, 21.

2. Henry Steele Commager, *The American Mind*, p. 346.

3. *Congressional Record*, 53 Cong., 1 sess., vol. 25, pt. 1, pp. 400-411; *ibid.*, 53 Cong., 2 sess., vol. 26, pt. 2, pp. 1655-1658. See also Bryan, *Speeches*, I, 78-145, 159-179. Hibben, *The Peerless Leader*, pp. 153-157; Allan Nevins, *Grover Cleveland, A Study in Courage* (New York, 1932), pp. 537-540; James C. Olson, *J. Sterling Morton* (Lincoln, Nebr., 1942), pp. 376-381.

4. Chicago *Tribune*, July 2, 1896.

5. Chicago *Record*, July 3, 1896.

6. Marietta Stevenson, "William Jennings Bryan as a Political Leader" (unpublished Ph.D. dissertation, University of Chicago, 1926), p. 139; Nevins, *Grover Cleveland*, pp. 707-708; Horace S. Merrill, *William Freeman Vilas, Doctrinaire Democrat* (Madison, Wisc., 1954), pp. 237-239.

7. Sullivan, *Our Times*, I, 292-293; William M. Springer to Bryan, n.d., *Springer Papers;* Charles S. Hamlin, Diary, I (October 13, 1896), p. 176, *Charles S. Hamlin Papers,* Division of Manuscripts, Library of Congress; William R. Morrison to [?] Wendling, October 28, 1896, *Morrison Papers;* Nevins, *Grover Cleveland*, p. 705; James A. Barnes, "Gold Standard Democrats and Party Conflict," *Mississippi Valley Historical Review*, XVII (1930), p. 435.

8. John P. Mallan, "The Warrior Critique of the Business Civiliza-

tion," *American Quarterly*, VIII (1956), pp. 216-219. For progressive attitudes toward the business community see also Leuchtenberg, "Progressivism and Imperialism." Perhaps the attitude of the business interests had as much to do with the failure of the boom for Admiral Dewey as did the political ineptitude of the unfortunate hero of Manila Bay. Had the conservative Democrats been able to accept imperialism, Dewey might have been a good stalking horse for those who hoped for the annihilation of Bryanism. For comments on Dewey's candidacy see *Public Opinion*, XXVIII (April 12, 1900), p. 455.

9. Ogden to Bryan, September 23, 1899, *Bryan Papers*.
10. Newlands to Bryan, June 28, 1900, Merriam to Newlands, June 16, 1900, *Bryan Papers*.
11. Baumgarten to Bryan, May 3, 1900, *Bryan Papers*.
12. After the election Bryan wrote Cockran a letter of thanks for his support. The defeated candidate commented upon "excellent reports" he had received on Cockran's writing during the campaign. Bryan to Cockran, November 10, 1900, *W. Bourke Cockran Papers,* New York Public Library. See also *The Public*, II (February 3, 1900), p. 2; James K. Jones to Cockran, August 21, 1900, *Cockran Papers*.
13. Cockran to Edwin Burritt Smith, August 14, 1900, *Cockran Papers*.
14. Cockran to Stephen P. Anderton, August 29, 1900, *Cockran Papers*.
15. Sulzer to Bryan, April 2, June 4, 1900, *Bryan Papers*.
16. Girdner to Bryan, April 21, June 16, 1900, *Bryan Papers*.
17. Mack to Bryan, July 19, 1900, *Bryan Papers*.
18. McGuire to Bryan, August 3, 1900, *Bryan Papers*. Other letters in the *Bryan Papers* support these conclusions. See especially James K. Jones to Bryan, April 21, 1900. James Creelman to Bryan, April 22, 1900. Arthur A. McLean to Bryan, July 17, 1900; Richard R. Kenny to Bryan, August 22, 1900. See also Edwin Burritt Smith to W. Bourke Cockran, August 6, 1900, and Charles L. Wedding to W. Bourke Cockran, July 13, 1900, *Cockran Papers*. It may be noted here that the return of the bolters was a development not confined to New York. Henry Watterson, for example, supported Bryan in 1900, and after the election he remained sympathetic. "I want you to know that I am your friend," he wrote, "and that throughout the campaign of 1896 I wrote no word and countenanced no word which was not wholly courteous and considerate. Our differences have related to one single issue and perhaps to some matters of expediency and method." If Marse Henry's memory was not entirely accurate, his intentions seemed good. Watterson to Bryan, November 30, 1900, *Bryan Papers*.
19. Cleveland to LeRoy Brooks, April 23, 1900, *Cleveland Papers*.
20. Cleveland to Olney, June 25, 1900, *Cleveland Papers*.
21. Quoted in *Public Opinion*, XXIX (July 26, 1900), p. 100.
22. Cleveland to Don Dickinson, October 12, 1900, *Cleveland Papers*.

23. Telegram, Cleveland to James K. McGuire, October 21, 1900, *Cleveland Papers.*

24. See various letters in the *Cleveland Papers:* Cleveland to Don Dickinson, October 12, 1900. Cleveland to Wilson S. Bissell, September 6, 1900; Cleveland to Commodore E. C. Benedict, October 16, 1900. Typical of the letters Cleveland received was one from Louis R. Ehrich of Colorado who wrote: "As bitterly as I opposed him [Bryan] in 1896 I felt perfectly sure as to his honesty and sincerity. I believe that he has made great strides in intellectual development during the last four years. I would trust him a thousand times rather than I would trust McKinley. I believe that every citizen who will not contribute his share to defeat our iniquitous policy in the Philippines will yet live to regret his action." Ehrich to Cleveland, August 20, 1900, *Cleveland Papers.*

25. Eckels to Cleveland, October 10, 1900, *Cleveland Papers.*

26. Morton to Cleveland, November 2, 1900, *Cleveland Papers.*

27. Quoted in *Public Opinion*, XXVIII (May 24, 1900), p. 646. Splitting into fusionist and middle-of-the-road factions, the Populists in 1900 made a sorry showing. Bryan and Charles A. Towne of Minnesota were nominated by the fusionists, Wharton Barker of Pennsylvania and Ignatius Donnelly by the middle-of-the-road element. Towne's candidacy on the fusionist ticket, thought many Bryan men, made him a contender for the Democratic vice-presidential nomination. Others, however, believed that Democrats should not accept their full ticket from a minority party. Archibald McNeil to Bryan, May 11, 1900, Thomas D. O'Brien to Bryan, May 14, 1900, Charles A. Towne to Bryan, May 15, 1900, C. Boyd Barrett to Bryan, May 25, 1900, *Bryan Papers;* J. M. Patterson to James B. Weaver, May 22, 1900, James K. Jones to James B. Weaver, May 19, 1900, *Weaver Papers;* John Lind to George Fred Williams, May 24, 1900, *Lind Papers.*

28. Bailey, "Was the Presidential Election of 1900 a Mandate on Imperialism?," p. 49. South Dakota's Richard F. Pettigrew, who lost his seat in the Senate, was exceptional in that he still could not comprehend the reasons for defeat after the results had been announced: "I cannot understand the labor vote of this country, neither can I understand how the farmers of this country are willing to submit to the taxation which must come from a large standing army, to the rule of trusts, which heretofore have fixed the price of everything they have to sell. It seems to me that the laborers and farmers are being ground out of existence by pressures from both directions, and I therefore cannot understand their vote." Pettigrew to Bryan, November 13, 1900, *Bryan Papers.*

29. Jones to Bryan, December 1, 1900, Sulzer to Bryan, November 14, 1900, Charles Shackleford to Bryan, November 30, 1900, William Rogers to Bryan, November 18, 1900, *Bryan Papers.*

30. Altgeld to Bryan, August 7, 1899, *Bryan Papers.*

31. Seymour to Bryan, January 23, 1900, *Bryan Papers*.
32. Eckels to Cleveland, September 6, 1900, *Cleveland Papers*.
33. Cleveland to Richard Gilder, May 8, 1900, *Cleveland Papers*.
34. Cleveland to Wilson S. Bissell, September 6, 1900, *Cleveland Papers*.
35. Cleveland to A. B. Farquhar, January 18, 1901, *Cleveland Papers*.
36. Cleveland to Dickinson, February 8, 1902, *Cleveland Papers*. Bryan, of course, had many supporters who looked upon conservative reorganization as somewhat less inspiring. See, for example, B. O. Flower to Bryan, December 10, 1900, Erving Winslow to Bryan, July 24, 1901, George C. Barnes to Bryan, November 11, 1901, William H. Biggs to Bryan, April 7, 1902, *Bryan Papers*.
37. Quoted in *Public Opinion*, XXXIII (July 3, 1902), p. 4. Even though Watterson was active in the harmony movement, he and Cleveland were not on speaking terms. Nevins, *Grover Cleveland*, pp. 491-492.
38. Frank Campbell to Cleveland, May 6, 1903, Walter N. Thayer to Cleveland, April 24, 1903, John Lowndes McLaurin to Cleveland, May. 7, 1903, *Cleveland Papers*.
39. Dickinson to Cleveland, September 24, 1903, *Cleveland Papers*.
40. Clipping in the *Cleveland Papers*. Although the name of the newspaper and the date are not indicated, Watterson probably wrote this diatribe in 1903. See *The Commoner*, April 10, 1903.
41. Roosevelt to Lyman Abbott, November 5, 1903, *Roosevelt Papers*.
42. Lamont to Cleveland, February 11 [?], 1904, *Cleveland Papers*.
43. Cleveland to William F. Vilas, January 24, 1904, Cleveland to Daniel S. Lamont, June 2, 1904, *Cleveland Papers*. One of Theodore Roosevelt's letters dealing with a newspaper story on Parker throws light on the character of the man who became his opponent in 1904: "How could any man be such a preposterous jack as to write that piece? Nothing in avowed caricature could come up to the delicious paragraph in which the author of the piece says of Parker that he regarded the Venus of Milo and the Winged Victory 'as very nice in their way,' but that Paul Potter's young bull was the real thing. There was an innocent podsnappery about it that passed belief." Roosevelt to Silas McBee, August 10, 1904, *Roosevelt Papers*.
44. New Orleans *Harlequin*, April 7, 1904; *The Public*, VII (April 16, 1904), p. 26.
45. *The Public*, VI (May 16, 1902), p. 267; Charles Shackleford to John Black, June 16, 1904, *John Black Papers*, Illinois Historical Library, Springfield; Richard Olney to Cleveland, July 25, 1904, *Cleveland Papers*; Nevins, *Grover Cleveland*, pp. 754-755. New Jersey boss Jim Smith, who played an active part in securing the nomination for Parker, went so far as to write prior to the convention that he intended to oppose Parker's nomination. Smith to Cleveland, June 30, 1904, *Cleveland Papers*.

46. Cleveland to Lamont, June 2, 1904, *Cleveland Papers*.
47. *The Commoner*, February 27, 1903.
48. *The Commoner*, July 25, 1902.
49. *The Commoner*, March 6, 1903.
50. *The Commoner*, February 12, 1904.
51. *The Commoner*, November 21, 1902.
52. *The Commoner*, March 15, 1901, February 5, 1904.
53. *The Commoner*, March 6, 1903. For other comments by Bryan on the reorganization movement see *The Commoner*, April 12, 26, 1901, March 28, May 9, 1902, January 4, February 6, 12, and March 11, 1904. See also Bryan to Carter Harrison, January 4, 1902, *Harrison Papers;* Pierce Butler to James Manahan, 1904 [?], Thomas D. O'Brien to Manahan, April 7, 1904, *Manahan Papers; The Public,* III (November 10, 1900), p. 136; *ibid.,* V (June 28, 1902), p. 177; *ibid.,* V (July 5, 1902), p. 202; *ibid.,* V (March 28, 1903), p. 811; *ibid.,* VI (September 19, 1903), p. 285.
54. Hamlin, Diary, I (July 25, 1902), p. 270, *Hamlin Papers*.
55. For the relationship between Bryan and Hearst see the following: Telegram, Hearst to Bryan, May 19, 1900, and Telegram, James Creelman to Bryan, June 6, 1900, *Bryan Papers;* Josephus Daniels, "Behind the Scenes with William Jennings Bryan," *Daniels Papers; Public Opinion,* XXXVI (April 7, 1904), p. 423; Milwaukee *Sentinel,* February 2, 1904; *The Commoner,* October 6, 1906; Abbot, *Watching the World Go By,* pp. 250-253, 264; Bryan, *Memoirs,* pp. 146-148, 153-154.
56. Hamlin, Diary, I (July 7, 1904), p. 346, *Hamlin Papers*.
57. Bryan, *Speeches*, II, 50.
58. Bryan, *Memoirs,* p. 154; Hibben, *Peerless Leader,* p. 248; Long, *Bryan, The Great Commoner,* pp. 184-185; M. R. Werner, *Bryan* (New York, 1929), pp. 143-145; Abbot, *Watching the World Go By,* p. 253.
59. Hamlin, Diary, I (July 7, 1904), pp. 339-343, *Hamlin Papers*.
60. Werner, *Bryan,* pp. 144-145; Abbot, *Watching the World Go By,* pp. 253-254; Long, *Bryan, The Great Commoner,* pp. 185-186.
61. Clipping, July 16, 1904, Mrs. Bryan's Scrapbooks, Nebraska State Historical Society, Lincoln.
62. Quoted in *Public Opinion,* XXXVII (July 14, 1904), p. 40; Philadelphia *North American,* July 9, 1904; New York *World,* July 8, 1904.
63. Cleveland to Olney, July 19, 1904, *Cleveland Papers*. Esopus, New York, was the home of Judge Parker.
64. Roosevelt to Henry Cabot Lodge, July 14, 1904, *Roosevelt Papers*.
65. Olney to Cleveland, July 25, 1904, *Cleveland Papers;* Pringle, *Theodore Roosevelt,* pp. 354-358.
66. Cleveland to Olney, July 19, 1904, *Cleveland Papers*. For the popular vote in the elections of 1896, 1900, and 1904, see Edgar E.

Robinson, *The Presidential Vote, 1896-1932* (Stanford, 1934), p. 46, from which the following is taken:

	1896	1900	1904
Democratic	6,379,830	6,356,734	5,084,223
Republican	7,098,474	7,218,491	7,628,461
Other	421,553	389,342	805,486

67. Daniels, "Behind the Scenes with William Jennings Bryan," *Daniels Papers.*

68. *The Commoner,* July 22, 1904; Bryan to Carter Harrison, July 20, 1904, *Harrison Papers.*

69. *Public Opinion,* XXXVII (October 20, 1904), p. 483; *ibid.,* XXXVII (November 3, 1904), p. 549; *ibid.,* XXXVII (November 17, 1904), p. 614; H. C. M. Burgess and A. B. Allen to Jonathan Dolliver, August 12, 1904, *Dolliver Papers;* Parker to Bryan, August 12, 1904, *Bryan Papers;* Theodore Roosevelt to E. Crumpacker, October 12, 1904, *Roosevelt Papers; The Public,* VII (November 12, 1904), p. 497.

70. Williams to Cleveland, October 6, 1904, clipping from the Richmond *News Leader,* October 5, 1904, *Cleveland Papers.*

71. *Public Opinion,* XXXVII (November 17, 1904), p. 614; *The Commoner,* November 11, 1904, January 27, 1905.

72. Abbot, *Watching the World Go By,* p. 256.

73. *The Commoner,* March 17, 1905, February 9, 1906; Charles W. Bryan to James B. Weaver, November 16, 29, 1905, *Weaver Papers.*

74. *The Commoner,* March 24, 1905.

75. *Harper's Weekly,* L (September 1, 1906), p. 1228.

76. Norbert Mahnken, "William Jennings Bryan in Oklahoma," p. 265; *The Commoner,* September 27, 1907.

77. Harvey to Ryan, July 5, 1896, printed in W. F. Johnson, *George Harvey, "A Passionate Patriot"* (Boston, 1929), pp. 119-122.

78. D. R. Francis to Watterson, June 8, 1906, Alex K. McClure to Watterson, July 14, 1908, George Harvey to Watterson, August 30, 1907, C. B. Carlisle to Watterson, February 6, 1908, John K. Hendrick to Watterson, February 6, 1908, *Watterson Papers.* Other correspondence in the *Watterson Papers* contains information on the relationship between Bryan and Watterson in 1908. See especially Bryan to Watterson, May 26, June 23, July 6, 16, 1908, Watterson to Bryan, July 2, 1908, Thomas T. Crittendon to Watterson, June 12, 1908.

79. Quoted in *Literary Digest,* XXXV (October 5, 1907), p. 470.

80. Quoted in *Literary Digest,* XXXVII (July 18, 1908), p. 69.

81. Chicago *Record-Herald,* August 30, 1906; *The Public,* IX (June 23, 1906), p. 265; *Literary Digest,* XXXV (November 23, 1907), p. 778.

82. Quoted in *Literary Digest,* XXXVII (July 18, 1908), p. 69.

83. The popular vote in 1908 was 7,675,320 for Taft, and 6,412,294 for Bryan. See Robinson, *The Presidenial Vote,* p. 46.

84. Rainey to Bryan, November 16, 1908, *Bryan Papers.* For other expressions of optimism see Edgar Lee Masters to Bryan, November 11, 1908, William J. Gaynor to Bryan, November 13, 1908, Henry M. Teller to Bryan, November 23, 1908, James S. Thomas to Bryan, February 6, 1909, *Bryan Papers;* Bryan to Thomas R. Marshall, November 9, 1908, *Thomas R. Marshall Papers,* Indiana State Library, Indianapolis; Judson Harmon to Henry Rainey, November 16, 1908, *Henry Rainey Papers,* Division of Manuscripts, Library of Congress.

85. Werner, *Bryan,* p. 159.

86. Charles S. Moore wrote Wilson after the convention of 1912: "I cannot for a second belief [*sic*] that he [Bryan] wanted the nomination for himself. I think that as a part of his political scheme he allowed the Wall Street crowd to be frightened with the idea that he might become a candidate. It is my firm conviction that he simply held that club back as a threat in order to lend additional strength against the Wall Street crowd for your nomination." Moore to Wilson, July 3, 1912, Trumbull White to Wilson, July 5, 1912, *Wilson Papers; The Commoner,* October 22, December 3, 1909, April 22, 1910.

87. *The Commoner,* March 22, 1912.

88. Arthur Link, *Wilson, The Road to the White House* (Princeton, 1947), p. 399.

89. Bryan, *Memoirs,* pp. 158-160; Ray Stannard Baker, *Woodrow Wilson, Life and Letters* (Garden City, N.Y., 1931), III, 199-206; Link, *Wilson,* pp. 25, 96-100, 117, 120; Henry Eckert Alexander to Wilson, December 20, 1910, *Wilson Papers;* W. H. Taft to J. C. Hemphill, May 3, 1911, *Taft Papers.*

90. Bryan to Wilson, January 5, March 1, 1911, *Wilson Papers; The Commoner,* December 16, 1910; Link, *Wilson,* p. 317.

91. *The Commoner,* January 26, 1912; Clipping from the Trenton, New Jersey, *True American,* January 23, 1912, *Wilson Papers;* Link, *Wilson,* p. 373; Louis F. Post to Marietta Stevenson, April 18, 1926, *Post Papers.* On the Harvey-Wilson feud, see also Johnson, *George Harvey,* pp. 186-200; Baker, *Woodrow Wilson,* III, 247-255; and Joseph F. Wall, *Henry Watterson, Reconstructed Rebel* (New York, 1956), pp. 264-280.

92. *The Commoner,* November 24, 1911; Louis F. Post to Marietta Stevenson, April 18, 1926, *Post Papers;* Henry Rainey to H. N. Wheeler, December 6, 1911, *Rainey Papers.*

93. Bryan to Clark, May 30, 1912, *Bryan Papers.* This letter is reprinted in Bryan, *Memoirs,* p. 163.

94. Bryan, *Memoirs,* pp. 335-336; Johnson, *George Harvey,* pp. 177-178; Baker, *Woodrow Wilson,* III, 324-325; Bryan to E. W. Rankin, May 29, 1912, *Wilson Papers.*

95. The best account of the convention is that in Link, *Wilson*, pp. 431-465. Also of value are Baker, *Woodrow Wilson*, III, 332-363, and Estal E. Sparlin, "Bryan and the 1912 Democratic Convention," *Mississippi Valley Historical Review*, XXII (1936), pp. 537-546. Bryan attended the Republican convention in Chicago before going to Baltimore and wrote a series of syndicated newspaper articles later collected under the title, *A Tale of Two Conventions* (New York, 1912). This work, together with his *Memoirs*, provides an account from the Commoner's point of view. Bryan's activities in the convention were very ably defended by *The Public*, XV (July 12, 1912), p. 650; *ibid.*, XV (July 26, 1912), p. 707. Although the suggestion that Bryan hoped to deadlock the convention and win the nomination himself cannot be conclusively refuted, it is extremely tenuous. If a Bryan did entertain such an idea, it was not William J., but his wife Mary. See Grace Bryan Hargreaves, Biographical Notes, *Bryan Papers*.

96. Abbot, *Watching the World Go By*, p. 283.

97. Link, *Wilson*, pp. 463-465.

98. Josephus Daniels, *The Wilson Era* (Chapel Hill, N.C., 1944), I, 50. Characteristically, Bryan had sent identical telegrams to Wilson, Clark, and several other candidates asking that they stand by him in his fight against Parker. Wilson replied affirmatively, saying, "You are quite right. . . . The Baltimore convention is to be a convention of progressives,—of men who are progressive in principle and by conviction." This unquestionably stamped Wilson as the most progressive of the "available" candidates. Wilson to Bryan, June 22, 1912, *Wilson Papers*. Bryan, *Memoirs*, pp. 161-168; Link, *Wilson*, p. 433.

99. Quoted in Bryan, *Memoirs*, pp. 174-175; Link, *Wilson*, pp. 442-443; Hibben, *Peerless Leader*, pp. 311-312.

100. Baker, *Woodrow Wilson*, III, 341.

101. Quoted in Link, *Wilson*, p. 437; Baker, *Woodrow Wilson*, III, 431.

102. Moore to Wilson, July 3, 1912, *Wilson Papers*. In a dispatch to the Des Moines, Iowa, *Register and Leader* dated June 30, its Washington correspondent wrote: "It is not yet plain who is going to be the nominee of this convention. It is plain as day, however, that Mr. Bryan is going to have his way. He may not do all the things he would like to do with this convention, but he has forced the convention into a position where it must do these things: Nominate a pronounced progressive; adopt a thorough going progressive platform." Des Moines *Register and Leader*, July 1, 1912.

103. Link, *Wilson*, p. 459. Even after Sullivan shifted to Wilson, four more ballots were required. It was not until the Oscar Underwood delegation gave up the fight that the nomination went to Wilson. Yet Sullivan's move was the break that started the landslide. For comments on the preconvention maneuvering in Illinois politics, see Lawrence B. Stringer to William F. McCombs, November 2,

1911, January 26, 1912, *Lawrence B. Stringer Papers,* Illinois State Historical Library, Springfield; Carter Harrison to Champ Clark, April 22, 1912, *Harrison Papers.* A full account is in Carter Harrison II, *Stormy Years, The Autobiography of Carter H. Harrison, Five Times Mayor of Chicago* (Indianapolis, 1935), pp. 319-328.

CHAPTER VIII

The Trumpet Soundeth

1. Agar, *The Pursuit of Happiness* (Cambridge, Mass., 1938), pp. 310-311.
2. A classic commentary on the disappointing results of progressive legislation is to be found in John Chamberlain, *Farewell to Reform* (New York, 1932), pp. 306-324.
3. For analysis of the disparity between public debate and legislative accomplishments, see Hofstadter, *The Age of Reform,* pp. 250-253, 264-269.
4. Baker, *American Chronicle,* p. 250.
5. *The Public,* XII (May 28, 1909), pp. 506-507.
6. Maurice F. Lyons took this address verbatim on January 8, 1912, but did not make a transcript until March 4, 1929. This transcript is in the *Lyons Papers.*

*

*   *   *

*

BIBLIOGRAPHICAL ESSAY

THE BOOKS AND SOURCES discussed in this essay do not, of course comprise a complete list of items relating to Bryan or to the period from 1896 to 1912. They do represent a selection from the materials consulted. The sources and secondary works included here (most of which have also been cited in the notes) are those that I have found most informative and/or suggestive.

Manuscripts

The William Jennings Bryan Papers in the Library of Congress are regrettably incomplete; yet they constitute the most important single collection used in this study. They have been supplemented with materials gleaned from other collections. Among the most important of these are the Papers of Josephus Daniels, Louis F. Post, and Henry Watterson, all in the Library of Congress. Post and Daniels were loyal Bryan men, and Watterson supported him in 1900 and 1908. The Woodrow Wilson Papers in the Library of Congress are invaluable for the years 1910-1912. The John Peter Altgeld Collection in the Illinois State Historical Library, Springfield, contains several items relating to Bryan's first campaign and his early years of opposition. The Papers of Ignatius Donnelly in the Minnesota Historical Society, St. Paul, are vital for an understanding of Populism and the relationship between Bryan and the agrarian movement. The Iowa Historical, Memorial and Art Department at Des Moines has a small but useful collection of the papers of James B. Weaver. Exceptionally valuable, especially for the campaign of 1896, are the James Manahan Papers in the Minnesota Historical Society.

The Henry T. Rainey Papers and the Maurice F. Lyons Papers in the Library of Congress contain a few items of interest. Congressman Rainey, like Bryan, was an alumnus of Illinois College. The Carter Harrison Papers in the Newberry Library, Chicago, include a number of letters from Bryan. The John Lind Papers in the Minnesota Historical Society are more useful for the period after 1912 than before, yet they contain several references to Bryan and to midwestern politics. The Thomas R. Marshall Papers in the Indiana State Library, Indianapolis, are very thin and of little importance. The Illinois State Historical Library has the papers of George A. Schilling, Lawrence B. Stringer, and William R. Morrison, all of which include several items of some interest and significance.

Bryan's relationships with the conservative eastern wing of his party are reflected in several collections. The W. Bourke Cockran Papers in the New York Public Library are particularly important for the campaign of 1900. The Grover Cleveland Papers, the Charles S. Hamlin Papers, and the Richard Olney Papers are all in the Library of Congress, and each collection has its particular value. The movement to reorganize the Democracy after Bryan's second defeat can be traced through various letters in the Cleveland Papers. The diaries of Charles S. Hamlin provide an insight into Democratic politics from a conservative viewpoint. The large Olney collection contains much that is helpful in understanding that viewpoint.

The papers of Republican leaders are, in general, more complete than those of prominent Democrats. Especially important are the William Howard Taft Papers and the Theodore Roosevelt Papers in the Library of Congress. Both are well arranged and easy to use. The Joseph Foraker Papers, also in the Library of Congress, have some items relevant to a study of Bryan. Two large and important collections are the Papers of Jonathan P. Dolliver in the Iowa Historical Society, Iowa City, and the Papers of Albert Baird Cummins in the Historical, Memorial and Art Department at Des Moines. They contain few references to Bryan but are invaluable for the study of middle western progressivism.

The Papers of Andrew Carnegie occupy a place of peculiar importance because of Carnegie's interest in world peace. He and Bryan exchanged several letters on the subject. Other collections of more than passing interest are the Papers of John Charles Black in the Illinois State Historical Library, the Papers of William Dudley Foulke in the Indiana State Library, and the Papers of William McKendree Springer in the Chicago Historical Society. Illinois College has in its archives a number of important holdings. Particularly interesting are the Minutes of the Board of Trustees of the College.

Only a few of the many important collections relating to the development of middle western culture have been fully exploited by scholars. The vast collection of Chautauqua materials in the State University of Iowa Library includes much that is important to the study of midwestern moralism. The Papers of William Allen White in the Library of

Congress reflect the views of a man who was representative of a certain middle western outlook. The Upton Sinclair Papers in the Special Collections of the Indiana University Library contain many items of interest to the student of American thought. The Newberry Library has the Sherwood Anderson Papers, a large and important collection. The Edgar Lee Masters Papers in the Illinois State Historical Library and the letters and poems by Masters in the Papers of Eunice Tietjens, Newberry Library, reflect that writer's revulsion against midwestern moralism.

Newspapers and Periodicals

Most of the major newspapers of the period were either hostile to Bryan or opposed to the policies he advocated. *The New York Times* was relatively free from bias and provided the most complete coverage of political news. The New York *World,* although Democratic and progressive, was never an enthusiastic supporter of the Commoner. The Chicago *Record Herald* kept up a running criticism of him which he frequently felt obliged to meet. The New York *Tribune* was partisan to Roosevelt and Taft. Hearst newspapers, of which the New York *American* and the Chicago *American* were the most important, supported Bryan until 1904. The Springfield *Republican* frequently disagreed with Bryan, but he held the paper in high regard nevertheless. The Des Moines *Register and Leader* was a progressive publication that often dealt with him sympathetically. The Omaha *World-Herald* was pro-Bryan. Other newspapers that have yielded useful comments on major issues of the period are the Chicago *Tribune,* the Milwaukee *Sentinel,* the Kansas City *World,* and the Springfield *Illinois State Register.*

Special mention should be made of four publications that have been particularly important to this study. The first is *The Commoner,* Bryan's weekly newspaper. Most of his speeches were reprinted here, along with editorial comment on news events. Scarcely less helpful than *The Commoner* is *The Public,* published in Chicago and dedicated to the fortunes of the reform element in the Democratic party. Up to 1906 *Public Opinion* and the *Literary Digest* both provided excellent summaries of press opinion. After 1906 the former publication was absorbed by the latter.

One of the striking features of the progressive period was the vast bulk of periodical literature offered the public. Among the most important of the magazines were *Collier's, Cosmopolitan, Everybody's Magazine, Harper's Weekly, The Independent, McClure's Magazine, The Outlook,* and *World's Work.*

Published Letters, Speeches, and Writings

Bryan wrote voluminously if not always felicitously. Most of his speeches were published either independently or in collected works. For his opposition career the best collection is *The Speeches of William Jennings Bryan* (2 vols., New York, 1909). A number of speeches, letters, and other materials were collected in Bryan's account of the 1896 campaign, *The First Battle* (Chicago, 1897). His *Second Battle* (Chicago, 1900) is not so valuable, but it too contains several speeches. No such work was compiled for the election of 1908. But for the campaign of 1912 Bryan turned out *A Tale of Two Conventions* (New York, 1912), a comparison of the Democratic convention at Baltimore and the Republican convention at Chicago. Bryan attended the Chicago convention as a reporter.

Bryan's Chautauqua speeches were in such demand that many were published. Among the most famous of these were *The First Commandment* (New York, 1917); *The Making of a Man* (New York, 1914); *Man* (New York, 1914); *The Prince of Peace* (Chicago, 1909); and *The Value of an Ideal* (New York, 1914). Somewhat larger works were Bryan's *Heart to Heart Appeals* (New York, 1917), selected from his speeches, and *The Old World and Its Ways* (St. Louis, 1907), based upon Bryan's personal observations abroad.

Other speeches and writings by Bryan deal with specific subjects. *British Rule in India* (Westminster, 1906), was a condemnation of imperialism. *Guaranteed Banks* (Chicago, 1908), outlined his plan for a bank deposits guarantee. Bryan's speech on prohibition at the Nebraska Democratic convention of 1910 was published under the title *A Defense of County Option* (n.p., n.d.). His article "A Remedy for the Trusts," *Public Opinion,* XXXVIII (April 25, 1905), presented his plan for limiting the growth of monopoly. Another, "The Next Awakening," *Public Opinion,* XXXVIII (May 27, 1905), provides a good example of his ideas on progress. Among the best of Bryan's publications is *The Forces that Make for Peace* (Boston, 1912), addresses delivered at the Mohonk conferences on international arbitration in 1910 and 1911. For other speeches, see *The Commoner* and the Democratic campaign textbooks for the Bryan campaigns.

The papers of many of Bryan's contemporaries have been published in part. Elting E. Morison and John M. Blum, eds., *The Letters of Theodore Roosevelt* (8 vols., Cambridge, Mass., 1951-1954), is outstanding not only for its selection of letters, but also for the incisive essays it includes. *The Works of Theodore Roosevelt* (20 vols., National Edition, New York, 1926), contains Roosevelt's most important speeches. See also Henry Cabot Lodge, ed., *Selections from the Correspondence of Theodore Roosevelt and Henry Cabot Lodge, 1884-1918* (2 vols., New York, 1925). Charles Seymour, ed., *The Intimate Papers of Colonel House* (4 vols., Boston, 1926-1928), has some material relevant to this study. Other published collections are Arthur H. Darling, ed., *The Public Papers of Francis G. Newlands* (2 vols., Boston, 1932); Ella Winter and Granville Hicks, eds., *The Letters of Lincoln Steffens* (2 vols., New York, 1938); Walter Johnson, ed., *Selected Letters of William Allen White, 1899-1943* (New York, 1947). The Papers of William Howard Taft have not as yet been published, but a number of Taft's speeches and writings are available. See especially *Four Aspects of Civic Duty* (New York, 1906); *Political Issues and Outlooks* (New York, 1909); *Present Day*

Problems (New York, 1908); *The Anti-Trust Act and the Supreme Court* (New York, 1914).

Memoirs and Biographical Studies

There is as yet no adequate biography of Bryan. Professor Paolo Coletta of the United States Naval Academy has been working on one for a number of years, however, and it may be the long-awaited definitive work. The best of the existing biographies is that by Paxton Hibben, *The Peerless Leader, William Jennings Bryan* (New York, 1929). Unfinished at the time of Hibben's death, it was completed by C. H. Grattan. It is highly critical of Bryan and in many respects fails to do him justice. Other biographies, Morris R. Werner, *Bryan* (New York, 1929), John C. Long, *Bryan, The Great Commoner* (New York, 1928), and Wayne C. Williams, *William Jennings Bryan* (New York, 1936), are useful but not penetrating. William Jennings and Mary Baird Bryan, *The Memoirs of William Jennings Bryan* (Philadelphia, 1925), is indispensable in spite of its many limitations. Bryan had not completed the work at the time of his death. His wife, with the help of professional writers, hastily gathered materials together and the book was rushed into print. The result is a rather unorganized compilation. It is, however, a valuable work for the point of view it represents. Marietta Stevenson, "William Jennings Bryan as a Political Leader" (unpublished Ph.D. dissertation, University of Chicago, 1926), contains little that cannot now be found elsewhere.

The major political figures of the years from 1896 to 1912 have all had their biographers. Allan Nevins, *Grover Cleveland, A Study in Courage* (New York, 1932), is a biography of the first rank. Ray Stannard Baker, *Woodrow Wilson: Life and Letters* (8 vols., Garden City, N.Y., 1927-1939), is the most extensive treatment of Wilson. But it is in large part superseded by the work of Arthur Link. Link's brilliant study of Wilson's course prior to his election, *Wilson, The Road to the White House* (Princeton, N.J., 1947), was particularly useful in the preparation of the present work. Herbert Croly, *Marcus Alonzo Hanna* (New York, 1923), contains information on the two Bryan-McKinley campaigns. See also Thomas Beer, *Hanna* (New York, 1929). Margaret Leech, *In the Days of McKinley* (New York, 1959), is an important work that treats McKinley sympathetically. Henry F. Pringle's two excellent biographies, *Theodore Roosevelt* (New York, 1931) and *The Life and Times of William Howard Taft* (2 vols., New York, 1939), are invaluable in themselves and as guides to research in the Papers of Roosevelt and Taft.

Other useful biographical studies include Claude Bowers, *Beveridge and the Progressive Era* (Cambridge, Mass., 1932); John M. Blum, *Joe Tumulty and the Wilson Era* (Boston, 1951); Elmer Ellis, *Henry Moore Teller, Defender of the West* (Caldwell, Idaho, 1941); Louis G. Geiger, *Joseph W. Folk*, "University of Missouri Studies," XXV (Columbia, 1953); Walter Johnson, *William Allen White's America* (New York, 1947); Willis Fletcher Johnson, *George Harvey, "A Passionate Patriot"*

(Boston, 1929); Belle and Fola La Follette, *Robert M. La Follette* (New York, 1953); Horace S. Merrill, *William Freeman Vilas, Doctrinaire Democrat* (Madison, Wis., 1954); James C. Olson, *J. Sterling Morton* (Lincoln, Nebr., 1942); Francis B. Simkins, *Pitchfork Ben Tillman* (Baton Rouge, La., 1944); George M. Stephenson, *John Lind of Minnesota* (Minneapolis, 1935); Nathaniel Stephenson, *Nelson W. Aldrich* (New York, 1930); Joseph F. Wall, *Henry Watterson, Reconstructed Rebel* (New York, 1956); C. Vann Woodward, *Tom Watson, Agrarian Rebel* (New York, 1938).

Memoirs and autobiographies are an important part of the literature coming out of the progressive movement. Ray Stannard Baker, *American Chronicle* (New York, 1945), Lincoln Steffens, *Autobiography* (2 vols., New York, 1931), and Ida Tarbell, *All in the Day's Work* (New York, 1939), all provide insights into the muckraking movement and progressivism in general. S. S. McClure, *My Autobiography* (New York, 1914), is disappointing. William Allen White, *The Autobiography of William Allen White* (New York, 1946), is rich in observations on the progressive movement. Edward A. Ross, *Seventy Years of It* (New York, 1936), is the work of one of the most controversial figures in academic life during the period.

Memoirs and biographical works concerned mainly with politics are Willis J. Abbot, *Watching the World Go By* (Boston, 1933); Carter Harrison II, *Stormy Years, The Autobiography of Carter H. Harrison, Five Times Mayor of Chicago* (Indianapolis, 1935); Champ Clark, *My Quarter Century of American Politics* (2 vols., New York, 1920); Richard F. Pettigrew, *Imperial Washington* (Chicago, 1922); Arthur Mullen, *Western Democrat* (New York, 1940); Arthur W. Dunn, *From Harrison to Harding* (2 vols., New York, 1922); Oscar King Davis, *Released for Publication* (New York, 1945); Charles W. Thompson, *Presidents I've Known, and Two Near Presidents* (Indianapolis, 1929); William Allen White, *Masks in a Pageant* (New York, 1928).

Midwestern Culture

Several general works dealing with American thought have sections that are helpful to an understanding of middle western culture. Ralph Gabriel, *The Course of American Democratic Thought* (New York, 1956), originally suggested several of the ideas and interpretations that I have attempted to develop in this study. Walter Webb, *The Great Frontier* (Cambridge, Mass., 1952), Henry Nash Smith, *Virgin Land* (Vintage Edition, New York, 1957), David Potter, *People of Plenty* (Chicago, 1954), Constance Rourke, *American Humor* (Anchor Edition, New York, 1953), are all imaginative and provocative. Henry Steele Commager, *The American Mind* (New Haven, 1950), has important chapters on American thought in the late nineteenth century. Alexis de Tocqueville, *Democracy in America*, trans. Henry Reeve (Vintage Edition, 2 vols., New York, 1956-1958), is *sui generis*.

Three works concentrating on the Middle West require special emphasis. R. Carlyle Buley, *The Old Northwest, Pioneer Period, 1820-1840* (2 vols., Indianapolis, 1950), is distinguished for the soundness of its scholarship as well as for the excellence of its style. Lewis Atherton, *Main Street on the Middle Border* (Bloomington, Indiana, 1954), provides an invaluable insight into the mind of small midwestern communities. John J. Murray, ed., *The Heritage of the Middle West* (Norman, Okla., 1958), contains a series of popular lectures by prominent historians and treats almost every aspect of the Middle West.

Nothing could be more important to analysis of middle western thought than understanding of American religious development. Fortunately this has been a subject of considerable investigation. Among the standard works in this area are those of William Warren Sweet. Particularly useful in the present investigation were *Religion in the Development of American Culture, 1765-1840* (New York, 1952), *Revivalism in America* (New York, 1944), and *American Culture and Religion, Six Essays* (Dallas, Texas, 1951). Colin B. Goodykoontz, *Home Missions on the American Frontier* (Caldwell, Idaho, 1939), emphasizes the work of the American Home Missionary Society but deals with the general missionary impulse of the nineteenth century. Peter Mode, *The Frontier Spirit in American Christianity* (New York, 1923), is in the tradition of Frederick Jackson Turner. H. Richard Niebuhr, *The Social Sources of Denominationalism* (Living Age Edition, New York, 1957), is a seminal work.

One of the outstanding contributions to recent scholarship in the field of American religion has been made by Sidney Mead. See especially "Denominationalism: The Shape of Protestantism in America," *Church History*, XXIII (1954), pp. 291-320, and "American Protestantism Since the Civil War," *Journal of Religion*, XXXVI (1956), pp. 1-16, 67-89. H. Richard Niebuhr and Daniel D. Williams, eds., *The Ministry in Historical Perspectives* (New York, 1956), contains suggestive essays. Winthrop S. Hudson, *The Great Tradition of American Churches* (New York, 1953), is a commentary on the significance of separation of church and state in the United States. Charles A. Johnson, *The Frontier Camp Meeting: Religion's Harvest Time* (Dallas, Texas, 1955), is a new look at a phenomenon of considerable importance. Three recent books on revivalism have made significant contributions: Timothy L. Smith, *Revivalism and Social Reform* (New York, 1957); Bernard Weisberger, *They Gathered at the River, The Story of the Great Revivalists and Their Impact upon Religion in America* (Boston, 1958); and William G. McLoughlin, *Modern Revivalism, Charles Grandison Finney to Billy Graham* (New York, 1959). Paul A. Carter, *The Decline and Revival of the Social Gospel: Social and Political Liberalism in American Protestant Churches, 1920-1940* (Ithaca, N.Y., 1954), and Norman Furniss, *The Fundamentalist Controversy, 1918-1931* (New Haven, 1954), explore problems that lie on the periphery of this study.

The McGuffey Readers and other textbooks of the nineteenth century deserve more careful consideration than they have received from students of American thought. Two books, Richard D. Mosier, *Making the American Mind: Social and Moral Ideas in the McGuffey Readers* (New York, 1947), and Harvey C. Minnich, *William Holmes McGuffey and His Readers* (New York, 1936), are helpful. Atherton, *Main Street on the Middle Border,* and Buley, *The Old Northwest,* already cited, also have valuable comments on the Readers.

By far the most significant scholarly work on the circuit Chautauqua is Donald L. Graham, "Circuit Chautauqua, A Middle Western Institution" (unpublished Ph.D. dissertation, State University of Iowa, 1953). Victoria and Robert Ormond Case, *We Called It Culture* (Garden City, N.Y., 1948), is a popular treatment. Other informative works on the movement are in the nature of memoirs: Gay MacLaren, *Morally We Roll Along* (Boston, 1938); Charles F. Horner, *Strike the Tents* (Philadelphia, 1954); and Harry Harrison and Karl Detzer, *Culture Under Canvas* (New York, 1958).

A number of studies help to relate some of the main themes of middle western culture to William Jennings Bryan. Of special importance are Paolo Coletta, "The Youth of William Jennings Bryan—Beginnings of a Christian Statesman," *Nebraska History,* XXXI (1950), pp. 1-24; George R. Poage, "The College Career of William Jennings Bryan," *Mississippi Valley Historical Review,* XV (1928), pp. 165-182; and Paul R. Anderson, "Hiram K. Jones and Philosophy at Jacksonville," *Journal of the Illinois State Historical Society,* XXXIII (1940), pp. 478-520. Charles H. Rammelkamp, *Illinois College: A Centennial History, 1829-1929* (New Haven, 1928), might well serve as a model for college histories. Donald Polzin, "Curricular and Extra-Curricular Speech Training at Illinois College: 1829-1900" (unpublished M.A. thesis, University of Illinois, 1952), and Helen Edith Marshall, "The Social Philosophy of William Jennings Bryan, An Interpretation" (unpublished M.A. thesis, University of Chicago, 1929), contain useful information.

Agriculture and Populism

The historical literature relating to the farmer is so extensive that this discussion must be confined to major works and to those which I have found particularly helpful. Any study of Populism might well begin with John D. Hicks, *The Populist Revolt* (Minneapolis, 1931), and Fred A. Shannon, *The Farmer's Last Frontier* (New York, 1945). For the background of Populism, Solon J. Buck, *The Granger Movement* (Cambridge, Mass., 1913) still has value. Farm problems of the twentieth century are treated in Theodore Saloutos and John Hicks, *Agricultural Discontent in the Middle West, 1900-1939* (Madison, Wis., 1951). An impressive number of scholarly articles supplement these works. See especially John D. Barnhart, "Rainfall and the Populist Party in Nebraska," *American Political Science Review,* XIX (1925), pp. 527-540; Hallie Farmer, "Economic Background of Frontier Populism," *Mississippi Valley Historical Review,* X (1924), pp. 406-427; Leon W. Fuller, "Colorado's Revolt Against Capitalism," *Mississippi Valley*

Historical Review, XXI (1934), pp. 343-360; Raymond C. Miller, "The Economic Background of Populism in Kansas," *Mississippi Valley Historical Review*, XI (1925), pp. 469-489; Fred Shannon, "The Status of the Midwestern Farmer in 1900," *Mississippi Valley Historical Review*, XXXVII (1950), pp. 491-510; Benton H. Wilcox, "An Historical Definition of Northwestern Radicalism," *Mississippi Valley Historical Review*, XXVI (1939), pp. 377-394.

Taking a unique approach, James C. Malin has made an outstanding contribution to the study of history as well as to the history of agriculture. The three works by Malin which I found most useful are *Winter Wheat in the Golden Belt of Kansas* (Lawrence, Kans., 1944); "The Turnover of Farm Population in Kansas," *Kansas Historical Quarterly*, IV (1935), pp. 339-372; and "Mobility and History: Reflections on the Agricultural Policies of the United States in Relation to a Mechanized World," *Agricultural History*, XVII (1943), pp. 177-191.

Recent scholarship in the area of agricultural history has either explored new ground or indicated the need for a reappraisal of earlier work. Paul W. Gates, *Fifty Million Acres: Conflicts over Kansas Land Policy, 1854-1890* (Ithaca, N.Y., 1954), is a thorough study of a neglected subject and is necessary for a proper evaluation of Populism. Allan Bogue, *Money at Interest, The Farm Mortgage on the Middle Border* (Ithaca, N.Y., 1955), is an admirable pioneer investigation of a crucial problem; it includes studies in depth of two townships, one in Kansas and the other in Nebraska. I am deeply indebted to Richard Hofstadter, *The Age of Reform, From Bryan to F.D.R.* (New York, 1955), for its brilliant and provocative treatment of Populism. For a further discussion of recent work, see Thomas LeDuc, "Recent Contributions to Economic History: The United States, 1861-1900," *Journal of Economic History*, XIX (1959), pp. 44-63.

Imperialism

The most satisfactory general work on expansion is Foster R. Dulles, *America's Rise to World Power, 1898-1954* (New York, 1955). Julius Pratt, *Expansionists of 1898* (Baltimore, 1936), is a valuable study of the groups that favored war with Spain. Albert Weinberg, *Manifest Destiny, A Study of Nationalist Expansionism in American History* (Baltimore, 1935), is an important work. Howard K. Beale, *Theodore Roosevelt and the Rise of America to World Power* (Baltimore, 1956), is a penetrating analysis based upon prodigious research. Walter Millis, *The Martial Spirit* (New York, 1931), is a deftly written account of the war with Spain. A suggestive discussion of the Philippine problem is Richard Hofstader, "Manifest Destiny and the Philippines," in *America in Crisis*, ed. Daniel Aaron (New York, 1952). A. Whitney Griswold, *The Far Eastern Policy of the United States* (New York, 1938), and Thomas Bailey, *Theodore Roosevelt and the Japanese American Crisis* (Stanford, Calif., 1934), are valuable. See also Harold U. Faulkner, *Politics, Reform and Expansion* (New York, 1959). Merle Curti, *Bryan and World Peace,* "Smith College Studies in History," XVI (Northampton, Mass., 1931), is invaluable for its analysis of Bryan's ideas on international relations.

Several important articles have provided suggestive interpretations of various phases of imperialism. See especially William E. Leuchtenberg, "Progressivism and Imperialism: The Progressive Movement and American Foreign Policy, 1898-1916," *Mississippi Valley Historical Review,* XXXIX (1952), pp. 483-504; F. H. Harrington, "The Anti-Imperialist Movement in the United States, 1898-1900," *Mississippi Valley Historical Review,* XXII (1935), pp. 211-230; F. H. Harrington, "Literary Aspects of Anti-Imperialism," *New England Quarterly,* X (1937), pp. 650-667; John P. Mallan, "The Warrior Critique of a Business Civilization," *American Quarterly,* VIII (1956), pp. 216-230; Paolo Coletta, "Bryan, McKinley, and the Treaty of Paris," *Pacific Historical Review,* XXVI (1957), pp. 131-146; and Ray Allen Billington, "The Origins of Middle Western Isolationism," *Political Science Quarterly,* LX (1945), pp. 44-64.

The Progressive Movement

One of the older general accounts of the progressive movement, Harold U. Faulkner, *The Quest for Social Justice, 1898-1914* (New York, 1931), is still one of the best. Eric Goldman, *Rendezvous with Destiny* (New York, 1953), is a well-written study of reform movements since 1865. Russel B. Nye, *Midwestern Progressive Politics* (East Lansing, Mich., 1951), has considerable merit. Mark Sullivan, *Our Times, 1900-1925* (6 vols., New York, 1926-1935), contains astute observations on the American scene. George E. Mowry, *The Era of Theodore Roosevelt, 1900-1912* (New York, 1958), is the impressive work of a painstaking and thoughtful scholar. Richard Hofstadter, *The Age of Reform,* provides a fresh and challenging interpretation of progressivism as well as of Populism. For an excellent account of the last phase of the progressive movement, see Arthur Link, *Woodrow Wilson and the Progressive Era, 1910-1917* (New York, 1954).

Particular phases of the progressive movement are treated in several valuable monographs. Alan Pendleton Grimes, *The Political Liberalism of the New York Nation,* "The James Sprunt Studies in History and Political Science," XXXIV (Durham, N.C., 1953), sets the background for urban reform. George Mowry, *Theodore Roosevelt and the Progressive Movement* (Madison, Wis., 1946), deals with the period following the Roosevelt administration. George Mowry, *The California Progressives* (Berkeley, Calif., 1951), has considerable general importance even though it focuses on progressivism at the state level. C. C. Regier, *The Era of the Muckrakers* (Chapel Hill, N.C., 1932), is a competent survey of reform journalism. Louis Filler, *Crusaders for American Liberalism* (New York, 1950), discusses the reforms initiated in part by the investigations of muckrakers. For a treatment of progressive economics, see Harold U. Faulkner, *The Decline of Laissez-Faire, 1897-1917* (New York, 1951).

Various attitudes associated with the progressive movement are reflected in books by progressives themselves. This is particularly true of Walter Weyl, *The New Democracy* (New York, 1914); Herbert Croly, *The Promise of American Life* (New York, 1909); and a work of lesser importance, Edward A. Ross, *Sin and Society* (New York, 1907). Lincoln Steffens, *The Shame of the Cities* (American Century Edition, New York, 1957), contains the important muckraking series on large American cities. Woodrow Wilson, *The New Freedom* (Garden City, N.Y., 1913), is a collection of speeches made during the campaign of 1912. Some of the disillusionment which came with the failure of progressivism is reflected in John Chamberlain, *Farewell to Reform* (New York, 1932).

Immigration posed one of the major problems of the progressive years. Carl Wittke, *We Who Built America* (New York, 1945), and Marcus Hansen, *The Immigrant in American History* (Cambridge, Mass., 1942), provide a general discussion of the subject. Oscar Handlin, *The Uprooted* (Boston, 1952), is perceptive in its appraisal of the immigrant mind. John Higham, *Strangers in the Land, Patterns of American Nativism, 1860-1925* (New Brunswick, N.J., 1955), is the best treatment of nativism. See also Oscar Handlin, *Race and Nationality in American Life* (Anchor Edition, New York, 1957).

Party Politics

The distinctive character of American politics is the subject of Daniel Boorstin's perceptive study, *The Genius of American Politics* (Chicago, 1953). Richard Hofstadter considers the problem of political leadership in *The American Political Tradition, and the Men Who Made It* (New York, 1948). Less interpretive but nevertheless useful are W. E. Binkley, *American Political Parties, Their Natural History* (New York, 1943); Edward Stanwood, *History of the Presidency* (2 vols., Boston, 1921); Herbert Agar, *The Pursuit of Happiness* (Cambridge, Mass., 1938). See also Charles E. Merriam, *Four American Party Leaders* (New York, 1926); Harold Zink, *City Bosses in the United States* (Durham, N.C., 1930); Matthew Josephson, *The Politicos* (New York, 1938); Matthew Josephson, *The President Makers* (New York, 1940); and Herbert Agar, *The Price of Union* (Boston, 1950).

Bryan's campaigns, particularly that of 1896, have been subjected to analysis in scholarly articles. Paolo Coletta has two articles on Bryan's early political activities: "The Morning Star of the Reformation: William Jennings Bryan's First Congressional Campaign," *Nebraska History,* XXXVII (1956), pp. 103-119, and "William Jennings Bryan and the Nebraska Senatorial Election of 1893," *Nebraska History,* XXXI (1950), pp. 183-203. Writing on the campaign of 1896, James A. Barnes corrects some common misconceptions in "Myths of the

Bryan Campaign," *Mississippi Valley Historical Review,* XXXIV (1947), pp. 367-404. Barnes also explores the position of Democratic conservatives in his "Gold Standard Democrats and Party Conflict," *Mississippi Valley Historical Review,* XVII (1930), pp. 422-450. Other aspects of the campaign of 1896 are treated in Harvey Wish, "John Peter Altgeld and the Background of the Campaign of 1896," *Mississippi Valley Historical Review,* XXIV (1938), pp. 503-518; Elmer Ellis, "Silver Republicans in 1896," *Mississippi Valley Historical Review,* XVIII (1932), pp. 519-534; and William Diamond, "Urban and Rural Voting in 1896," *American Historical Review,* XLVI (1940), pp. 281-305. Thomas A. Bailey, "Was the Presidential Election of 1900 a Mandate on Imperialism?" *Mississippi Valley Historical Review,* XXIV (1937), pp. 43-52, answers the question in the negative. Edgar A. Hornig is sympathetic to Bryan in two articles on the campaign of 1908: "The Indefatigable Mr. Bryan in 1908," *Nebraska History,* XXXVII (1956), pp. 183-199, and "Campaign Issues in the Presidential Election of 1908," *Indiana Magazine of History,* LIV (1958), pp. 237-264. Estal E. Sparlin, "Bryan and the 1912 Democratic Convention," *Mississippi Valley Historical Review,* XXII (1936), pp. 537-546, should be consulted. The remarks by Senator George Norris in his "Bryan as a Political Leader," *Current History,* XXII (1925), pp. 859-867, reveal as much about Norris as they do about Bryan.

A BRYAN CHRONOLOGY

March 19, 1860	Born in Salem, Illinois
1875-1881	Attended Whipple Academy and Illinois College, Jacksonville, Illinois
1881-1883	Studied law, Union College of Law, Chicago
1883-1887	Practiced law, Jacksonville, Illinois
October 1, 1884	Married Mary Baird
October 1887	Moved to Lincoln, Nebraska
November 4, 1890	Elected to Congress
November 8, 1892	Re-elected to Congress
September 1, 1894	Became editor, Omaha *World-Herald*
June 9, 1896	Delivered "Cross of Gold" speech at the Chicago convention of the Democratic party
June 10, 1896	Nominated for President by the Democratic party
November 3, 1896	Defeated by William McKinley
July 13, 1898	Assumed command of the Third Nebraska Volunteers
December 12, 1898	Discharged from the Army
July 5, 1900	Received second nomination for President
November 6, 1900	Defeated by McKinley a second time
January 23, 1901	Published first issue of *The Commoner*
November 1903-January 1904	Traveled in Europe, visited Tolstoy
July 6-10, 1904	Attended Democratic convention in St. Louis
January 17, 1905	Elected Chairman of the Board of Trustees, Illinois College
February 12, 1906	Resignation from Illinois College Board of Trustees accepted
September 1905-August 1906	Traveled around the world
August 30, 1906	Feted at a reception in New York on return to the United States
July 10, 1908	Nominated for President a third time
November 3, 1908	Defeated by William Howard Taft
December 1909-April 1910	Toured Latin America
July 26, 1910	Defeated on county option at Nebraska Democratic convention
June 25-July 2, 1912	Attended Democratic convention at Baltimore
March 4, 1913-June 9, 1915	Served as Secretary of State under Woodrow Wilson
July 10-21, 1925	Assisted prosecution in Scopes trial
July 26, 1925	Died in Dayton, Tennessee

*

* * *

*

ACKNOWLEDGMENTS

The author is grateful to the following publishers for permission to quote passages as cited in the notes:

Abingdon Press, for permission to quote from Peter Cartwright, *Autobiography,* ed. Charles L. Wallis

American Book Company, for permission to quote from Harvey Minnich, ed., *Old Favorites from the McGuffey Readers*

Columbia University Press, for permission to quote from Woodrow Wilson, *Constitutional Government in the United States*

Cornell University Press, for permission to quote from Paul Carter, *The Decline and Revival of the Social Gospel*

Harcourt, Brace and Company, for permission to quote from Lincoln Steffens, *The Autobiography of Lincoln Steffens.* (Copyright 1931 by Harcourt, Brace and Company, Inc.; renewed by Peter Steffens. Reprinted by permission of the publishers.)

Harper and Brothers, for permission to quote from Harold U. Faulkner, *Politics, Reform and Expansion,* and *Harper's Weekly*

Houghton-Mifflin Company, for permission to quote from Herbert Agar, *Pursuit of Happiness;* Claude Bowers, *Beveridge and the Progressive Era;* Edward A. Ross, *Sin and Society;* Walter Webb, *The Great Frontier*

Indiana University Press, for permission to quote from Lewis Atherton, *Main Street on the Middle Border*

Alfred A. Knopf, Inc., for permission to quote from Thomas Beer, *Hanna;* Eric Goldman, *Rendezvous with Destiny;* Richard Hofstadter, *The Age of Reform;* Richard Hofstadter, *The American Political Tradition;* H. L. Mencken, *Notes on Democracy;* William L. Riordan, *Plunkitt of Tammany Hall,* ed. Roy V. Peel; Alexis de Tocqueville, *Democracy in America,* trans. Henry Reeve

Fleming H. Revell Company, for permission to quote from William Jennings Bryan, *The Making of a Man;* William Jennings Bryan, *The First Commandment*

Rutgers University Press, for permission to quote from John Higham, *Strangers in the Land*

Charles Scribner's Sons, for permission to quote from Ray Stannard Baker, *American Chronicle*

University of Chicago Press, for permission to quote from Daniel Boorstin, *The Genius of American Politics.* (Copyright 1953 by the University of Chicago. All rights reserved. Copyright 1953 under the International Copyright Union.)

University of Minnesota Press, for permission to quote from John D. Hicks, *The Populist Revolt.* (Copyright 1931 by the University of Minnesota. Copyright renewed by John D. Hicks, 1959.)

Yale University Press, for permission to quote from Henry S. Commager, *The American Mind*

The author also wishes to acknowledge his indebtedness to Mrs. Willis J. Abbot, for permission to quote from Willis J. Abbot, *Watching the World Go By;* to Brandt and Brandt, for permission to quote from Gay MacLaren, *Morally We Roll Along;* and to Mr. William Jennings Bryan, Jr., for permission to quote from William Jennings Bryan, *Speeches of William Jennings Bryan,* William Jennings Bryan, *The Value of an Ideal,* and William Jennings Bryan, *Man.*

*

* * *

*

INDEX

Abbot, Willis, 67-68, 170
Adams, Samuel Hopkins, 128
Agar, Herbert, 176
Agrarian discontent, 33, 43-44, 48-51.
  See also Populism; Farmers
Agricultural prices, 46-47, 188-189,
  190
Alaska, 59
Alcott, Bronson, 24
Aldrich, Nelson W., 73, 166
Alger, Horatio, 35
Allen, William V., 55
Altgeld, John Peter, 30, 51, 59, 144,
  148
American Akademe, 23
American Bible Society, 6
American Home Missionary Society,
  7, 8, 180
American Magazine, 128
American Mercury, 16, 19
American Sunday School Union, 6
American Tobacco Company, 200
American Tract Society, 6
Anderson, Sherwood, 1
Anthracite strike, 124
Arbitration of international disputes.

See International disputes, arbitra-
  tion of
Arminianism, 4
Australia, 59

Baker, Ray Stannard, 120, 129, 130,
  131, 132, 133, 171
Baltimore, Maryland, 170, 171, 173
Bangor, Maine, 155
Bank deposits guarantee, 92-93
Baptist church, 3, 4, 27
Barnes, James A., 54
Bates, "Sunshine," 19
Baumgarten, D. L., 144
Beauchamp, Lou, 19
Beecher, Lyman, 4, 6, 7
Belmont, August, 170-171, 178
Bennett, Philo S., 35, 185-186
Bennett, William Rainey, 18
Beveridge, Albert, 71, 125
Boers, 70, 196
Boorstin, Daniel, 201
Bossism, 63, 64-65, 116-117, 175, 176.
See also Political parties
Boston, Massachusetts, 5
Breckenridge, W. C. P., 142